The Poverty of Rights

Human Rights and the Eradication of Poverty

About CROP

CROP is a response from the academic community to the problem of poverty. The programme was initiated in 1992, and the CROP Secretariat was officially opened in June 1993 by the director-general of UNESCO, Dr Federico Mayor.

In recent years poverty alleviation, reduction or even eradication has moved up the international agenda, and the CROP network is providing research-based information to policy-makers and others responsible for poverty reduction. Researchers from more than 100 countries have joined the CROP network, with more than 40 per cent coming from so-called developing countries and countries in transition.

The major aim of CROP is to produce sound and reliable knowledge which can serve as a basis for poverty reduction. This is done by bringing together researchers for workshops, coordinating research projects and publications, and offering educational courses for the international community of policy-makers.

Crop Publications

Poverty, Research Projects, Institutes, Persons, ed. Tinka Ewold-Leicher and Arnaud F. Marks, Tilburg, Bergen and Amsterdam, 1995, 248 pp.

Urban Poverty: Characteristics, Causes and Consequences, ed. David Satterthwaite, special issue of *Environment and Urbanization,* Vol. 7, No. 1, April 1995, 284 pp.

Urban Poverty: From Understanding to Action, ed. David Satterthwaite, special issue of *Environment and Urbanization,* Vol. 7, No. 3, October 1995, 284 pp.

Women and Poverty – The Feminization of Poverty, ed. Ingrid Eide, The Norwegian National Commission for UNESCO and CROP, Oslo and Bergen, 1995 (in Norwegian), 56 pp.

Poverty: A Global Review. Handbook on International Poverty Research, ed. Else Øyen, S. M. Miller and Syed Abdus Samad, Scandinavian University Press and UNESCO, Oslo and Paris, 1996, 620 pp.

Law, Power and Poverty, ed. Asbjørn Kjønstad and John H. Veit-Wilson, CROP Publications, Bergen, 1997, 148 pp.

Poverty and Participation in Civil Society, ed. Yogesh Atal and Else Øyen, UNESCO and Abhinav Publications, Paris and New Delhi, 1997, 152 pp.

Poverty and Social Exclusion in the Mediterranean Area, ed. Karima Korayem and Maria Petmesidou, CROP Publications, Bergen, 1998, 286 pp.

Poverty and the Environment, ed. Arild Angelson and Matti Vainio, CROP Publications, Bergen, 1998, 180 pp.

The International Glossary on Poverty, ed. David Gordon and Paul Spicker, CROP International Studies in Poverty Research, Zed Books, London, 1999, 162 pp.

Poverty Reduction: What Role for the State in Today's Globalized Economy?, ed. Francis Wilson, Nazneen Kanji and Einar Braathen, CROP International Studies in Poverty Research, Zed Books, London, 2001, 372 pp.

Poverty and the Law, ed. Asbjørn Kjønstad and Peter Robson, Hart Publishing, Cambridge, 2001

For more information you may contact the CROP secretariat:
CROP Secretariat, Fosswinckelsgate 7, N-5007 Bergen, Norway
tel: +47 55 58 97 39   fax: +47 55 58 97 45
email: crop@uib.no   CROP on the internet: http://www.crop.org

The Poverty of Rights

Human Rights and the Eradication of Poverty

Edited by

WILLEM VAN GENUGTEN

CAMILO PEREZ-BUSTILLO

ZED BOOKS
London and New York

The Poverty of Rights: Human Rights and the Eradication of Poverty
was first published in 2001 by
Zed Books Ltd., 7 Cynthia Street, London N1 9JF, UK and
Room 400, 175 Fifth Avenue, New York, NY 10010, USA

Distributed in the USA exclusively by Palgrave, a division of
St Martin's Press, LLC, 175 Fifth Avenue, New York, NY 10010, USA.

CROP International Series on Poverty

Copyright © CROP, 2001

Cover design by Andrew Corbett
Designed and set in 10½/12 pt Bembo
by Long House, Cumbria, UK
Printed and bound in the United Kingdom
by Biddles Ltd, Guildford and King's Lynn

The rights of the authors of this work have been asserted by them
in accordance with the Copyright, Designs and Patents Act, 1988

A catalogue record for this book
is available from the British Library

ISBN   Hb 1 85649 977 4
Pb 1 85649 978 2

Library of Congress Cataloging-in-Publication Data
The poverty of rights : human rights and the eradication of poverty / edited by Willem
van Genugten and Camilo Perez-Bustillo
    p. cm.
  Includes bibliographical references and index.
  ISBN 1-85649-977-4 -- ISBN 1-85649-978-2
  1. Distributive justice. 2. Human rights. 3. Poverty. 4. Social justice. 5. Political
participation. I. Genugten, Willem J. M. van. II. Perez-Bustillo, Camilo, 1955–

HB523.P68 2001
323.3'2942--dc21   00-043902

Contents

About the Contributors

Patricia Helena Massa Arzabe is Master of Law, University of São Paulo, and Public Defender in the State of São Paulo, Brazil. She is presently working on the issues of inequality and alternatives for social inclusion. In 1994, she taught constitutional law at undergraduate level at the Universidade de Mogi das Cruzes; in 1995, she taught economic law in graduate level at the Universidade São Francisco.

Juan Antonio Blanco is Professor of Philosophy at the University of Havana, Cuba, where he also became a PhD in History. He serves as a member of the Tribunal of the National Board of Sciences, Cuba, to evaluate doctorates in History. Blanco has lectured at several universities and institutions, including Yale, Berkeley, La Paz and Havana, and serves as diplomat for the United Nations. At the moment, he is working at the Human Rights Internet in Canada (http://www.hri.ca). Blanco has written numerous articles and essays for journals in North America, Latin America and Europe. His most recent book is *Reflections on the Third Millennium* (1997).

Eduardo S. Bustelo holds a degree in Political and Social Sciences from the National University of Mendoza, Argentina, where he was awarded the prestigious gold medal. He is a Magister in Political Science and Public Administration at the Latin American Faculty of Social Sciences (FLACSO) and Master of Economics and Political Science from the London School of Economics. He has been a visiting professor at universities in Argentina and abroad, and lectured on the methodology of social indicators, evaluation of projects and policy, and social planning. From 1978 onwards he has been acting as a consultant for several United Nations agencies. From 1989 to 1993 he was Director of UNICEF in Argentina. Bustelo has written numerous articles for scientific and academic magazines and has co-authored several books, including the recent *Todos Entran, una Propuesta para Sociedades Incluyentes*. He is currently Director of the Master's programme in Social Policy at the University of Buenos Aires.

Willem van Genugten is Professor of International Law at Tilburg University and Professor of Human Rights at Nijmegen University. He is also Chair of the Board of the Dutch Research School of Human Rights, which is a joint initiative of the universities of Maastricht, Utrecht, Rotterdam and Tilburg. He is also a member of the Advisory Council on International Affairs of the Dutch government. He has published a series of books and articles, mainly in the field of human rights.

Claudio González-Parra is an Associate Professor of Rural Sociology at the University of Concepción in Chile. His research and teaching over the past 20 years has concentrated on human rights, especially cultural rights. Since 1994, he has conducted research with the Pehuenches in the highlands of the Bío Bío river as well as with other Mapuche groups in Chile. He has served as a consultant to the National Corporation of Indigenous Development (CONADI) as well as to national and international NGOs and the World Bank. Most recently he has undertaken research in intercultural education and resettlement in Mapuche communities. His publications include *La Educación Intercultural Bilingüe. Desarrollo y Propuestas para las Escuelas de Collico y Lleu Lleu*, Chapingo University, 1998.

Maribel Gordon C. holds a Master's degree in economics and politics. She is a professor and researcher at the Economy College, University of Panama. She also belongs to the poverty research team, the non-governmental organization PRODESO. She has written several papers and essays including *Panama: Basic Necessities Unsatisfied* (1992), *Community Rights* (1997) and *Economic, Social and Cultural Rights in Panama* (1999).

Héctor Gros Espiell is Professor of Constitutional Law and International Law at various universities in Uruguay. He has taught at several universities in America and Europe and at the Academy of International Law in The Hague. He has served as Uruguay's Minister of Foreign Relations and as ambassador of Uruguay to France. He has been Permanent Delegate of Uruguay to UNESCO, Executive Director of the Inter-American Institute of Human Rights, delegate to the United Nation's Commission of Human Rights and Member of its

Sub-Commission on the Protection of Minorities and Prevention of Discrimination. He is also a member of the Institute of International Law. Gros Espiell is author of several books in the field of international and constitutional law and international politics, including *Derechos Humanos y Vida Internacional* (1995).

Chris Jochnick is the co-founder and Advocacy Director of the Center for Economic and Social Rights (CESR) and coordinates CESR's Latin America programme from Ecuador. He has organized and participated in numerous conferences and workshops on economic and social rights and has made oral and written presentations to the Inter-American Commission on Human Rights, the African Commission on Human Rights and the UN Committee on Economic, Social and Cultural Rights. He is a graduate of Harvard Law School, the former Editor-in-Chief of the Harvard Human Rights Journal and a former research Fellow of the MacArthur Foundation. He has published numerous articles and reports on human rights and teaches a graduate course on economic and social rights at FLACSO in Ecuador.

Luiz Hernandez Navarro is a social anthropologist and is coordinator of the editorial pages of *La Jornada*, a Mexican daily newspaper. He is also a consultant to the Coordinadora Nacional de Organizaciones Cafetaleras (CNOC) and a researcher at the Centro de Estudios para el Cambio en el Campo Mexicano (CECCAM) in Mexico City. He has written extensively on rural issues and social and peasant movements in Mexico. Among his recent publications are *Chiapas: la guerra y la paz* (1995) and *Chiapas: la nueva lucha india* (1998).

Camilo Perez-Bustillo is Research Professor at the State of Mexico campus of the Instituto Tecnológico y de Estudios Superiores de Monterrey (ITESM), where he gives courses in media studies, law and international relations. He is also a resident scholar at the Permanent Seminar on Chicano and Border Studies of the Social Anthropology Division of Mexico's National Institute of Anthropology and History (DEAS–INAH), the representative in Mexico of the US-based National Lawyers' Guild, and adjunct professor at the Mexico City campus of the United States International University (USIU), based in San Diego, California.

Marco Aurelio Ugarte Ochoa holds a doctorate in social anthropology. He has worked as professor and researcher at the Universidad Autónoma de Puebla, Mexico, and as professor at the Universidad Nacional de San Antonio Abad del Cusco. He is President of the

Peruvian Association ATD/Fourth World Order and member of the ATD/Fourth World Order International Council. He won the first prize in the Joseph Wresinski competition in Paris in 1988 and serves as member of the Joseph Wresinski Foundation. Ugarte Ochoa is author of *La Convención El Trabajo y sus Luchas Sociales* (1986).

Patrick van Weerelt holds a Master of Law degree from Maastricht University in the Netherlands and a Master of International Law degree from the University of Lund/Raoul Wallenberg Institute for Human Rights and Humanitarian Law, Sweden. He has previous work experience with the University of Maastricht and the Netherlands Ministry of Foreign Affairs. At the time of the CROP/ALOP workshop in Chile he worked at the United Nations Office of the High Commissioner for Human Rights in Geneva. He is currently working as Governance Programme Officer at the United Nations Development Programme in Pretoria, South Africa.

Preface

Camilo Perez-Bustillo

This book is a compilation of selected papers from two workshops in Latin America sponsored by the Comparative Research Programme on Poverty (CROP),* and held respectively at the facilities of Sur/Centro de Estudios Sociales y Económicos in Santiago de Chile in September 1997, and at the Universidad Iberoamericana and the State of Mexico campus of the Instituto Tecnológico y de Estudios Superiores de Monterrey (ITESM) near Mexico City in March 1999. Some 20 papers were presented at the Human Rights and the Eradication of Poverty workshop in Chile, with participants from Argentina, Bolivia, Brazil, Chile, Colombia, Costa Rica, Cuba, Ecuador, France, Mexico, the Netherlands, Norway, Panama, Peru, Switzerland, Uruguay, USA and Venezuela. The background paper for the workshop – the first of its kind organized in the Latin American region by CROP – was written by the co-editor of this volume, Professor Willem van Genugten of Tilburg University in the Netherlands. Two chapters draw upon those papers presented at the Mexico workshop, on the much broader theme of Poverty and Social Justice in Latin America, which were most closely related to the book's theme of human rights and poverty.

An important part of this book, of the collaboration and exchange which it nurtured between the co-editors and the authors, illustrates CROP's exemplary commitment to fostering meaningful, often empirically based research and dialogue between North and South and across traditional disciplinary borders which in many cases unduly compartmentalize and fragment effective policy analysis, research and action regarding global poverty issues. CROP's increasing Latin American

* CROP's major focus is scientific. CROP has been responsible for the preparation of this book, but the views expressed in the Preface do not necessarily reflect the focus of CROP.

activities have the potential to make an important contribution from Mexico City to Buenos Aires.

This collection is then itself an (inevitably incomplete) expression of the need for and complexities of such a dialogue. Many of the chapters were written originally in Spanish or Portuguese, or by, and from the perspective of, researchers whose mother tongues are indigenous to the Americas (as well as from countries as diverse in their cultures as Norway, the Netherlands and the United States). What is striking, therefore, is the extent to which these perspectives, which are so diverse in terms of discipline, culture, historical, economic, political and social context, converge in their insistence on the need for renewed reflection and urgent actions to redress deepening patterns of globalized poverty, marginalization and exclusion. An important sub-text is the need for reformulation and revitalization of the imperatives for global democracy as a category specifically encompassing economic, social and cultural rights, and breaking with unidimensional affirmations of the ostensible primacy of civil and political entitlements which characterized much of western discourse during the Cold War.

An epistemological rupture of this kind is especially necessary in the context of Latin America, the specific focus of much of this volume. Latin America is both the single region in the world with the greatest inequities in the distribution of wealth and income, according to the World Bank and the United Nations Development Program, and a relatively wealthy region in terms of GDP in comparison to Africa, South Asia or most of the Middle East. This combination of relative wealth and absolute inequity renders it at the same time one of the world's most explosive and most hopeful arenas for meaningful social transformation. Potential regional 'super-powers' such as Brazil and Mexico (in the same category as, for example, Nigeria, Egypt and South Africa in Africa, or Indonesia, Pakistan, Bangladesh, the Philippines and Malaysia in Asia) reflect both the region's most tragic dimensions in terms of affronts to human dignity, and its best aspirations and most imaginative efforts – from the Movimento Sem Terra of landless peasants in Brazil to the predominantly Mayan indigenous Zapatista National Liberation Army based in Chiapas, Mexico – to overcome these conditions. Such efforts shine especially brightly amid the devastating human and economic costs imposed by the new post-Cold War variants of US hegemony in settings as diverse as the International Monetary Fund, the Persian Gulf and the Balkans.

It is this duality which led us to frame the book's title in terms of the potential role that can be played by the vigorous advocacy of compliance with international human rights' norms, one of this volumes two major themes. The other major theme concerns the explicit incorporation and actionability of such standards as minimums in national constitutional and legal frameworks as an integral part of the overall struggle to ensure the reduction and ultimate eradication of global poverty and social injustice. 'Law is not a panacea', as the concluding chapter states, but can in fact provide an indispensable basis and/or complement to successful social mobilization, when armed with the best, and most critical, sociological analysis. At the same time, evolving international human rights standards can provide a basis for transcending the limitations of domestic law where national legal frameworks regarding poverty-related issues are inadequate, outmoded or largely unimplemented, or where authoritarian regimes have undermined, as currently in Mexico, Colombia, Peru and Ecuador, or for recent extended periods in fact eclipsed the rule of law, such as in Brazil, Chile, Uruguay, Argentina, Nicaragua, El Salvador, Guatemala, Honduras and Paraguay during much of the 1970s and 1980s. Efforts of this kind are especially important in countries undergoing processes of ostensible 'transition' to democracy, including many of those listed above. In other countries, such as Venezuela and Cuba currently, and Nicaragua during the period of Sandinista rule, the issue is whether a multidimensional democracy committed to the rule of law can function under conditions of revolutionary transformation, especially when complicated by US intervention (such as economic and trade sanctions and the financing, training and arming of counter-revolutionary movements, acts which themselves violate international law).

All of this seems less theoretical when observed from conference rooms in Santiago de Chile or Mexico City. It is interesting to note that the Chile workshop took place shortly after the twenty-fourth anniversary of the bloody military coup which overthrew the democratically elected socialist government of Salvador Allende and put General Augusto Pinochet in power on 11 September 1973. Many of those attending the workshop had never (or never after the Allende period) been to Chile, because of their abhorrence for Pinochet's dictatorial regime. A few of us were able to combine participation in the workshop with private pilgrimages to places such as the Salvador Allende Foundation, the now-reconstructed Moneda Palace, the traditional residence and office complex of Chile's presidents, which was bombed by the Chilean Air Force during the coup, and the recently reopened home of Chile's 1971 Nobel Laureate in Literature, poet Pablo Neruda, in Isla Negra.

All of the above acquired renewed significance when news came of Pinochet's arrest in London in October 1998 on a Spanish warrant for his extradition to face trial on an indictment for the commission of crimes against humanity and the instigation of multiple acts of state terrorism. Following two historic decisions in November 1998 and March 1999 by the House of Lords and by the British Home Secretary Jack Straw, authorising the essence of the matter to proceed towards possible extradition, it became clear that regardless of the ultimate judgements reached in his case, a new era had dawned in international law just around the fiftieth anniversary of the Universal Declaration of Human Rights. CROP is an indispensable actor in the overall effort to help make international human rights norms a reality in the lives of the poor of Latin America, an effort which is intimately related to the need to ensure that no regime like that of Pinochet ever blights again the face of this luminous continent. NUNCA MAS!

Mexico City and Bergen

PART I
Citizenship, Democracy and Participation

Contemporary Challenges and New Paradigms

1

Expansion of Citizenship and Democratic Construction

Contemporary Challenges and New Paradigms

EDUARDO S. BUSTELO

And you think you're going to fix the world?
Discepolo, Quevachache

It appears that the key substantive question in discussions of contemporary social policy, paradoxically after more than two centuries of industrial development, continues to be the issue of equality. In general terms, and although certain social indicators may be moving in a generally positive direction – infant mortality, life expectancy at birth, levels of education, etc – the distribution of income and wealth continues to evidence dramatic disparities, and, in the case of Latin America, represents the highest levels of inequality in the world. This is not to suggest that such improvements in basic social indicators should be trivialized. The point is that, given the contemporary context of open economies and the current phase of free capital flows, we are building societies which are increasingly unjust and which could end up reversing the social progress achieved so far, even in terms of basic human survival.

It is on this basis that this chapter seeks to reflect on four questions which appear important regarding contemporary Latin America: (i) Is it possible to conceive of social policy alternatives capable of producing higher levels of equality? (ii) is there now an historic opportunity to bring this about, based on popular choice? (iii) is it possible to build a more just society and to do so democratically? and (iv) if democracy is not just a system of government, what is it?

Models of Citizenship

When a particular style or model of social policy becomes hegemonic, one of its primary tendencies and functions is to negate any rival alternative that might imply a threat to its conceptual dominance. In the case of Latin America, the implementation since the 1980s of a neo-conservative macro-economic policy that implies, as we will see below, a very particular vision of social rights and citizenship, has brought about an apparent social-policy consensus which rules out differing, viable, equitable and efficient alternatives.

To discuss development with seriousness is to differentiate among its ultimate possible purposes. Put simply, to do so is to arrive at an agreement about fundamentals, such as whether the production of wealth is a means or an end of development; in other words, is the ultimate objective of a process of material accumulation to serve people and not just the creation of wealth in and of itself? Addressing these dilemmas is important in a region that is implementing an economic and social policy which guarantees that millions of people are, and will be, left out of the benefits of progress. This is not just a debate about the poor, because we confront a model of accumulation which is potentially of importance but that is crystallizing a social modality that incorporates only a minority politically, socially and economically. This modality simultaneously augments a zone of vulnerability where a significant proportion of society has to make dramatic efforts so as not to become disengaged from economic development and technological innovation which ultimately abandons millions in poverty. The question is: can we develop an economy without a society, or one that is in fact anti-social?

Situating this debate at the level of values that animate a particular model or objective of development makes sense because in instrumental terms many of the policies characteristic of the new economic and social model may to some degree even be persuasive. One could, for example, agree with decentralization as a social policy objective, even though it can be postulated on the basis of diametrically opposed value judgements. In one case, decentralization may be about diluting the public sphere and supplanting state authority in favour of local power, fragmenting demand for public services, and restricting public participation to specific problems of immediate concern. From another, competing, perspective decentralization means expanding 'public space' by encouraging the exercise of plenary citizenship and democratic participation. This is why discussion about social policy's instrumentality makes little sense if it evades more fundamental debates about the essence of social policy: what happens to equality understood as access to the fruits of development and technological progress? What happens to the possibility of building a society which is socially and economically inclusive, and where no one is left out?

We can think about social policy along the lines suggested by T.H. Marshall (Marshall 1975, 1981, 1992), as the development of a process of expansion of citizenship from civil rights (liberty, freedom of thought and speech, the right to contract, property, due process, etc) to political rights (participation in political life, to elect and be elected), and finally, social rights (from the right to a minimum standard of economic well-being and security to the right to share in the heritage and lifestyle of a civilized person according to the values prevalent in the society in which one lives). According to Marshall, citizenship is a status due and accorded to all fully-fledged members of a community, which in turn guarantees them an equality of rights and obligations. There is no universal principle in his view that determines which rights and obligations are inherent in citizenship in a given society, but in those settings where the social order is considered to be of an evolving nature an 'image of an ideal citizenship' emerges and becomes the goal to which people aspire as well as the benchmark against which progress is measured.

It is not surprising that Marshall's notion of a citizenship process assumes an inherent logic tending towards equity, which derives from the inclusion of social rights in his definition of citizenship. This approach drastically subverts the logic of capitalism, which as we know produces deep social inequalities. The internal logic of capitalism is, however, also rooted in a conception of rights which is essentially indi-vidualistic. This is why under capitalism civil rights trump the others. There is then a form of citizenship which is itself wedded to a capitalist rationale, where it is the individual who has moral value and not the family, the community or the society. As a result, social rights are non-existent because they cannot be ascribed to individual subjects and are thus not implementable. If there are poor and marginalized people, they do not enjoy the status of citizens, because civil and political rights are merely formal recognitions. What difference would recognition of the right to property make to those who possess nothing, or the right to vote if its exercise is ineffectual in changing the situation of social exclusion? According to this logic the poor should be assisted in their development and could thus come to be conceived of as possessing a 'dependent' citizenship. According to the same logic, the political insti-tutions dedicated to assisting the poor should also be marginal and as far as possible transitory, subject to evaluation on the basis of individual welfare and freedom, and not on the basis of whether they promote public well-being. Participation in political life for the purpose of resolving social problems is not an important priority from the stand-point of this model of citizenship. Citizenship is here outside politics, as are also both happiness and the ultimate meaning of life. On the other hand, from the Marshallian perspective on citizenship, rights only have meaning to the extent that they are given form by a sense of belonging to a particular community, and cannot be exercised in violation of that community's interests. Here social and economic rights have primacy in the sense that they are recognisable because one is a member of that society, and because they grant one that status. In other words, it is social and economic rights that emancipate people from the most demanding material needs and enable their access to the civility of enjoying civil and political rights. In other words, social citizenship is the citizenship which enables the development of society's civil and political dimensions.[1]

Returning to the Latin American context, and taking into account the rationales described above, it seems that there are two basic ways of thinking about the politics of citizenship in terms of the three most important social problems that afflict the region and which are reflected in its current levels of inequality, vulnerability and social exclusion. These two conceptions – 'dependent citizenship' and 'emancipated citizenship' – can be understood in terms of two rival models which today contend for the role of guiding social policy in Latin America. Before describing these models of citizenship I should first clarify what I mean by a model.

The word 'model' is used here in the sense of its being a paradigm, a simplified representation of a pattern of values and concepts which have been structured to a certain degree of consistency. A model makes it possible to recognise and define an overall pattern of representative dimensions which characterize a particular paradigm with relative precision. Now, of course, models are not reproduced in a pure state in reality, which by definition is much more complex. Despite this limitation, models make it possible to differentiate among varying expressions of social policy in the real world, and to reference or catalogue them in terms of their greater or lesser proximity or relationship to different paradigmatic forms of citizenship. In the same way, all social policy can be conceived of as the sum total of instruments which operationalize and implement different models of citizenship. It is important to stress that the nature of the relationship between a particular model and a particular social policy enables us to discern the deeper significance of a specific policy by shedding light upon the ultimate ends it pursues, and at the same time to assess, as I have indicated, the degree of correspondence between the policy as means and the extent to which it may constitute a set of values – a model of citizenship – as an end.

Returning to the foregoing analytical framework, I propose to differentiate among the two predominant models of citizenship (dependent and emancipated) reflected in contemporary Latin American social

Table 1.1 • Models of citizenship

Type of citizenship	Dependent	Emancipated
Equality	High social stratification. Social inequality is 'natural'. Government policies are distribution-neutral.	An important goal. Everything examined in light of its distributive impact. Public policy orients the process of accumulation.
Solidarity	Handled within each social stratum. High competitiveness. Possessive individualism prevails. 'Welfare' for the poor.	Non-competitive social solidarity. Co-operation, reciprocity and social symmetry. Altruism prevails.
Social mobility	Competitiveness: 'Let the best one win.' Individuals 'ascend' through 'recognized' channels of mobility, e.g., the educational system	Strong. Equality of opportunities in education, health, due process. Knowledge of concepts and 'codes' necessary for social ascent is instilled.
Society	Atomized. Priority given to individual, particularized interests. Society in effect reduced to social relations.	Society is Us/We. Robust public sphere. Systematic behaviour is characterized by complementarities and reciprocity.
Inclusion	The market as vehicle. Restricted participation, and then only to resolve specific problems. The excluded become 'subsidized'.	Considered fundamental, through equal access to productive work. Widespread participation: social, political and economic. Emancipated citizenship and active democracy.
Poverty	The poor as object of governmental policy intervention. Targeting of programmes for the poor.	Constituted as autonomous social subjects. Priority given to income and wealth distribution: rich and poor.
Gender	Among higher strata, incorporation of women into the dominant male paradigm. In lower strata, women are pre-citizens.	Gender equality. Women enjoy full citizenship.

Table 1.1 cont.

Type of citizenship	Dependent	Emancipated
Social rights	Recognition of civil and political rights. Social rights not 'actionable'.	Citizenship is broad. Integral approach to political, economic and social rights. Social rights have priority.
State-market relations	The state is minimal and marginal. The market distributes resources and what is respectively social and political. Negative rights and liberties prevail.	The state is active and democratic. Robust public sphere. The market is an instrument and not an end in itself. Market and efficiency are compatible with democratic regulation. Positive rights and liberties.
Social and economic policy	Economic policy is hegemonic priority. Social policy is marginal and subordinate. The economy is an end in and of itself. Citizenship is subordinate (dependent).	Social and economic policy are integrated. Economic policy is instrumental and not an end in itself. It is subject to democratic regulation. Economy is constructed from society, not the reverse. Development of 'social' citizenship.

policy in terms of ten dimensions which are relevant from the perspective of the historical development of citizenship. These models are presented schematically in Table 1.1.

The dimensions and conceptualizations of the models described above have taken into account the pioneering work of Richard Titmuss in the United Kingdom (Titmuss 1958, 1974) and that of Oscar Varsavsky in Latin America (Varsavsky 1971), as well as some subsequent elaborations (Bustelo 1990; Demo 1995). What follows is a succinct description of these.

The dependent citizenship (DC) model can be located in the most conservative social and economic policy tradition and can be found most recently in the theoretical formulations of Friedrich von Hayek (von Hayek 1944) and Milton Friedman (Friedman 1962). It is the hegemonic conception associated with the economic adjustment and 'open' economy models which prevail in contemporary Latin America, especially those related to the so-called 'Washington Consensus' (Williamson 1996).[2] This approach flows from an atomistic conception of society in which sole recognition is given to individuals with interests as the basic organizing principle of all human associations. The archetype behind this model is that of 'economic man' who, by maximizing his personal benefit, automatically benefits society as a whole.

The negative freedoms, masterfully explored by Sir Isaiah Berlin in his *Four Essays on Liberty* (Berlin 1969), are the deepest theoretical elaboration of this concept. Negative freedoms are those which are the vehicle for the full exercise of individual rights without interference by the state or others, or, in general, by means of arguments invoking a public interest in doing so. The state should thus be minimal in nature and neither alter nor interfere with the basic self-regulating mechanism of the market, where the interests of millions of buyers and sellers come together and can be made optimal. The market is conceived of as a self-regulating entity, autonomous from politics and social policy, and its logic is hegemonic over the formulation of public policies: this is why we must always 'listen' to market forces.

There are no viable, advantageous models of cooperation: the prevailing style is that of the 'free rider' so well described by Mancur Olson in his book *The Logic of Collective Action* (Olson 1965). In the absence of any other public good but that of the market, entitled to greater weight than that of individual interests, there is no possibility of public policies. Citizenship is conceived of essentially as of a civic character. Political citizenship consists only of formal rights, principally that of voting and being voted into office. Social rights are not actionable in a positive sense unless they have a fiscal basis (e.g., an individual social security insurance account consolidating each person's contributions and with benefits calculated in actuarial terms). Social rights, in those limited instances when they are reducible to social services, are subject to the availability of resources. This is why they are actually 'conditional opportunities' (Barbalet 1988).

There is no concern for income and wealth distribution since inequalities are natural and the fruit of the survival and triumph of the fittest. State policies should thus be marginal and distributively neutral. Those denominated as social policies should be targeted on poverty and socially vulnerable groups, forming 'networks of contention' for resources, and not directed at income distribution. At this point the social policy approach characteristic of DC coincides with that of traditional electoral clientelism, social paternalism and patrimonialism (that of subordinated citizenship managed by a boss), traditionally prevalent in Latin America. In the current context of economic adjustment policies rooted in an 'open' economic model, social policy is perceived of as a necessity in order to guarantee the sources of governability capable of assuring the legitimation of reforms demanded by the market.

Varying forms of income transfer to the poor imply a social policy rooted in an ethic of compassion that underlies a subsidy approach: social citizenship essentially becomes 'subsidized citizenship'. From the standpoint of economic calculus subsidies are disincentives, and so their use should be marginal and transitory in nature. It is possible to develop minimalistic state health and educational policies based on human capital, whose structure does not escape a private logic: individuals invest in themselves, calculating future returns on these investments. Individuals also ought to capitalize their income in private funds or securities that follow an individual actuarial logic. Here, social policy closes the circle with economic policy since such practices provide the funds necessary to increase the savings which can be channelled for financial investment in the capital markets.

The emancipated citizenship (EC) model draws on another conceptual framework traceable back to the early utopian thinkers (including the socialists). It culminated in what we now define as the welfare state, expressed in the social reforms promoted by the Fabians and Beveridge in England, by G. Moller in Sweden and, in the academic realm, by Thomas Marshall and Richard Titmuss. For this tradition the central theme is social equality as the key value, understood principally as the right of people, conceived of as members or stakeholders in a common cooperative social framework, to have equal opportunities of access to socially and economically meaningful benefits. Equality then implies equity, i.e. proportionality in the degree of access to the benefits and costs of development, and also redistributive justice, grounded in collective solidarity.[3]

A social cooperation scheme implies the existence of an 'us' or a 'we' that is the underpinning of a particular human social order. Individuals are not negated, but there is a society and as a result a public sphere, understood as a concern for matters of common interest and for the interests of the society as a whole. This 'we' coincides with the 'social' as associates, like a corpus of partners joined in an effort for mutual cooperation. This 'we' as a concrete project is also a shared community of discourse and argument, consisting essentially of a sense of direction about where the society is headed and how its various partners want to get there. This sense of 'we' then becomes the basis upon which a society can compete more effectively with social and productive endeavours from other national spaces in a globalised context. Individual freedoms in their negative form are important, but equally relevant are positive rights, which broaden the field of those persons able to accede to opportunities necessary for their development and for the improvement of their living conditions. In this context equality is not just a levelling project, but a way to build.

Thus conceived, the EC model is by definition a socially inclusive project. All individuals form an equal part of a discourse through which a community of shared arguments develops. Some of these arguments are essential in order to reduce the multiple ways in which exclusion can be reproduced: access to productive employment, to quality education and to the socially relevant codes that permit women and men to participate and to broaden the field of their rights and responsibilities. In the EC model people are not patients – objects of public treatment or intervention – but actors in their dual individual and social dimensions. Emancipation remains individualized in form, because individuals are autonomous, *but emancipation is not achieved one by one, and is neither solitary nor unique.* All of this again implies a shared community of arguments, and a shared responsibility for the whole: this is why this is a project of emancipation which is democratic in character.

The market and the logic of profit are not penalized in themselves but are clearly subordinated to other priorities. Here all political, economic and social institutions are judged in terms of their impacts on people, on women and men, on new generations, as to whether they contribute to emancipation or to the generation of dependency, as to whether they degrade, humiliate, exploit, or tend to concentrate power and wealth to the detriment of all those who should enjoy equality of opportunities.

As we can see from the analysis above, conceptually speaking there are at least two rival models of citizenship which imply two distinct modalities of social policy. These models do not exist in a pure state. They are stereotypes that inform the content of concrete social policies, and appear in reality in approximate and even mixed forms. Both models could in principle be implemented along the spectrum of possible social policy and circumstances in contemporary Latin America. Having disposed in this way of the argument that there are no alternatives to what is currently being done or that there is no other way to make social policy, let's confront the other argument used to try to invalidate the emergent new citizenship: that which dismisses the EC model as utopian or idealistic.

In the first place, there is a natural and permanent tension between societies as they are and as they should be, according to values of equality and solidarity, triggering opportunities which are invitations to work and participate. This is why the EC model, which is neither closed nor finished, can be constructed socially and democratically. As Veca (1996) explains, this presupposes 'an attitude of reasonable, not promethean, confidence in the possibility of designing, reforming, correcting, and renovating political, economic and social institutions in a direction consistent with the idea of equality'. This model's characteristic of being susceptible to a democratic process of social construction also implies going beyond a reductionist or transitory individual commitment and the good intentions ridiculed by R. Rorty as having the pretence only that people be 'nicer, more generous and less egotistical' (Rorty 1992).

In the second place, the EC model has no pretension either of enabling the return of a 'grand' project or of being a 'great' experiment, much less of being a way to resurrect the various collapsed varieties of grand narratives or mega-discourses. There is no ineluctable march of history nor the promise of definitive human redemption. The EC model can be built democratically as a process of (not necessarily lineal) expansion of a shared conversation about how to include women and men equally in a 'we' that can emancipate all from different forms of economic, social and political exclusion. Once we have discussed these two basic models of citizenship and articulated EC as a viable alternative model to what exists, the question becomes: do we face an historical moment that enables us to move forward in this direction?

The Emergence of the Public

Since the early 1980s, Latin America has undergone a powerful transformation from a reliance on the import-substitution economic model, stressing development of internal demand and a strong guiding state role in development, to an export-led 'open' economy model, focused on insertion into the global market and on a dynamic role for the market. This has led to a new relationship between the state and private sphere, based on the crisis of the previous modality which was characterized by the predominance of the state administrative apparatus over that of civil society. Internally, the axis of this process has fostered destabilizing waves of inflation, macro-economic imbalances and their direct impacts in the form of low levels of capital accumulation and economic growth and, above all, depressed levels of general welfare. Externally, this has led to widespread technological change through constant pressure to innovate, and to an emphasis on value-added growth and increases in productivity. It is undisputed that in Latin America today the private sphere has become a dominant priority.

Albert O. Hirschman has undertaken a provocative analysis of the oscillation in popular preferences between the public and the private and back again, affirming that both acts of private consumption and those of participation in public life are attempted because people seek satisfaction of needs which, if unrequited, generate disillusion. Hirschman makes an historical analysis of these mood swings, tracing them back to the emergence of the private with the development of commerce and industry in the seventeenth and eighteenth centuries, when the proposition that 'the pursuit of our private material interests is a completely valid form of human conduct, which in effect may be preferable, from the standpoint of society, to a life of intense participation in public matters' became legitimized (Hirschman 1986).

The point here is not whether or not history is characterized by pendular shifts (Heller and Fehér 1992), though in the case of Latin America the shift from an import-substitution model to an open economy model is in fact related to a movement between the state and the private sphere. The term 'state' and not 'public' – the latter defined in terms of matters of general interest – is deliberately employed here since in reality in this region social disillusion targets the state in particular rather than the public sphere as such, given the predominant role of the former in the import-substitution model. At the same time it would be erroneous to claim that there has emerged in Latin America a clear enthusiasm for the primacy of the private. What has characterized the shift that has occurred is the sum of the two following continuous disillusions: disillusionment with the state, due to the displacement of the import-substitution model, followed by disillusionment with the private, which in turn could lead to a return to the kinds of state intervention and macro-economic policies which characterized the import-substitution model.

A large part of the swing in the general perception regarding the state–private dichotomy flowed from a disillusion with two extreme cases. The belief that the state could exclusively direct socio-economic processes, invading economic spheres where the private sector had clear comparative advantages, and intervening in social spheres where democratic community-based participation would have been much more effective, has encouraged neither sustainable development nor greater social well-being. Extreme instances of state incompetence, bureaucratic arbitrariness and inefficiency in public management, accompanied by the impunity of increased illegalities of conduct and corruption, the protection of corporatist privileges and monopolized reserves of power, led in Latin America to a vast disillusion with the dimensions of state power. The effects of public policies promoting the sole primacy of the state included the stimulation of inflationary pressures that heightened the difficulties of distributive policies, thereby contributing to an ever greater concentration of wealth and income in fewer hands. This, together with the low prevailing rates of productivity and innovation, fed the idea of a retreat to the private – for some, to family, friends and private associations with very narrow purposes, and for others, a focus on the pursuit of material interests – and constituted an adequate response to changing circumstances, preferably from a social perspective to intense participation in public affairs. To these endogenous factors can be added those exogenous ones noted above, flowing principally from patterns of technological transformation, processes of globalization and new emergent opportunities in international trade.

Latin America has in effect swung from one extreme to another with the currently prevailing stress on the exclusive affirmation of the private. In this way, substantive processes of reducing the state role through decentralization, deregulation and rampant privatization are dominant. Market mechanisms have been reinstituted not just as a means of optimizing resources but as an hegemonic economic logic in processes of public sector decision-making. At the same time, all kinds of incentives and guarantees for the capture of external investments and savings have proliferated. Even when the private sector has not responded as expected in certain instances, such as in the finance sector, in various countries in the region impressive rescues have arisen that transfer public financial resources to restore the impaired private functioning. Capital markets have been expanded by means of privatized pension funds which have implied the transfer of substantial resources from public to private hands. All of this has flourished in the context of a powerfully promoted anti-public discourse, accompanied by the marketing of all kinds of private interests and gains, and even of their ostensible social benefits, abstracted from any ethical responsibility for the circumstances of the markets' origin and extreme rates of accumulation.

From an economic point of view, the implementation of the ten adjustment modalities which add up to the Washington Consensus (Williamson 1996) initially had positive macro-economic effects, such as contained inflation, increased exports and productivity, as well as renewed economic growth. But the limitations of the overall approach have begun to emerge because other problems, such as the traditional problem of low investment rates in the region, insufficient technological development, and the virtually null generation of productive quality employment, remain unresolved. In addition, important transfers of resources from the public to the private sector have been financed by increased levels of internal debt. Latin American economies continue to be highly vulnerable to swings in the international capital markets whose great volatility has direct effects, including that of inducing cycles of recession. The dramatic effects of this approach in terms of social exclusion have been documented elsewhere (Bustelo and Minujin 1997).

In this context it is important to evaluate the initial hypothesis that there are indications in Latin America of an increasing disillusion with the prevalence of the private that open up possibilities for the emergence of public space. Several concrete reasons point in this direction, even in the heterogeneous contexts of the various countries of the region:

1. There is increasing evidence that the prevailing social policies which have accompanied the implementation of the open economy model have not and will not promote the social, economic and political inclusion of vast sectors of the population. The boundaries of social inequality expand continuously and the possibilities of obtaining productive employment decrease. There is an emerging, increasingly generalized concern that the priority in Latin America should be that of redistribution and not just the combating of poverty, which in turn demands the expansion of social solidarity and public responsibility.

2. There is increasing concern about the loss and near-disappearance of public spaces: education, health and different forms of social protection. A vigorous current of public opinion is re-emerging which demands a serious discussion about the public character of these and other key public spaces as spheres for democratization of the overall society.

3. Public services which have been privatized with continued monopoly guarantees have left consumers in virtual helplessness in terms of verifying the costs of their services (e.g., that of telephones and electricity) so as to be able to justify rate hikes. Efforts at organized forms of consumer protection have not yet attained the vigour or the power that they have in the developed world, although they have begun to emerge. The idea here is not of a return to the former state role as such, but rather of an increased popular percep-

tion of the need to define adequate public regulatory frameworks for the protection of consumer rights.

4. Expectations that the black market, informal economy and illicit enrichment would be reduced and that corrupt practices would be eliminated with the shrinking of the state have not only not been satisfied, but such phenomena have tended to increase. Traditional lack of confidence in governing political élites has been augmented by a growing perception of unscrupulous entrepreneurs dedicated only to the promotion of their own interests through the exercise of economic power. Behind every corrupt politician there is a corrupt entrepreneur who promotes him. The affirmation of individual interests or incentives for economic gain independent of ethical constraints or codes has rendered corrupt practices implicitly acceptable (IDS Bulletin 1996). Once again, there is a vigorously growing demand for public regulatory frameworks to govern private economic activity as well as that of public officials, and especially for an independent judicial power capable of guaranteeing compliance with the rule of law and of sanctions for those who do not comply.

5. Increased 'new' wealth together with its ostentation has helped generate a perception of its concentrated and exclusive character and, as a result, a disenchantment with prevailing policies. Even though access to increased consumption is an important goal for the majority of the population, there is an increasing awareness that not everybody consumes, and certainly not to the same degree. The concentrating character of prevailing policies has been accentuated as well by the non-transparent way in which many privatizations have been carried out. There is an increasingly generalized perception that those who sold services to the state in the import-substitution model have managed to retain the monopoly possession of important public services, with new income guarantees of a vitally important character.

6. There is increased awareness that increases in spontaneous functioning of markets will not in themselves resolve the principal challenges which arise within the open economy model. The experiences of East Asian growth, despite its recent crises, demonstrate clearly the significant positive role that the state can play in fostering development through industrial and export-promotion policies. At the same time, there is a growing conviction about the strategic comparative advantage inherent in generating greater social capital so as to effectively compete in the context of globalized economies with similar

approaches to development, and to promote insertion in the global market.

7. Finally, current rates of population growth and specifically the numbers of those entering the labour market in Latin America ensure a continuing tendency in the growth of the demand for public goods.

Each of the above affirmations is supported by numerous studies of public opinion throughout the Latin American region.[4] These evident tendencies do not, however, imply a general shift back towards preference for the former statist approach of the import-substitution model, nor a renewed or increasing confidence in ruling élites, but rather indicate a substantial and growing consensus about the need to restore the public sphere (Arendt 1958) and a renewed interest in issues of common concern in the context of greater civic participation.

In terms of economic policy debates, the ideological character and technical limitations (Stewart 1996) of the hitherto virtually uncontested Washington Consensus have begun to be demystified. The emergence of proposals for a new 'practical neo-structuralism' (Rosenthal 1996) posits the development of a more realistic alternative capable of generating an increasing level of state activity consistent with market dynamics, regulation of the degree of openness in the overall economy, and reflecting a greater stress on endogenous forces of development, incorporation of the demands of the public sphere, and of the need to address issues of income and wealth redistribution in a much more decisive and concrete manner.

Given the circumstances and opportunities available, which evidence the tendency towards the re-emergence of the public sphere, it seems that we confront an historical moment when it is possible to reinitiate the process of expanding citizenship in the majority of the countries in the Latin American region. This possibility puts us on the road to being able to redress the stark prevailing patterns of inequality and the devastating deficit of citizenship in the region.

The next section considers the space or domain most apt for anchoring the individual or collective striving towards the goal of expanded citizenship.

Democracy and Social Rights

The process of expanding citizenship cannot be conceived of as one characterized by lineal advancement based on an understanding of history as a semi-automatic motion towards fulfilment. The history of social processes is much more complex when understood as social constructions, and much more difficult when the intention is to accord them meaning. The approach here is to reassess the possibility of changing and transforming reality pursuant to a practical premise: that it is in fact possible to construct a society better than what we have. Reality is not a trap which disables us from doing anything but contemplating it in perplexity. Perplexity can be useful as a moment of surprise, as a sudden or sharp breakdown of an expectation, but useless to the extent that it fosters impotence or stasis. We cannot always remain perplexed in the face of what happens to us, because otherwise history would always be what happens to us and not what we want.

So what is the key aspect in the process of expanding citizenship in Latin America, in the region of the world where the greatest disparities in the distribution of income and wealth prevail? From my perspective, that role corresponds to the category of social (and economic) rights, because their domain is the place where the concept of citizenship converges with that of equality. Let us recall that for Marshall equality of citizenship is an equality of status which does not contradict the inequality produced by the capitalist system. But although Marshall did not advance in his analysis in terms of exploring greater possibilities for expanding citizenship in the direction of equality, he was emphatic in understanding that here lies the greatest point of tension between the citizenship process and the capitalist system itself.[5]

It is surely uncontested that democracy is a system where increasing levels of equality could be more easily realized. What is debatable is whether democracy is capable of imposing limits or controls on the expansion of individual interests and on profit as the fundamental motivation underlying all human activities. Or is it, on the contrary, capitalism itself, the market and the system of inequalities which they engender that will be able to brake that expansion? It is at this conjuncture that the crucial issue of governability arises. In the case of Latin America and in the context of currently prevailing economic and social policies, governability is understood as the reduction of politics to the mere art of governing the imperatives of the market and the logic of profit. Determinism of this kind negates all possibilities for human freedom. In the opposing domain of emancipated citizenship, the market and the economy as a whole are subject to democratic regulation to the extent that governability is understood in precisely the inverse sense, that is, as the democratic control of markets. At issue here is a titanic, tension-filled struggle, whose resolution essentially corresponds to the realm of political dynamics. This point will be returned to.

To advance the agenda of social policy in the region in the sense of achieving a mode of development in which there is room for everybody, avoiding social exclusion and inequalities, implies advancing towards social citizenship, which means advancing towards a governing conception of social rights.

There is a whole discussion about whether social rights are really rights and as to whether they are actionable.[6] In one tradition, rights are only worthy of the name to the extent that they inhere in individuals, and citizenship is restricted only to those rights which are civil and political in character. In the Marshallian tradition, the rights of members of a community have their origin in the simple fact of their belonging to that community. If this is so, social rights are not procedural in nature but rather recognise the autonomy of actor-subjects. Marshall conceded that equality of status does not necessarily imply equality of power. Because of this, social rights were conceived of as capacities for participation in struggle, and their fulfilment is essentially the outcome of social struggle.[7] This is why social rights are not defended primarily in courts but fundamentally in the political sphere, in civil society, in political parties, the legislature, in unions, neighbourhoods, streets, and all the democratic spaces where the forces that brake or detour the possibilities of expanding citizenship can be derailed.

The social effort necessary to expand citizenship with a substantive impact on reaching the historically elusive goal of greater social equality demands an overarching commitment to the expansion and strengthening of democracy. However laudable it may be to have a personal commitment to such goals, it is not from a non-governmental organization (NGO), a church, a neighbourhood organization, a union, or from any other isolated instance alone that changes of such dimensions can be obtained. Such initiatives, however valuable and altruistic, and even though they may give meaning to individual lives, do not have the potential nor the possibility of changing prevailing relations of power. That power which was referred to by Marshall is played out in the democratic sphere, in its expansion towards governing the market, in the democratization of the economy and of all decisions related to the movements of the great macro-economic protagonists (decisions to invest and to become indebted), and regarding the understanding and dissemination of the social and economic information necessary so that citizens can analyse, debate and participate in the definition of the overall direction of social and economic development. Instruments of democracy include public participation in electoral processes and political parties, in legislative debates and processes and in the mass media, struggles for public control of those who hold public office, for an independent judiciary, etc. It is these which have the potential of turning the corner in the process of expanding citizenship and of ensuring advancement towards that objective. All of this implies a healthy politicization of all resources, including those which are technical and scientific in character, which are conducive to maximizing the process of critical public discussion in order to broaden the spaces for citizen participation and activating the overall process of the expansion of citizenship.

In summary, the social policy necessary in order to guarantee the enjoyment of social rights, which implies belonging to a society committed to advance towards equality, implies power, and thus the need to construct power democratically as an instrument of struggle and fulfilment. For this simple reason social policy is politics and not merely the administration of social sectors.

Democratic Construction

If we situate democracy as the political domain where the fate of the social policy that could enable the expansion of citizenship is determined, what kind of democracy are we then talking about? Democracy is not only a system of government, but fundamentally a kind of society where a set of reciprocal relationships prevail among its constituents. I should pause here to clarify, if only briefly, what I am talking about, since this is crucial to my arguments about the relationship between capitalism and democracy. Here for reasons of simplification I follow the inspiring insights of C.B. MacPherson (MacPherson 1973, 1977),[8] who posited two different assumptions upon which democracy should be founded – what kind of human being the system is intended to serve and what ethical theory of validation it follows – and who suggests that there are four different models of democracy.

The first model is that of Protective Democracy, whose principal concern, as its name indicates, is to protect the governed from the oppressions of authority. The underlying theory is that of utilitarianism which considers the 'greatest happiness of the greatest number' to be the only valid rationale for legitimating governance, and which is understood to mean maximizing the amount of pleasure an individual can enjoy once pain is subtracted. Happiness is then the individual accumulation of material goods and money the best measure of pleasure and pain. The happiness of a society is the aggregated happiness of its individual members, and wealth can thus be disaggregated in terms of the respective happiness quotas of its members. Human beings are maximizers of pleasure, who obtain it by accumulating wealth, but in order to achieve it need power in order to dominate others. Society is then a collection of individuals incessantly seeking power over others in order to fulfil their individual needs. In this context, a framework of civil and criminal laws is necessary so that society does not disintegrate, and their goal too must be to produce the greatest happiness for the greatest number.

MacPherson identified this model as the founding model of western democracy, and considered Jeremy Bentham and James Mill to be its principal exponents. Its democratic assumptions flow from the premise of 'one man one vote', which was only firmly established as a concession to the emerging working class when it was understood by its architects not to represent any threat to private property. This model, which emerged at the beginning of the nineteenth century with the onset of the industrial revolution, indulges in no enthusiasm about the idea of democracy in itself nor regarding its transformative moral potential. Democracy is merely a requirement in order to govern individuals whom it assumes to be the insatiable pursuers of individual benefit. Human beings are potentially infinite individualized consumers and their basic motivation is to maximize their pleasure and their possession of all the material goods useful for expanding their wealth. Society is a mere aggregation of individuals, and government a functional requirement to protect individuals, especially from government itself. This is the crude summary description of a basic model of democracy, which corresponds to early industrial capitalism and its idea of individual people cut to the measure of a market-centred society. It is not surprising, therefore, to encounter its contemporary equivalents in conceptions of governability as the adaptation of democracy to the logic of the market.

An attempt to overcome the initial model was attempted by John Stuart Mill and his humanist followers in the twentieth century, and takes concrete form in the concept of a Developmental Democracy that sees the system of democratic governance as a medium for individual self-development. Mill, in distinction from the initial model, conceived of democracy as rooted in morality contributing to the development of humanity in order to build a society of 'free and equal' persons that has not yet been achieved. This development is understood to be the enlarged outcome sum and complement of the self-development of all the persons of a particular society, as reflected in the progress of the community in intelligence and virtue, as well as in efficiency and a practical sense of life. Human beings are capable of developing their capabilities and competencies. They are not just high-living consumers but also architects of themselves, capable of developing and enjoying the fruit of their talents. That government is good which expands the domain for the development of competencies among its people and which opens up their spectrum of potential individual development.

Both Mill and his followers saw no incompatibility between inequalities in the distribution of power and wealth resultant from capitalist production relations and the kind of equality demanded by the functioning of democracy itself. They considered democracy ingenuously capable of being overcome by invocations to morality, or by the development of higher levels of knowledge and social communication. With respect to voting, there was a step backward in Mill's reasoning, since he considered it naive to assume that the 'common man' could be capable of transcending the horizons of his own interests, seeing the interests of others and that of the future of society and of humanity as a whole, and so he considered it to be false that 'one man could equal one vote'. But since the idea of universal suffrage was essential for the development of human capabilities through political participation, Mill got himself out of this trap by affirming that all should have the vote, but some should have more votes, with the result that the inequalities flowing from capitalist relations of production would then be reproduced by inequalities in democratic practice.

MacPherson and later followers of Mill such as E. Barker, R.M. MacIver and John Dewey accepted universal suffrage and generally resolved the problem of the inequality in social relations inherent in capitalist society and their relationship to democracy by depoliticizing the issue. They had hopes that in the search for democratic consensus, class conflicts would evaporate, either because they would be eclipsed by the emergence of pluralistic social groups (e.g., the disabled, women, immigrants, etc) or because they would be reduced by welfare-state policies, and democracy could thus be rendered compatible with a market society. They thought, in sum, that distributive matters were the subject of constant adjustment, as reflections of the extent to which conceptions about justice evolved, and as dominant interpretations of what is meant by liberty and equality expanded continuously.

In MacPherson's view these authors had an implicit image of a democracy that functioned like a market, and as a system in which interests compete with each other and which adjusts itself in semi-automatic fashion. They did not make the analogy with the market explicitly, because to do so would have been too materialist. It is for this reason that this model was finally transcended by that of Equilibrium Democracy, where the democracy–market analogy is explicitly employed.

The Equilibrium Democracy model is the prevailing contemporary version, also described by MacPherson as the balanced pluralistic-élitist variant. It is pluralistic because it assumes that a society with a modern democratic system incorporates a pluralistic system of social relations, that is, a society in which individuals pursuing their own interests push in different directions with constant changes. It is élitist because it accords a great weight to the role of leadership groups which anoint candidates in the political process. It is, finally, as well a model of equilibrium, because it conceives of the political process as a market in equilibrium between the supply and demand dynamics of political goods.

The difference between the two latter models is that in the equilibrium model democracy is solely a mechanism to elect and give a specific mandate to a government, which does not imply the construction of a particular kind of society nor activities guided by moral intentions. At the same time, this mechanism consists of a competition between two or more groups of political leaders that designate themselves as candidates, organise themselves into political parties to be elected and govern until the next election. Democracy is thus itself simply a market mechanism wherein voters are the consumers, politicians are the entrepreneurs, and wherein a stable government is produced by means of the equilibrium between the supply and demand of political merchandise. The purpose of democracy is merely to register the preferences of consumers as they are, not as they should be. It is the model of an amoral democracy.

As MacPherson explains so effectively, this representation of what democracy is produces an equilibrium in inequality, because it does not alter in any way the relations of production characteristic of the capitalist system. Nor does it even satisfy the ideal of consumer sovereignty which it propounds, since in the case of the voters their demands do not in fact structure a 'truly' competitive market. In the case of the political market, the only 'effective' demand is that of those who have purchasing power and not the consumers as such. The dominant interests are those of the sectors with the money necessary to organise a political party or pressure group, finance an electoral campaign or buy promotional spots in the mass media. Similarly this formulation does not take into account the various different kinds of restrictions which frequently arise in the spaces of activity of consumer-citizens confronted by obstacles such as oligopolistic political parties, or 'packets of prefabricated desires' promoted by sophisticated political marketing techniques. At the same time, the social and economic inequality which this model leaves intact generates an equivalent inequality in the political realm that in turn produces a generalized disbelief among the majority of citizens in the possibility of real participation in, and control over, the political process. Thus, this modality of democracy functions on high doses of citizen apathy which end up feeding the growth of the 'party of indifference'. This model corresponds quite closely and ruthlessly to that present in many of the countries in the Latin American region today.

Lastly, we have according to MacPherson the model of Participatory Democracy, a model which is still in the process of being developed and which results from a combination between direct and representative democracy. Even though we can advance in some directions in terms of its conceptualization, this model is still a model to be built, for the simple reason that contemporary societies have only undertaken a partial reconciliation between capitalism and democracy (Esping-Andersen 1996). The model implies above all the passage to an active democracy which transcends a formalistic one. This means among other things, but beginning with the obvious, the following: improvement in the functioning of existing institutions and independence of the branches of government (especially the judiciary); the promotion of citizen participation in legislative organs and the development of new institutional forms of deliberation in civil society; the creation of new mechanisms of equilibrium and control over executive decisions; the democratic opening-up of political parties as well as mechanisms that guarantee their adequate financing and that of electoral campaigns; decentralization so as to foster possible efficient instances of direct democracy; and strict norms to control the probity, frugality and ethics of public officials.

But if one had to conceive of two basic but substantive characteristics necessary for the institution of a participatory democracy in the context of vastly unequal societies, the following could not be ignored: first, a stress on the function of the educational system in promoting the formation and development of a culture of citizenship consisting of rights and obligations, of an education to prepare successful competition but above all education in the values of cooperation, team work, and relations of reciprocity and complementarity; and second, the democratization of the economy, which is historically the more difficult challenge. In the first instance a key point is the education of youth in the sense of reconciling politics with public ethics, and not its identification, as now predominantly, with crime and corruption. The most important thing is, however, that participatory democracy implies a learning society, since education is the root of emancipation itself.

Everything in such a society should be for the purpose of educating, while recognizing that everyone educates because all can learn, and that learning and education are life-long activities. Participation and education in this sense are almost interchangeable terms: to participate is to educate and to learn, and, equally, to educate is to participate and to learn. In the second case, the objective is to achieve higher levels of equality, participation and social inclusion through democratic processes and to the fullest extent of its available vehicles. The idea is not the satanization of the market and of its mechanisms, but it is well-known, as has been argued throughout this chapter, that it is impossible to advance in the expansion of the process of citizenship without facing up to the political struggle necessary to make markets governable.

In any likely scenario the obstacles to be overcome are so big, and the interests of the market so powerful, that overcoming them will require political coalitions with a broad social base. Finally and no less importantly, in order to crystallise the building of coalitions and/or political poles on the part of the social forces committed to the advancement of citizenship and democracy, something no less complex will also be necessary: a legitimate vocation for power and for searching out and creatively broadening the field consisting of all the political options which are possible, guided by an attitude of tolerance and generosity at the moment of designing its electoral configuration.

Summary and Conclusion

In this chapter an attempt has been made to conceptualize social policy in terms of two rival models of citizenship and to demonstrate the possibility for alternatives to its present configurations that predominantly foster and reflect a dependent form of citizenship in Latin America. This dominant model of social policy must be transformed if we want to advance the process of the expansion of citizenship and the emancipation of people. Since the three central problems in Latin America are social inequality, the increasing vulnerability of majority sectors of the population and increasing social exclusion, social rights are the gateway in order to build citizenship. Varying models of democracy have been discussed leading to the conclusion that the participatory democracy model is the most useful, if our commitment is to the political struggle for social rights and the expansion of citizenship.

In order to expand citizenship in Latin America, we have to match our efforts for greater equality with those in the struggle towards the implementation of social rights, thereby constituting citizens who are subject-actors. Democracy, understood as a system of equality, is the privileged domain capable of enabling the expansion of citizenship, since historically democracy has been juxtaposed to the system of inequalities which are the direct result of capitalist production relations. The regional agenda calling for the building of more equitable societies is dependent on the need to deepen democracy and its institutional expressions. Equality cannot be produced automatically nor accidentally. Historically, no one has ever been given equality as a gift, nor has it ever been won in a lottery: social rights have to be fought for if they are to be obtained at all. In order to struggle effectively for those rights, it is necessary to build democratic power, and to build power is essentially to be political. This is why the new social policy paradigm which is needed in Latin America suggests a new model of development with room for everybody. It implies not just the social administration of an historical process but, more fundamentally, a much bigger game capable of reconciling the social with the political. In other words: social rights must be conceived as part of the process of building a participatory democracy, and a political practice capable of bringing this about.

In this era of total capitalism, isn't it unduly idealistic to propose the disciplining of the profit motive, or, even more ingenuously, to believe that it is possible to build a good capitalism? Here I have to echo Discepolo, a fine poet and composer of militantly sceptical tangos, in acknowledging that all of this is not about changing the world nor the supposed nature of all things. It is only about having the reasonable confidence that there is something we can do, that there are possible viable options and that in the same sense even freedom itself is a definite possibility. History is an open range of possibilities, and in the face of an hegemonic development model which is so exclusionary it is worth the effort to renounce historical quietism and the solitary game of being mere spectators and to at least attempt the challenge of building a society in which there is room for everybody.

Notes

1. Regarding rights and citizenship, reading of N. Bobbio (1990) is virtually obligatory.
2. An intelligent orthodox economic reading of social policy can be found in G. Esping-Andersen (1990) *The Three Worlds of Welfare Capitalism,* Polity Press, Cambridge, UK.
3. A similarly concise and clear work regarding the equality dimension in social and

economic policy can be found in G. Esping-Andersen (1994) *Changing Classes: Stratification and Mobility in Post-Industrial Societies*, Newbury Park, London, and Sage Publications, California.

4. Various different public opinion surveys undertaken by Latinobarometro, by public opinion research centres in various countries of the region and by the Estudio Graciela Romer y Asociados in Argentina have been taken into account here.

5. An especially interesting analysis regarding the nature of social rights and the relationship between capitalism and democracy can be found in the article by Francesco Paolo Vertova (1994).

6 Jack Barbalet (1988) argues that social rights depend on the availability of resources for the funding of social services. In this sense social rights are not really rights and are not justiciable as such. In this view social rights are merely 'conditional opportunities'.

7. Zincone (1992).

8. All of the citations in this section refer to two books by MacPherson included in the bibliography. A complementary discussion regarding MacPherson's vision can be found in Held (1987).

References

Arendt, Hannah (1958) *The Human Condition*, The University of Chicago Press, Chicago.

Barbalet, J.M. (1988) *Citizenship: Rights, Struggle and Class Inequality*, Open University Press, Milton Keynes, UK.

Berlin, Isaiah (1969) *Four Essays on Liberty*, Oxford University Press, Oxford, New York.

Bobbio, N. (1990) *L'età dei Diritti*, Einaudi, Turin.

Bustelo, Eduardo S. (1990) 'Mucho, Poquito y Nada: Crisis y Alternativas de Política Social en los 90', in E.S. Bustelo and A.E. Isuani, *Mucho Poquito o Nada*, UNICEF, Buenos Aires.

Bustelo, E. and A. Minujin (1997) 'La Política Social Esquiva', *Espacios, Revista Centroamericana de Cultura Política*, July/December, No. 8, San José, Costa Rica.

Demo, Pedro (1995) *Cidadania Tutelada e Cidadania Assistida*, Editora Autores Associados, Campinhas, Sao Pablo, Brasil.

Esping-Andersen, G. (1996) 'After the Golden Age? Welfare State Dilemmas in a Global Economy', in G. Esping-Andersen (ed.) *Welfare States in Transition. National Adaptations to Global Economy*, Sage Publications, London.

Friedman, Milton (1962) *Capitalism and Freedom*, The University of Chicago Press, Chicago.

Hayek, Friedrich von (1944) *The Road to Serfdom*, The University of Chicago Press, Chicago.

Held, D. (1987) *Models of Democracy*, Polity Press, Cambridge, UK.

Heller, A. and F. Fehér (1992) *El Péndulo de la Modernidad*, Ediciones Península, Barcelona.

Hirschman, Albert O. (1986) *Interés Privado y Acción Pública*, Fondo de Cultura Económica, Mexico.

IDS Bulletin (1996) *Liberalization and the New Corruption*, Vol. 21, No. 2 (April),

University of Sussex, Brighton, UK.

MacPherson, C.B. (1973) *Democratic Theory, Essays in Retrieval*, Oxford University Press, Oxford.

MacPherson, C.B. (1977) *The Life and Times of Liberal Democracy*, Oxford University Press, Oxford.

Marshall, T.H. (1975) *Social Policy in the Twentieth Century*, Hutchinson, London.

Marshall, T.H. (1981) *The Right to Welfare and Other Essays*, Hutchinson, London.

Marshall, T.H. (1992) 'Citizenship and Social Class', in T.H. Marshall and T. Bottomore (eds) *Citizenship and Social Class*, Pluto Press, Chicago (originally published in 1950).

Olson, Mancur (1965) *The Logic of Collective Action: Public Goods and the Theory of the Groups*, Harvard University Press, Cambridge, USA.

Rorty, Richard (1992) 'Cantaremos Nuevas Canciones?', in Bosetti Giancarlo (Comp.) *Izquierda Punto Cero*, Paidos, Barcelona.

Rosenthal, Gert (1996) *Development Thinking and Policies in Latin America: the Way Ahead*, Development Thinking and Practice Conference, Washington DC.

Stewart, Frances (1996) *John Williamson and the Washington Consensus. Comments on John Williamson's Paper*, Development Thinking and Practice Conference, Washington DC.

Titmuss, R.M. (1958) 'The Social Division of Welfare', in R.M. Titmuss, *Essays on the Welfare State,* Allen and Unwin, London.

Titmuss, R.M. (1974) *Social Policy: An Introduction*, Allen and Unwin, London.

Varsavsky, Oscar (1971) *Proyectos Nacionales*, Ediciones Periferia, Buenos Aires.

Veca, Salvatore (1996) 'La Igual Dignidad', in *Izquierda Punto Cero,* Bosetti Giancarlo, Paidos, Barcelona.

Vertova, Francesco Paolo (1994) 'Cittadinanza Liberale, Identitá Collecttive, Diritti Sociali', in D. Zolo (ed.) *La Cittadinanza: Appartenenza, Identitá, Diritti*, Laterza, Rome.

Williamsom, J. (1996) *The Washington Consensus Revisited*, Development Thinking and Practice Conference, Washington DC.

Zincone, G. (1992) *Da Sudditi a Cittadini*, Il Mulino, Bologna.

2
Human Rights
A New Paradigm

PATRICIA HELENA MASSA ARZABE

The human rights discourse is quite new. The Universal Declaration of Human Rights has completed just over fifty years, a short time for changing cultures and law practices. Its most representative historical bases are the French and American revolutions as well as the Industrial Revolution. In general, one can say that the construction of civil and political rights was influenced by the former, while the issues of social and economic rights were influenced by the latter. Many difficulties for their full implementation remain. The impact of the 1948 Declaration in describing human rights, and its definite contribution to their protection and promotion, has not been sufficient to transform a culture that tolerates many forms of human rights violations. Although present in most Latin American state constitutions, the human rights rules remain highly rhetorical and conditioned to economic and political interests at both national and international levels.

Another point that indicates the difficulties for the full implementation of human rights relates to their indivisibility and interdependency. The pre-eminence given in recent decades to civil and political rights over social, economic and cultural ones is rooted in a liberal culture which holds the latter to be a consequence of the free exercise of the former. This dissociation of the two groups of rights legitimates a view of human rights which contributes to the maintenance of social exclusion and extreme poverty, as will be shown later. It also allows for the permanent violations of social rights, these being perceived as normal in our societies, with the victims of such violations barely aware of their status as victims.

The full exercise of human rights at both national and international levels depends not only on the existence of rules – the international and regional covenants and treaties and the states' constitutions and

29

regulations – but also, or mainly, on the legal and political culture that transforms these rules into action. The legal system, in so far as it is based on the liberal principles of autonomy, free will, universality and abstraction, does not allow special treatment for the extremely poor. The response of the legal and political system to social problems seems related to the leading social paradigm of the day. The extreme levels of inequality faced today around the world can be viewed either as mere externalities of the system, that is to say, as natural consequences of the social order, or as an important problem to be tackled by public and private institutions. Beyond this, but still linked to paradigm considerations, is the question of which conception of the effectiveness of human rights, formal or substantive, is aimed at. The same is true for the significance of human rights in the construction of citizenship and democracy.

Human Dignity and Democracy

The Universal Declaration of Human Rights affirms that the 'recognition of the inherent dignity and of the equal and inalienable rights of all members of the human family is the foundation of freedom, justice and peace in the world'. The International Covenant on Economic, Social and Cultural Rights recognises that 'in accordance with the Universal Declaration of Human Rights, the ideal of free human beings enjoying freedom from fear and want can only be achieved if conditions are created whereby everyone may enjoy his economic, social and cultural rights, as well as his civil and political rights.' According to these documents, a dignified existence implies the simultaneous enjoyment of freedom and of social, economic and cultural rights. The expression 'freedom from fear and want' indicates the way of understanding the specific difference between human rights and other legal norms. Human rights require not only formal access but also public and private efforts for their promotion and protection to turn access into reality. The human rights system spins on the concrete needs for the dignity of a person or of a people.

The human rights discourse (the legal norms, the guarantees, the speech of the human rights operators) introduces a new and different legal approach that sets the human being, the communities and peoples as the central point of the system. Concerns common to legal categories and relations such as seller/buyer, employer/employee and supplier/consumer are inadequate in the human rights system. Here, the main concerns relate to a different type of relation: gender, race, age, national or social origin, ethnic groups, economic status.

Human rights norms are intended to ensure every person the means for the full development of his/her personality and citizenship in the social system, and are necessary for productive interaction in a democratic society. These are the rights without which the person will not be able to exist completely nor have her/his dignity fully respected, because of unsatisfied needs or unavailable possibilities of self-development.

Such needs, and the shape of human dignity, are historically and spatially conditioned. Human rights must not be considered natural rights inherent in the human being regardless of social structure. They result from social struggles between interests and between groups. Individual and social needs change over time, as do the rights that ensure the possibility of *being* human with dignity. The human rights system evolves, adding new rights that formerly were not considered necessary for the correct development of each one's personality in society.

The key words in understanding the extension and the intention of human rights rules is human dignity, whose meaning does not remain restricted to the abstract sense. Its basis must be concrete. As human dignity is related to the conditions necessary for a social and participatory life for each person in both private and public spheres, it follows that the enforcement of the human rights rules shall not simply be formally enforced, as regarding an abstract person, who is simply non-existent, but fully enforced, as regarding concrete persons.

This perspective creates the conditions for individual and social autonomy, as long as it permits the inclusion of all members of society in the effective access and exercise of human rights. As a consequence, the possibility arises for the creative participation of all in democracy. Democracy itself can only be improved when at least a greater part of the members of a society is able to contribute actively to the improvement of the social system. Democracy with the participation of a few has another name. The effectiveness of democracy – regardless of its extent or form, whether it is representative or participative – is in fact bound to the material fulfilment of human rights. The necessary participation is, however, not only in the individual aspect but also in the collective. The participation of non-governmental organizations, minorities and indigenous communities must, therefore, be strengthened to face the challenges of our society and to strive for the fulfilment of human rights. The signification of individual and social autonomy, of freedom and of the search for forms of collective freedom, corresponds to the democratic, emancipatory and revolutionary project, as Castoriadis (1997) noted.

The range of human rights principles and rules is far beyond ensuring survival. The right to life is not only, but necessarily, the right to be alive. It must be related to the right to worthy living, to the quality of life – not to be confounded with material conditions – which includes, for example, the right to work, the right to education, the right to health, the right to culture. Take into consideration, for example, a poor person, who suffers an illness or has a suffering relative, that has difficulties in accessing treatment, or one who is unemployed and is not certain of having food for the family the following day or week. How can he or she exercise civil rights? How many who have had no access to education beyond primary level can effectively exercise freedom of opinion or freedom of speech?

According to this logic, the human rights system is not hierarchically structured, with the prevalence of civil and political rights over social, economic and cultural ones or the prevalence of these latter over the former. The conception of generations of rights has led many to see human rights as succeeding or substituting for other rights or, the other way round, to insist on civil and political rights as more fundamental than those which historically came afterwards. Cançado Trindade (1996) points out that it is not a question of a succession of rights but the expansion, cumulation and strengthening of established rights, revealing the complementary nature of all human rights. He asserts that 'against the temptations of the powerful to fragment human rights into categories, postponing under several pretexts the fulfilment of some of these (e.g., social and economic rights) for an indefinite tomorrow, Human Rights Law rebels, and states the fundamental unity of conception, the indivisibility and the justiciability of all human rights (p. 20). This indivisibility, which bears out the idea of an essential complementary and dynamic interaction between the rights, leads to the conclusion that the right to liberty vanishes when the right to equality is not ensured and, in its turn, that the right to equality vanishes when freedom is not assured. Flávia Piovesan argues, along the same lines, that civil and political rights are reduced to formal categories without the effective realization of economic, social and cultural rights, and that without the fulfilment of civil and political rights, economic, social and cultural rights will have no real significance. There is no way to think of liberty divorced from social justice (Piovesan 1996: 160–61).

Taking the indivisibility and the reciprocal complementarity of all human rights as a starting point, claiming that social, economic and cultural rights must come together with, and not after, civil and political rights, and arguing that effective democracy depends on effective human rights, the importance of the state in treating the causes of poverty and in ensuring the effectiveness of human rights norms arises.

This approach recalls the consideration of the social means of production and reproduction and the capitalist view of the market. The capitalist rationality changes the relationship between freedom and equality. The unbalance of this relation, with pre-eminence of freedom over equality, is directly linked to the present levels of extreme poverty.

Market, Poverty and State

Inequality is central to capitalism's functioning. The state contributes to this process by enacting the necessary laws for the circulation of money, while the contract, the autonomy of the will and the property institution are its foremost pillars. Globalization affects this process and increases inequality in the means of production, especially labour. The revision of social rights seen in some countries, often those under supervision of the International Monetary Fund, are weakening the human rights framework. The loss of work opportunities owing to technology cannot be repaired by cheaper workers. Workers who cost less in the market system are citizens with lesser access to social rights and, consequently, to all human rights. Policies undertaken by the state to promote more employment by strengthening the market create better conditions for the market system, i.e., industries and service sectors, excluding agriculture and agribusiness in peripheral countries, but often worsen the conditions for workers and potential workers, that is, for the major part of the population.

Jürgen Habermas clearly puts public policies against unemployment and for better welfare in the range of payment for social costs of the market system. He shows how the state is of crucial importance to the maintenance and reproduction of the market and the capitalist structure, pointing out that the state apparatus regulates the overall economic cycle by means of global planning and improving the conditions for the utilization of capital. This global planning, Habermas says, manipulates the marginal conditions of decisions made by private enterprises in order to correct the market mechanism by neutralizing dysfunctional side-effects. The state, however, supplants the market mechanism wherever the government creates and improves conditions for utilizing excess accumulated capital. It does so by

- 'strengthening the competitive capacity of the nation', by organizing supra-/international economic blocks, by an imperialistic safeguarding of international stratification;

- by unproductive government consumption (armament and space-travel industry);

- by the politically structured guidance of capital in sectors neglected by an autonomous market;

- by improving the material infrastructure (transportation, education and health, vocation centres, urban and regional planning, housing etc);

- by improving the immaterial infrastructure (promotion of scientific research, capital expenditure and development, intermediary of patents etc);

- by increasing the productivity of human labour (universal education, vocational schooling, programmes of training and re-education etc);

- by paying for the social costs and real consequences of private production (unemployment, welfare, ecological damage) (Habermas 1984: 137).

This implies that market systems do have social costs, and a necessary question is how much *laissez faire* in these globalization days is worth deep inequality. Another question is: shall the free function of the market, with the state support, be a supreme value even when extreme poverty turns into a rule for living in many countries? The utilitarian perspective announces that more consumers are better than a few and in order to have more consumers, more life quality, education, health and wealth are necessary. So, even for the sake of the reproduction of the market system, state intervention becomes a necessity.

Habermas' conception of the state's functions is probably true regarding the quality of state promotion of welfare. The promotion of scientific research, for instance, is often tuned to market possibilities. Education, which is of the utmost importance for democracy, may be seen as necessary to prepare people for the market. But education is also as essential to the exercise of some human rights, and the fight for them, as are political rights (e.g., participation in the public sphere) and civil rights (e.g., freedom of speech). Education also needs to be offered in a critical perspective, that is, in a way that allows people to think and act *critically* and *creatively* in their milieu. The entitlement to civil and social rights is an important step on the human rights road, but not enough if one is deprived of the conditions for sound and active participation in society.

The presence of the state in economic processes is justified in the difference between market rationality and the premises of quality of life linked to the conditions for development of the human personality on the one side, and the need for adjustments in the deficiencies and dysfunctions of the market on the other (Massa 1995: 4). The state must intervene to correct the side-effects of the market system in the society, this being essential for the market's continuation. Alongside the economic order, however, the state must be present in the social order for the promotion of social welfare, for the control of social conflict as well as the collection of taxes to fulfil its aims. The recognised rights must reach each person, whatever policy may be necessary for their full effectiveness, and each person must have access to the conditions to build his/her full citizenship and participation in democratic decision-making. The dilemma is that the market system, in its present form, is not the way to eliminate extreme poverty because it is also a main promoter of inequality and poverty.

Historically, formal equality in law was designed to confront the privileges of the nobility and clergy, to justify the access to their rights of the bourgeoisie. This was a necessary principle for the security and certainty before the state in trade relations. However, formal equality also brings about several deeply unfair situations when the formally equal are materially unequal. Formal equality excludes solidarity. The space left for solidarity is likely to remain in the field of pity.

Paradigm of Continuous Economic Growth versus Paradigm of Human Dignity

A capitalist system which aims at more and more profit above all other interests is centred in what can be called the paradigm of continuous economic growth. Thomas Kuhn (1996) defined the paradigm as a criterion for the choice of problems, which can be considered to have possible solutions. The choice of problems under a given paradigm leads to the choice of their respective solutions. The prevalence of the paradigm of continuous economic growth considers poverty as a natural consequence of economic activity, as an externality. Thus, poverty is not considered an important problem of the system. It does not merit efforts for its solution. Within this concept, people are poor, or become poor, due to their incapacity for dealing with the capitalist moral (e.g. absence of ambition, of economic instinct). They are disabled for, not by, the system. Social Darwinism comes to the support of this thesis.

Despite its dominance, the paradigm of progress and economic growth is facing a process of crisis. The stress on economic growth has not brought a better quality of life for many societies. Moreover, all technological advances that could solve the problem of famine and extreme poverty world-wide have not succeeded. The incapability of this paradigm to answer current problems is still more evident in the field of environmental damage caused by exploitation of natural resources. While the conclusion has been reached that without natural resources the market system will not survive, the concern for human beings and future generations is still lacking.

A framework for an alternative paradigm that holds the dignity of the person, individually and collectively, as the most important aspect of a society, can be found in the International Bill of Human Rights, in international and regional human rights treaties and covenants, and in several national human rights provisions. The human dignity paradigm grows through cultural and political acceptance and enforcement of the international human rights treaties and covenants as well as from the constitutional provisions relating to human rights. The main difficulty lies in the dominance of the economic structure over the political, ideological and legal ones. Although the economic growth paradigm does not have the same explicit legal support as the human rights do, the economic perspective is culturally and politically more deep-rooted and penetrating.

If the paradigm of human dignity is incorporated into the economic perspective, the protection and promotion of human dignity may arise as defining criteria for the identification of problems, thereby determining adequate solutions for the protection and promotion of human dignity and human rights, and moving away from solutions that lead to human degradation in the interests of profit. The dominance of a paradigm reveals the relevant or convenient circumstances and facts for a certain time and society. A change in paradigms is, therefore, difficult and requires efforts and vehement demands from all concerned groups.

Globalization and the Grievance of Extreme Poverty

The problem of extreme poverty seems even further away when the question of the so-called globalization problem is examined. As Zygmunt Bauman (1998: 38) states, 'the deepest meaning conveyed by the idea of globalization is that of the indeterminate, unruly and self-propelled character of world affairs: the absence of a centre, of a controlling desk, of a board of directors. It is a new world disorder with another name'. Globalization is reducing states' sovereignty and affecting states' ability in political self-determination.[1]

Sovereignty as a principle was becoming relative from the beginning of the twentieth century, but more so after the Second World War. The human rights system is consolidating and has been benefiting from this relativization, since human rights violations that were held, until the League of Nations and even until the coming into existence of the United Nations, to be internal matters of a sovereign country are now considered of international concern. On the other hand, the loss of sovereignty has, for economic reasons had some undesired effects. The difficulty of states in dealing with the reduction of sovereignty, due to economic blocks or to the intervention of international financial institutions such as the World Bank or the IMF in national economic and monetary policies is in many cases increasing extreme poverty. Other political problems such as corruption and civil war evidently contribute to this grim view. Even under these circumstances, it can be said that the absence of the state in providing social policies for the effectiveness of civil, political and social rights facilitates such deviations.

Between Exclusion and Inclusion

The exclusion of parts of society enlarges the levels of extreme poverty. People who were at the margin of the society now risk social exclusion. However, in the theories of the social contract, the state emerged to increase the possibility of life in society for all of its members. The actions of the state must achieve the totality. No space and no one is to remain outside, taking into consideration the ideal origin of the state. States, however, move towards answering to the most expressive societal groups, that is to say those with the economic power to influence the structure and organization of the society, thus creating a structure which does not benefit the poorest sectors of the population. Policies of aid are not policies of inclusion, because they do not bring the whole set of human rights to these groups, only parts of it.

If this is so, and if there is consensus that extreme poverty is unbearable, then the paradigm of economic growth needs to be rethought. What is it for? What or whom does it serve? How does it relate to the paradigm of human dignity? How can policies of diginified inclusion be possible? And what does it take to implement human rights principles in order to fulfil the demands of the paradigm of human dignity?

Legal principles are, on the whole, the central part of law, working as the key for the interpretation of rules and the whole legal system. This being so, human rights principles, which concern the fundamental values of the human being, stand as the guideline to the interpretation of all other principles and rules. A human rights-directed hermeneutics would bring to the law and to the judiciary an important means for the reduction of social inequalities. The bridge between the legal texts and the reality of deep inequalities cannot be impartial under the premises of formal freedom (freedom of contract and autonomy of will) but must be impartial under the premises of material equality and freedom. The commitment to the world of facts expressed through the human rights/human dignity hermeneutics can lead to the effectiveness of the principle of human dignity which binds together liberty, equality and solidarity. The principle of solidarity is the necessary mediator between liberty and equality for it is its absence that creates the false idea of their contradiction. This perspective can be exercised in private or public law, in micro or macro questions.[2] The judiciary can make the right to access to justice formally or substantially effective. This choice depends more on the other parties than on the judiciary itself, which is conservative by nature, with honourable exceptions. Non-governmental organizations have to play their important role. Organized demands for the effectiveness of human rights cannot be undertaken individually.

If the internalization of human rights into cultural patterns isn't a question to be solved in a few years – the 50 years of the Universal Declaration of Human Rights haven't changed such patterns drastically enough – compliance with human rights laws by the judiciary can be obtained in lesser time. Judges are also immersed in the social culture of their societies and the solution to conflicts between human rights and rights as property, labour questions, gender and race questions, can be conducted under formal equality as well as under material (substantial) equality. Therefore, it ought to be the duty of engaged lawyers and NGOs to stress national and international human rights provisions in courts and to form a legal culture that makes these instruments a means of reducing social inequalities and the denial of rights.

Notes

1. For a brief account of the tendencies in law and state structure brought about by recent transformations of capitalism, see José Eduardo Faria (1997) 'Para onde vai o direito?' *O Estado de São Paulo*, 15 August, p. A2.
2. The *Sem-Terra* Movement for land distribution in Brazil can be seen, in an 'impartial' perspective, as illegal, both in criminal and in civil law. But the illicit character can be relieved considering the legitimate demands supported by the

1966 human rights covenants. NGOs can also take to the judiciary demands for social policies (education, health, work conditions), for the protection of collective rights such as indigenous rights and *quilombos'* rights (*quilombos* are the remaining communities of escaped slaves, all having more than a century of existence far from the cities and the rest of society).

References

Bauman, Zygmunt (1998) 'On glocalization: or globalization for some, localization for others', *Thesis Eleven*, No. 54, Sage Publications, London.

Cançado Trindade, Antônio Augusto (1996) 'Presentation', in Flávia Piovesan, *Direitos Humanos e o Direito Constitucional Internacional*, Max Limonad, São Paulo.

Castoriadis, Cornelius (1997) 'The crisis of the identification process', *Thesis Eleven*, No. 49, May, Sage Publications, London.

Habermas, Jürgen (1984) 'What does a legitimation crisis mean today? Legitimation problems in late capitalism', in William Connoly (ed.) *Legitimacy and the State*, New York University Press, New York.

Massa, Patricia Helena (1995) 'Algumas Observações sobre Meio Ambiente e Mercado', Masters Dissertation, Universidade de São Paulo, São Paulo, unpublished.

Kuhn, Thomas (1996) *The Structure of Scientific Revolutions*, 3rd ed., University of Chicago Press, Chicago.

Piovesan, Flávia (1996) *Direitos Humanos e o Direito Constitucional Internacional*, Max Limonad, São Paulo.

3

Natural History and Social History

Limits and Urgent Priorities which Condition the Exercise of Human Rights

JUAN ANTONIO BLANCO

The process which has brought about what we understand to be modern civilization from the perspective of social history has violently undermined the critical equilibrium of natural history. It may be that the latter may now seek a readjustment in search of a new kind of equilibrium, which could result in exclusion of the conditions necessary for the continued existence of the human species.

The fundamental problem lies in the political, social and economic institutional frameworks within which the development and use of our technologies evolve. The environmental crisis which surrounds us is indissolubly linked to patterns of social exclusion, to such a degree that the environmentalist cause and that in defence of human rights are but two faces of the same coin. One battle cannot be won if the other is lost. In order to reconcile the current bifurcation between natural and social history, a holistic vision of environmental problems is necessary which connects them to the current challenges confronting us in terms of human rights across all of their civil, political, economic, social and cultural dimensions.

Not an Era of Transformations, but a Transformation of Eras

The reign of instrumental reason which emerged during the sixteenth and seventeenth centuries and brought industrial civilization to the world is today in crisis. We are beginning to experience the transition to a new era whose central challenge is the uncertainty that it poses regarding the possibility of continuing survival for our species. For hundreds of thousands of years our processes of genetic evolution contributed to our ability to adapt ourselves successfully to the challenges confronted by our species as part of natural history, and today we experience a new existential cross-roads. The natural history of our planet, of its ecosystems and of the species which inhabit it is being violently destabilized by processes which have become dominant in the realm of our social history. Human society has achieved technological powers comparable only to those traditionally attributed to God; today we have the ability to create new forms of life or destroy all those which currently exist.

But the new technological civilization which has emerged has not been preceded by a new social culture and ethics capable of ensuring the full realization of the potential which it contains and at the same time of protecting us from the dangers which are inherent in it. The Bible, understood as a book of wisdom independently of religious beliefs, alerts us in this respect: 'No one puts new wine into old wineskins; if he does, the new wine will burst the skins and it will be spilled, and the skins will be destroyed. New wine must be put into fresh wineskins.' We persist, nonetheless, in pouring our new technological reality into old institutional vessels no longer able to contain it. In this way, to put it as Hegel did, the rational becomes irrational. The century we have just left behind us was witness, on innumerable occasions, to the barbarous application, in both social and environmental terms, of the technological progress we had achieved.

Humanity remains caged in an institutional architecture incapable of responding effectively to the challenges of a reality which has been fundamentally transformed. But above all we are trapped in our modern mindset, civilizational axioms and cultural myths. Those who assumed from the perspective of the traditional lexicon of the modern left that the problem consisted only of vanquishing the classes whose interests prevail in the current planetary status quo by now must have realised that the challenge was much more complex. The issue was not really about seizing state power in order to mend the world as the slogans assumed.

At the beginning of this new century and millennium there is not a single political tendency, or ideological programme, radical or conservative, from right or left, which has not been tested in the exercise of power somewhere in the world, but nonetheless nothing proceeds as had been expected anywhere. The issue was not then to seize existing structures of power in order to exercise it with the same axioms employed by the societies which it had been the intention to transcend, but instead to construct a new kind of power with a different character and meaning. After confronting the limits and failures of the political revolutions of the twentieth century we should be able to perceive clearly that the most urgent revolution needed is in our thought processes. As Einstein puts it, everything has changed, except our ways of thinking. This continues to be the drama in our process of epochal transition.

The Spanish thinker Ortega y Gasset, usually considered to be conservative, reminded us that the duty of philosophy is to identify the radical problems of its epoch and to define the radical solutions necessary in order to confront them. The radical issue of our time is the prevailing tension between natural and social history. If our societies continue to be organized during the next 50 years on the basis of the same logic and assumptions which have prevailed over the last 200 years, it will no longer be possible to reverse the critical damage wrought to the ecosystem which sustains the living conditions of our species. If we persist in this way beyond the critical point that lies before us presently we may well have to face the inevitability of the end of our social history. The planet and its ecosystems will seek a new point of equilibrium and will regulate themselves in such a way as to exclude our species, which occasions them so many inconveniences.

This is not the end of history conceived of by Francis Fukuyama, but there is a corollary to his argument which is operational here. If the current global status quo is assumed to be the one best organizational mode for the world community, we will then blindly accelerate in the self-destructive direction in which we are now headed. In the absence of a new culture and ethic of responsibility in political, economic and social terms, it will not be possible to fashion a technological civilization capable of acting in an environmentally responsible manner.

The environmental problems which we confront, and upon whose resolution the survival of our species depends, have no technological solution. Only a radical reorganization of our societies and a profound revision of our cultural values and our institutional functioning will be able to re-instil an authentic sense of progress to our technological advance. In the past, genetic transformations were necessary in order to adapt ourselves successfully to changes in the environment. Today, only a radical process of cultural transformation is capable of guaranteeing our survival throughout the next millennium. 'More of the same' can only lead us towards new totalitarianisms, social conflicts, famines, massive uncontrolled migrations, ecological disasters, the prevalence of violence and a spiritual vacuum, accelerating the definitive rupture of our process of social history from that of natural history. There are old formulas, from an also-aged left, that propose to change the present by promoting 'more of the same'. But life has transcended the logics that once seemed effective to defend the various different interests at war with each other. To wed ourselves blindly to these would be the equivalent of acting like the steward who time and time again rearranged the fallen chairs on board the Titanic as the ship was sinking.

In the struggle for human rights we cannot restrict ourselves to softening the hard edges of the tensions dominant in the world today, but must instead promote the conceptualization and implementation of new models of social organization. We urgently need a new civilizational and cultural paradigm that is politically participatory, economically inclusive, culturally pluralist, environmentally responsible, ethically rooted in notions of solidarity and equitable in terms of assuring equal access to opportunities for social advancement. The fundamental challenge of our times is to define and bring about the prevalence of this new paradigm. This is the only guarantee we have that we will be able to find an holistic and simultaneous solution to the needs we must confront in terms of both the environment and human rights. If we do not secure the integral, indivisible and interdependent observance of civil, political, economic, social and cultural rights, our species is not likely to survive long enough to witness the end of the new millennium of natural history.

Ethics and Society

Socialism has demonstrated itself to be the false promise of the twentieth century, but late twentieth century capitalism does not even bother to make any promises. In the wake of the collapse of the one-party bureaucratic totalitarianisms, we are witnessing the emergence of a new market-based totalitarianism which puts itself forward as the only possible school of thought.

Jesus expelled the moneychangers from the temple because they had dared to occupy the sacred spiritual space set aside for prayer. He did not expel them from Jerusalem, where he apparently thought that for better or worse they performed a useful social function, but rather from the temple, a space that he apparently thought needed protection and its due autonomy and significance in the face of the denaturalization of its function when employed for the purpose of mercantile transactions. During the present century the market has invaded the temples of politics, information, culture and many others from which it must retreat in order to occupy adequately its natural economic space, which must at the same time be shared democratically with other diverse actors. Market totalitarianism can be as pernicious and destructive as that of a political bureaucracy. The human rights of contemporary and future generations cannot be submitted to the logic of maximizing profits which today prevails over all other logics, including especially those of social equity and environmental responsibility. Vast expanses of social life must be set free from the singularly dominant constraints of the profit motive and democratized if we aspire to achieve the plenary and indivisible exercise of human rights in their most complete expression and the functioning of an environmentally sustainable economy.

The maximization of profits is the dominant philosophy of a human culture which has situated us at the very edge of an unprecedented social and environmental crisis on a planetary scale. The world we live in can no longer be, nor continue being the 'only possible world', and one which is thereby beyond the reach of any process of ethical judgement. The kind of market economy which prevails today is notably different from others that preceded it, and surely from future forms into which it could be restructured. Not every society with a market becomes a market society in which mercantile logic permeates and conditions the full range of human conduct and relations. The existence of the market and of the multiple modalities which it has assumed are historically contingent.

Markets have existed and co-existed under multiple forms throughout human history, which means that they can be moulded and reoriented in ways alternative to those which characterise its current configuration. Their structures and functions respond to human options assumed more or less consciously, which cannot escape from the ethical judgements which correspond to each of them and to their consequences. Economics does not study the immutable physical relations of the natural world, but rather the diverse ways of organizing production relations among human beings.

Market totalitarianism nonetheless proposes to degrade the humanistic essence of economics in order to reduce it to an apologetic vision, both uncritical and a-historical, of the dominant mode of production at this particular moment of social history. Economists, more than any other turn-of-century specialists, are subjected to a pedagogy which has the pretence of educating them into a unidimensional mode of thinking that defines as the sole mission of the profession the maximization of profit and not the improvement of the quality of life of our societies. We must begin by freeing our schools of economics from the ideological fundamentalism which is today hegemonic among them in its promotion of a new generation of technocrats. These new authentic

Talibans conceive of the market as a supreme deity which they are called upon to defend by brutally suppressing all unbelievers who do not worship it in the same way.

We must begin by redefining the way in which relations among civil society, the market (as a form of economic technology), and the government (as a form of political technology) are currently structured. Their current design invariably implies zero-sum exchanges in social relations. We have to redesign our societies along the lines of a logic of win-win. But this will demand the same kind of creativity, wisdom and audacity with which the bourgeoisie was able over a period of 200 years to imagine and construct a new civilization and culture, and which was able to demonstrate as well that feudalism was not the only nor best of all possible worlds.

The false dichotomy that some propose to impose upon us between the market and the state must be transcended so that there can be a redefinition of each of their functions and limits, as well as of their reciprocal connections. All of these must in turn be submitted to the democratic participatory control of the whole of civil society. What we must do now is urgently reflect about what kind of market, government and civil society can enable the successful transition to a new civilization and human culture within the framework of a new kind of state. It would be suicidal to assume that the current global organizational structure can remain unaltered, and that thereby new technologies will be able to handle the levels of both existing poverty and environmental destruction, which are inextricably linked to each other by means of the logic of maximizing profits. To assume that the current status quo will become eternal because it possesses the means to coopt or crush its opponents is not only ingenuous but dangerous. For the first time, given the critical point of tension which has been attained by the breach between natural and social history, the ethics of solidarity and of responsibility have ceased to be one option among many and have become a necessity for the survival of our species. The vision of the world which we urgently need in order to redesign contemporary global reality demands a humanistic ethic as a point of departure. The earth is one common vessel in which we all live, and vessels of this kind have no lifeboats.

In this time in which we live there is an invisible common thread which connects the most powerful with the most marginalized, which it is necessary to make visible and strengthen. The Uruguayan armed revolutionary movement known as the Tupamaros once said that 'either there will be a homeland for all or there won't be a homeland for anybody'. The critical point to which the current status quo has brought us in terms of natural history should help us understand that in global terms 'either there is a future for all or there won't be a future for anybody'. There cannot be winners and losers when we are battling on the deck of a gigantic ecological and social Titanic.

Humanistic ethics and bioethics provide us with the compass necessary to understand the current state of the relationship between natural and social history, and reorient our current direction in the universe. Nonetheless, at the beginning of the third millennium, the three greatest deficits borne by humanity are in terms of wisdom, imagination and hope.

Human Rights and the Environment

The definition of human rights which emerged with modernity was restricted to relations among members of our own species and was based on certain false premises. We now know that (i) human well-being cannot be found in nor based on the unlimited accumulation of material wealth; (ii) technology does not have an opportune and effective response for every challenge; (iii) nature has a limited capacity to provide us with resources and for the recycling of waste; (iv) civil and political human rights are indivisible from and interdependent with economic, social and cultural rights; and (v) social exclusion is inextricably linked to environmental deterioration.

We need to come closer at the beginning of this new millennium to the definition of a social criterion rooted in notions of solidarity which is at the same time environmentally sustainable, and which together would be capable of grounding our search for fulfilment as a species. The new technologies which are today at our disposal can be used for the purpose of ecological pillage and social domination or for the preservation of the environment and the promotion of human rights.

We should make a break once and for all with the assumptions and conventional logic which brought us to a world where one of every four mammal species is in danger of extinction, in which the human population increases at a rate of 3 per cent each year while the production of food increases at a rate of 1.3 per cent, and where less than 20 per cent of the population concentrates more than 80 per cent of all the world's acquired wealth.

The struggle in defence of the environment, and the cause of human rights, are today two faces of the same coin. It is not possible to win one if we lose the other. The time has come for the environmentalist movement and the human rights movements to coordinate their actions and strategies locally and on a global scale. Both movements have already demonstrated their ability to exert external influence over governments and multilateral forums. Now they must combine their strengths and acquire negotiating skills that could enable them to participate effectively and directly in the deliberations and negotiation processes of the UN system and other international forums.

It is before these forums that we must converge to reveal the critical nexus between natural history and social history; to insist that social exclusion and environmental degradation go hand in hand; to put a limit on the Talibans of the totalitarian market by submitting the logic of maximizing profit to the ethics of human rights and to demand that they incorporate themselves definitively to the monitoring and denunciation of the violations of the civil, political, economic, social and cultural rights of individuals, social groups and nations, amounting to the vast majority of human beings who inhabit the world today, and which are carried out throughout the world on a massive and brutal scale.

Ethics and Possible Futures

There is no reason for us to assume that our struggle can rely on the certainty of the eventual triumph of just causes which animated the determinist left in the past. The fact that we are living during a period of social transition to a new era, in which the only certain thing is uncertainty itself, does not relieve us, however, of the ethical obligation to distinguish good from evil, nor from the conviction that to struggle for a more responsible world characterized by greater solidarity than the world we now live in is, above all, an obligation for all those who wish to reaffirm their human condition.

To forge convictions from a standpoint of uncertainty may turn out to be more difficult than to do so from the basis of false certainties that a teleological sense of history once accustomed us to. The challenge is to bring together all the wisdom, imagination and hope needed in order to correct in a timely fashion the self-destructive direction of our social history. Today, more than ever, we must engage in politics on the basis of an ethical criterion which is responsible and rooted in solidarity. There is not one but many possible futures. We are called upon to distance ourselves from those that threaten our survival as a species and to struggle to bring into being those other, alternative, futures that today reside potentially in the historical crossroads that confronts us. Advocates and activists for human rights and for the environmentalist cause are often told to resign themselves to the understanding that no other future is possible, a view that would mean making the present eternal. At the dawn of the third millennium politics is therefore the art of the impossible.

PART II
The Vicious Circles
of Poverty

4

Poverty and Human Rights in the Light of the Philosophy and Contributions of Father Joseph Wresinski

MARCO AURELIO UGARTE OCHOA

One of the persistent concerns which have oriented my work as an anthropologist has been the effort to seek explanations and solutions for the prevailing economic, social and political inequities in my own country, Peru. My own origins in a poor rural family helped spur a great commitment to such issues, and strengthened my option of work and service on behalf of the poor of the southern Andean region of Peru. On this occasion I would like to share with you my experiences and reflections regarding the conceptualization and treatment of poverty issues which are the fruit of long years of work with poor families and also of my knowledge about the philosophy and actions of Father Joseph Wresinski.

During the 1960s, at the beginning of my professional career and relationship with the Andean communities of the Cusco region, my understanding was that poverty among rural families was the product of backwardness and of their inability to integrate themselves into the larger society. I assumed that poverty could be overcome through schemes that would enable the integration of such families, and it is for this reason that I collaborated with projects of applied anthropology in the rural community of Kuyo Chico, in the Písaq district, sponsored by Cornell University, the national ministries of Labour and Indigenous Affairs, and the Universidad Nacional de San Antonio Abad del Cusco. Our theoretical framework assumed that overcoming poverty required the implementation of development projects that could capitalize on the dormant capacities of these kinds of communities.

In order for such a process to be unleashed, we had to begin with those in the community who were most propitious for involvement, and could thereby ensure quick success for our efforts. Our emphasis was on the promotion of centres of development which could then serve as models for other, equally backward, communities so that in this way development could spread by means of contagion or influence. With time we came to realise that our rationale proceeded from ethnocentric assumptions which led us to differentiate between modern and traditional societies, that is on the one hand societies closed to change and innovation, and on the other, societies open to western conceptions of development, science and technology, understood as fundamental prerequisites of development itself. As an example I could cite how in Kuyo Chico our applied anthropology project promoted the construction of new stoves which were a metre high off the ground, assuming that this would benefit women in such rural communities. But the stoves were never used by these women because Andean peasant culture provides for ground-level cooking fires, which enable women to sit on the ground, gather the food to be cooked around them and tend the fire as well as converse with visitors, without having to get up or change position. Another factor weighing against acceptance of the new stoves is the traditional belief that fires at waist level or higher may directly impact the womb and cause sterility, a very negative consequence. Women's activities beyond cooking include tending gardens and domestic animals, and ground-level cooking fires protect their unsupervised children from being hurt in the way they might be if a pot located at a greater height were to be knocked over.

The failure of our efforts for such reasons helped us to understand that we could not denigrate the knowledge, culture and rationality of such communities. If we wanted to promote development, we had instead to build on such elements by respecting their culture, values and conceptions of life and of the world. Years later I came to understand the full significance of this recognition while working on research and development projects for the Aide à Toute Détresse (ATD)/Fourth World Movement. Such experiences also led me to realise that poor people have typically been studied as objectified others akin to natural phenomena alien to and outside of the framework of reality of social researchers and development workers. This is a grave error which not only distorts reality but also creates a sharp distancing effect from those who are supposedly to be benefited by our actions, which also creates serious resistance to our efforts on their part.

By the late 1970s and early 1980s, driven by my questioning of these initial experiences and by a Marxist conception of how to proceed, I undertook further work incorporating the assumption that all social phenomena have a reflexive quality which links together the researcher and the social phenomenon to be studied in a dialectical way. This in turn leads to a stress on the participatory nature of research. Within this framework the idea is that both the researcher and the researched must be transformed, and that the researcher should identify completely with those extremely exploited and poor peasants who were the objects of study, helping transform them into researchers of their own reality and making them more independent and more able to engage in struggle by seeking to resolve their own problems, in turn contributing to the transformation of the social structures responsible for their poverty. In this way abstract academic models that assumed that the creation of knowledge is the sole province of universities and researchers could be overcome.

These were the principles that continued to guide my work as an anthropologist until I met Father Joseph Wresinski in June 1987, when I was invited to participate in a seminar on Family, Extreme Poverty and Development organized by UNESCO and the ATD/Fourth World Movement. It was the life and work of this priest, a person of the Fourth World, that influenced me greatly and caused me to reformulate the perspective I had held until then about development and poverty. I discovered that in everything I had previously done I had neglected the most destitute among the poor, limiting my work only to one limited sector. This was due to my prejudiced assumptions about the poorest of the poor, whom I considered in effect to be people devastated by misery and incapable of transcending their own situation, still less capable of contributing to the development of the country.

In 1956, Father Joseph Wresinski arrived in Noisy-le-Grand, one of the poorest suburbs of Paris, where 252 families lived in conditions of extreme poverty. There he understood that if he wanted to do something to pull them out of such misery, he should not distribute clothing or food among them, or carry out any other kinds of charitable actions. Father Wresinski knew, because of his own experience, how denigrating it is for a person to receive alms, but above all he knew that what was most humiliating was for no one ever to ask poor people for their opinion, nor to recognise their values, their experiences, and much less to permit them to express their hopes. It was his awareness of these things which led him to trace out the path he was to follow: first, to do what he could so that these persons or families who appeared before the rest of society as people without an identity of their own, or as isolated cases, could appear as a people, with a recognisable name, that of the Fourth World, with commensurate rights and responsibilities to be recognized by all. Then he would demand of the rest of society and of international organizations that they accept the existence of the inhuman condition of extreme poverty and assume responsibility in the struggle to eradicate it.

In order to do so, they would have to constitute themselves as a movement, but as a movement born in the depths of the poorest families, a movement rising up from the bottom of the social ladder, a movement capable of testing the energies, courage and hopes of the families of the Fourth World, and capable of demonstrating that these families, despite their denigrating situation, are not lost or irreparable cases. It is because of these insights that Father Joseph Wresinski is indissolubly linked to his Fourth World people.

As a result of this encounter with the philosophy of the ATD/Fourth World Movement, I realized that successfully overcoming social problems depended on constant practical efforts alongside those of the poorest families. This led to a commitment to link my work to this perspective and to the decision by thirteen of us to found the Peruvian branch of the movement, which by now includes Fourth World families, volunteers, allies and friends, with whom we carry out grassroots projects in both urban and rural areas. These include street libraries and training workshops through which participating families can express and channel their life experiences and original thoughts. Together with these families we develop life histories which are testimonies of their experience from which we draw our lessons and where we find the guiding thread to continue with our efforts.

The attempt to eradicate extreme poverty and forge a more just and equitable society depends necessarily on developing a new awareness of misery, highlighting its human dimensions and overcoming reductionist emphases which conceive of poverty as a simple problem of material deprivation. Father Wresinski's work and philosophy enable us to understand that human dimension. The fundamental aspects of what we consider to be the necessary new understanding of extreme poverty are set out below.

The Human Dimension of Poverty

The magnitude of poverty in our societies demands a new conceptualization stressing its human dimensions, enabling a vision of the poor not as ciphers or statistical data but rather as human beings, with a story to tell and a dignity that must be respected. Life testimonies can assist us in exploring these dimensions which are ignored by so many. Dario, a youth from the Province of Cusco tells us:

> I live alone with my mother. I never knew my father. My mother works hard to support us and to send me to school. We live as caretakers at the construction site of a house, where there is no water or electrical services. In

school I always had a lot of problems, was held back several times, and labelled by the teachers as a 'bad student' because I rarely finished my homework and when I did complete my assignments, I did so the wrong way. I also had a lot of problems learning and doing schoolwork, because I don't have any books and no one who could lend them to me. My mother can't help me with that, because she doesn't know how to read or write, and works all day washing clothes.

A father, who had abandoned his wife and children, when asked about his behaviour, responded:

I love my family. Every day I left the house early to look for work and to bring back something to eat for my wife and my children, but I couldn't find anything. When night fell I had to go back home. I didn't know how my wife would manage to find something to cook, but I couldn't eat, the food stuck in my throat. I felt useless, and my presence just meant one more mouth to feed. I was a burden on them; this is what led me to go away.

David and Vilma, 8 and 10 years old, two orphan siblings, also have a story to be shared. Their mother died last year, leaving them alone. While she was alive they used to spend the night in a room in the Cuesta de la Almudena, and after she died they were kicked out of there. These children give us the following testimony:

They say my mother died of a strange illness. The room we used to stay in was just for sleeping, as soon as the sun rose my mother would wake us up and take us with her to work. Her work was peeling potatoes in a guest house, and her pay was leftover food from the day before. But one day she got sick and the neighbours took her away to the hospital.

David and Vilma always remember what their mother told them: 'Don't ever split up, stay together, and always love each other'. They continue: 'When we went to the hospital they told us my mother had died, we never saw her again'. Since then David and Vilma's home has been in the street.

These testimonies are evidence of how extreme poverty results from a lack of compassion by others, and how it is characterized by instability and by the efforts of the extremely poor themselves to resist their misery, all typical scenarios among the families of the Fourth World. It is for this reason that we should not look at the poor as mere ciphers or statistical artefacts. An emphasis on the human dimension should enable us to focus on poverty from the standpoint of the capacities demonstrated by those who live in poverty, transcending those approaches that reduce poverty to a matter of material deprivation. The latter approach generally leads to efforts tending towards charity or welfare dependency. A capacity-centred approach permits us to focus on the following key inquiries: (i) to what extent do we have the knowledge we need about the daily efforts engaged in by the poor to emerge from their misery, and about their constant struggles to transcend that condition; and (ii) how can we join together with them in defence of the concept of the indivisibility of human rights?

Gathering together the life testimonies and oral histories of families trapped in extreme poverty on a day-to-day and long-term basis permits us, through the verification of these experiences jointly with them, gradually to build, bit by bit, the history of the Fourth World. By returning this history to them in written form, the poorest of the poor cease to be invisible and recover their right, equal to that of any other citizen, to participate in the political, cultural, economic and social life of the community.

Poverty is not Destiny

Our stress on the human dimension of poverty demonstrates in turn that poverty is not a fatality nor is it an accident since, as Father Wresinski has pointed out, families in extreme poverty generally come from poor origins. It takes a long time to create an extremely poor population in any country, since it is not so easy to drag people down into the abyss voluntarily. Misery is generational in character, transmitted from parents to children, by means of shared conditions and experiences. In the words of Father Wresinski: 'If the Fourth World is transmissible from parents to children, it is because the world that surrounds them reproduces in each generation the same rejection and lack of understanding' (Wresinski 1987: 92).

This generational characteristic of extreme poverty is graphically evident in Sebastiana's testimony:

> Misery did not separate us, because my mother refused to hand us over to the landowner, who offered so many advantages in return. Our only protection was our work, first that of my grandparents in *haciendas* in the Puno region, then the work of my parents, which took us from Llave to Santa Rosa, from Taquile to the Tiquina Strait, from Yunguyo to Moya de Ayaviri, and from there to Cusco. It was there that my father worked on building the Huatanay River canal, helped build the regional hospital, worked in the railway station, and also as a bricklayer and journeyman. My mother sold food on the street, sold everything she could, was a labourer like me, my brothers, and now like my male children.

This generational aspect of poverty transforms its experience into a kind of 'vicious circle' from which it is difficult to extricate oneself. The following is testimony from a participant in the Seminar on Extreme

Poverty as a Denial of Human Rights at the United Nations Head-quarters in New York in October 1994:

> When you live in extreme poverty and lack education, it is not easy to find work. Without resources it is impossible to find decent housing to pay one's bills. Our family was left without electricity and even without water. It is hard for us to feed ourselves adequately. Under such conditions, my children find it difficult to complete their studies (quoted by Despouy 1996: 30).

Since misery is not predetermined, it has its explanation in the injustice of the prevailing economic, political and social systems which enable a situation of privilege and wealth for some, and of exclusion and poverty for the vast majority. In the case of Peru, this pattern of social inequality is expressed in the abysmal gaps which characterise the distribution of national income: according to the periodical *CUANTO* (Santiago de Chile, July–August 1995) the distribution in 1994 was as follows: 10 per cent of the households concentrate 31.3 per cent of all income, while the bottom 60 per cent, or more, obtain only 30.8 per cent of the total income.

Leandro Despouy's Final Report regarding *Human Rights and Extreme Poverty* notes that 'the term Fourth World was coined by Father Joseph Wresinski in order to give a positive social identity to all those people in the world living in extreme poverty' (Despouy 1996: 56). A representative of the Fourth World families of Cusco who participated in the Second Congress of Fourth World Families held in New York and Washington in October 1994 said upon his return:

> What I learned there I transmitted to my community, so that they would know that in other countries there is poverty too, and that there were people sleeping in the streets, alcoholics begging for money, people selling trinkets and singing in the metro. I also let them know that we, the poorest of the poor, can be found on all five continents, and that despite differences of race or language, we are one people, and that we have important things in common such as our stories, and our commitment to solidarity with each other which is being lost among the richer societies because of individualism.

New Paths to Bring us Closer to the Poor

A new conceptualization of poverty cannot be arrived at without taking into consideration what the most poor think, feel and want. To do this means transcending the already ingrained tendency to think of the poor as passive subjects, without initiative, incapable of thinking about and overcoming their situation, and still less so of contributing to the development of their country and of the international community.

In the already cited report, Despouy tells us:

> Those who suffer the most painful consequences of the problem of extreme poverty…dedicate virtually every hour of the day to the struggle to satisfy the basic needs of their families. It is indispensable to support the efforts of the poorest who will continue to struggle, as they always have, to satisfy their basic needs, by means of their own efforts. Without an understanding of this struggle, of this constant rejection of misery, it would not be possible to break with a fatalistic understanding of misery (Despouy 1996: 47).

This path was first walked by Father Joseph Wresinski and by his people of the Fourth World, who once again placed on the table the indivisibility and interdependence of human rights in the light of the experience of the most poor, affirming that misery is the negation of human rights and posing extreme poverty as the central problem of humanity at the dawn of a new millennium. To continue along this path is the challenge of our time. The highest-ranking cultural institutions have the historical responsibility of recognizing and accepting the experiences, thoughts, wisdom and knowledge of the families trapped in extreme poverty, not as a data bank but rather as the basis upon which to pursue the elimination of misery and to place human rights at the service of humanity.

Jean Diene, upon being received by the Pope in Rome as part of a delegation of Fourth World families, stated on 27 July 1989:

> Our first concern is our children, our youth and their future. Our children are deprived of their infancy. They have their heads and their hearts filled with our worries. We want our children to go to school. We want them to have real work, and that the doors of the future be opened to them. If not, tomorrow, like us, they won't be respected. We are not idle ourselves, but frequently no one recognises our efforts. We sacrifice everything we have for the future of our children. Others have to come to share with us the most beautiful, the best of their knowledge. They will have to go to the most distant corners of our neighbourhoods, so that the whole world can learn then in respect and friendship.

The Family and its Role as a Basis for Social Cohesion amid Poverty

Every human being needs the protection and security that a family can provide. But one of the greatest harms that misery can engender is the deterioration or destruction of the family: women abandoned, children living on the street, alcoholism, promiscuity and child abuse are among the many ills which tear apart families trapped in misery. But at the same time we cannot ignore that even amid misery the family fulfils a key role as a factor of cohesion and resistance. The testimonies we have gathered demonstrate the deep-seated need for the family which exists among the extremely poor. Martina, a mother who became ill with an affliction that was misdiagnosed as contagious tuberculosis, left her children in an orphanage as recommended by her doctor. Here she tells what happened when she went to pick them up.

> The people who worked in the orphanage did not want to give them back. They asked me why I wanted to take them away since they were ok, each of them had a bed, ate three times a day and the place where they were was good and safe. But I insisted, I refused to give up the hope of getting them back, and had to deal with a lot of paperwork to achieve this. I talked to the director of the orphanage and finally persuaded him. Finally now they've been restored to me and we live together in our room, many things are lacking but the most important thing is that we're together.

As Father Joseph Wresinski said, to place the necessary restored value on the family and to give it its due place in the fight to eradicate extreme poverty is basic:

> The family is the only refuge of the person when everything else fails, only there can you find someone to take you in, only there do you continue to be somebody. In the family you can find your identity. Your own, your children, your spouse, your companion … are for you, in such a situation, the last refuge of freedom (Wresinski 1996: 18).

Proposal for an Integral Definition of Poverty

In 1987, Father Wresinski proposed a definition of poverty and extreme poverty, later adopted by France's Economic and Social Council, which we believe provides the means to focus on this problem in an integral manner, linking it to the exercise of rights and responsibilities in a way also suggested in Despouy's report. Wresinski suggests that social vulnerability is the absence of one or more assured capacities which permit individuals and/or their families to carry out their basic responsibilities and enjoy their fundamental rights. The insecurity which results from such a condition leads frequently to extreme poverty and tends to prolong itself over time, becoming persistent and gravely compromising the ability to recover the exercise of these rights and responsibilities within the foreseeable future (Wresinski 1987). The value of this approach is that it was developed in conjunction with Fourth World families and permanent grassroots volunteers. It provides us with a theoretical framework appropriate for focusing in on the problem of poverty and extreme poverty, reflecting both the proximity and the difference between both conditions. It also establishes poverty and extreme poverty as human rights problems, problems related to rights to life, education, health care, housing, etc. At the same time, by stressing that extreme poverty is the final outcome of a series of vulnerabilities, Father Wresinski's approach demonstrates that the vindication of rights in a decontextualized way is not enough to enable the extremely poor to recover the full enjoyment of all of their rights. This definition takes us, therefore, to the terrain of the indivisibility and interdependence of all human rights.

This new conceptualization enables an ongoing search to find among those who are impoverished those who are the poorest, the most excluded. To search out the extremely poor is the expression of a commitment to eradicate extreme poverty. Misery cannot be limited somehow to certain countries, cities, towns or communities as poverty maps would have us believe. We must be conscious of the fact, as Father Joseph Wresinski stressed: 'Behind any poor community is another which is poorer. Behind a poverty-stricken street is another even worse, and behind a poor family we can almost always find another poorer' (Wresinski 1996).

Poverty as the Negation of Human Rights

All of the above leads us to call for the re-evaluation of research regarding poverty and extreme poverty from the perspective of the human rights–centred approach set out here. It has become a general practice in Latin America to reduce human rights to the terrain of political rights and civil liberties, ignoring the original objective of such rights which was to guarantee and defend human dignity in an integral way, as the Universal Declaration of Human Rights does by stressing their indivisibility and interdependence. In this way extreme poverty, which denigrates, excludes, mutilates and kills, has become the single greatest violator of human rights in the world today.

Human rights lose their meaning and their force if we separate them from each other. The life testimonies of the extremely poor demonstrate that we are subject to a chain of vulnerabilities from which there is no exit if they are not confronted in a holistic manner. To struggle for the human rights of all poor people, respected in the most integral way, is to undertake the most effective action to eradicate extreme poverty.

A fundamental step forward in the battle against extreme poverty and in its understanding as a matter of human rights was taken by Joseph Wresinski on 17 October 1987 when he spoke at the unveiling of a plaque in commemoration of the historical victims of extreme poverty in the Human Rights and Liberties Square of Paris, France:

> On that day the poorest people of the entire world demonstrated to other citizens that they were the first to reject extreme poverty. In this way they affirmed their conviction that poverty is not predestined, and proclaimed their solidarity with all those who struggle throughout the world to destroy it.... The plaque issues a call to all people to unite against misery.

This approach demonstrates that human rights are being violated wherever there are human beings condemned to live in misery. To unite to ensure their respect is a sacred duty.

Conclusions

The scale of poverty in the contemporary world challenges us to develop new research able to permit a more integral conception of poverty, overcoming general or reductionist approaches and highlighting its human dimension. This leads us to place it in the context of human rights, highlighting the fact that poverty implies not just levels of material deprivation but above all the negation of rights.

When we place poverty in the context of human rights, we must be aware of the latter's indivisible and interdependent character. The decontextualized vindication of a right is not enough to enable the poor to enjoy their remaining rights.

References

Despouy, Leandro (1996) *Informe Final Sobre los Derechos Humanos y la Extrema Pobreza*, UN Commission on Human Rights, Geneva.

Lewis, Oscar (1977) *Antropología de la Pobreza*, FCE, Mexico.

Mendoza, Oswaldo Baca (1995) *Estudio Comparativo sobre Extrema Pobreza en Zona Rural y Urbano Marginal (Informe Final de Investigación)*, Centro de Investigación Multidisciplinario, UNSAAC, Cusco, Peru.

Mendoza, Oswaldo Baca (1996) *Extrema Pobreza: Denegación de los Derechos Humanos (Informe Final de Investigación)*, Centro de Investigación Multidisciplinario, UNSAAC, Cusco, Peru.

Mendoza, Oswaldo Baca (1997) *Desarrollo y Extrema Pobreza (Informe Final de Investigación)*, Centro de Investigación Multidisciplinario, UNSAAC, Cusco, Peru.

Ugarte Delgado, Alberto (1994) 'Extrema Pobreza: Concepciones y Metodologías de Focalización', *Revista de Antropología*, Universidad Nacional Mayor de San Marcos, No. 1, September.

Ugarte Ochoa, Marco Aurelio (1993) *Extrema Pobreza Reto de Nuestra Epoca*, ATD/Fourth World Movement, Cusco, Peru.

Wresinski, Joseph (1987) *Pobreza Extrema y Precariedad Económica y Social*, ATD/Fourth World Movement, Paris.

Wresinski, Joseph (1996) *Los Pobres son la Iglesia*, Fourth World Movement, Spain.

5

The Promotion of Economic, Social and Cultural Rights as a Formula to Face Poverty

The Case of Panama

MARIBEL GORDON C.

General Characteristics

The Republic of Panama has an area of 75,517 km², a population of 2,329,329 inhabitants according to the National Population and Housing Census of 1990, and a population density of 30.8 inhabitants per km². Of the total population, 53.7 per cent (1.3 million) live in the urban area and 46.3 per cent (1.1 million) in the rural area. Panama is thus a relatively small country with respect to both its geographical area and its population.

Historically, Panama has depended on its tertiary sector (services/commerce), which explains the hypertrophy of its economic structure. From 1990–94 the annual growth rate of the economy was 6.5 per cent. The growth rates for 1995 and 1996 reached 1.9 per cent and 2.5 per cent, respectively. For 1997, the growth rate was estimated at 3.6 per cent (official figure, questioned by some economists). In order to reduce unemployment significantly, growth rates of between 6 and 7 per cent are required. During this period, however high growth rates have resulted in only modest advances in terms of unemployment (on average the unemployment rate has been 15 per cent).

Levels of Poverty in Panama[1]

Fifty per cent of the families in Panama live in poverty and 34 per cent in extreme poverty. Poor families have specific socio-demographic and occupational characteristics: increased family size, a high proportion of minors, lower income per capita and higher levels of unemployment and underemployment than amongst non-poor families. According to data from the National Population and Housing Census (1990),

Panamanian families reflect a decrease in their average size (1970: 4.8 members per family, 1980: 4.6 members and 1990: 4.4 members). There is, however, a regional differentiation in average family size, which reflects a higher fertility rate in the major poverty areas: in the urban and rural areas families have 4.2 and 4.7 members respectively, while in the indigenous areas this number reaches 8.0 members.

The unemployment rate for poor families is 30 per cent, amongst those living in extreme poverty 36.5 per cent and amongst the non-poor 12.9 per cent. Accounting for this pattern is income distribution, as a result of which 20 per cent of the poor to receive 2.75 per cent of the national income, while 20 per cent of the richest receive 60.3 per cent. Of the national working population, 26 per cent receive incomes lower than the minimum wage (the minimum average wage is US$0.97 per hour), 32.5 per cent receive wages that do not cover the cost of the minimum food basket (that is, monthly salaries of under US$250), while 73 per cent cannot afford the cost of the minimum food basket. Panama ranks second in Latin America regarding unequal income distribution.

The female labour force represents 47.9 per cent of the working population. The rate of female unemployment reaches 20.5 per cent, an alarming figure, taking into account the fact that 23 per cent of households are female-headed. The female labour force has constituted itself in a retaining force of wage levels since it is hired only as low-wage labour. This force constitutes a restraint to social upheaval, creating a false appearance that wage levels are sufficient to meet basic family needs when in fact, in order to maintain the same buying power, it is necessary for the man and the woman, or at least more than one family member, to work.

Mortality is 24.8 per 1,000 of the population; child mortality 18.9 per 1,000, and maternal mortality 0.5 per 1,000 live births. There are 879 inhabitants per doctor, 983 inhabitants per nurse and 4,779 inhabitants per odontologist. In rural areas the conditions are dismal, with 3,572 inhabitants per doctor, 3,929 inhabitants per nurse and 13,404 inhabitants per odontologist. Social security coverage has also narrowed: in 1980 it reached 49.9 per cent of the population, in 1990 48.2 per cent. Many medicines have, simultaneously, been removed from the basic medication list, reducing by 10 per cent the number available per patient under social security.

Hunger and nutritional problems affect 34 per cent of all families. 22.8 per cent of adult men and 24 per cent of women are undernourished. Amongst pre-school children, 30 per cent suffer from malnutrition and growth deficiencies. The country's neo-liberal economic policy, through its measures to liberate prices, led to a 35.2 per cent increase in the cost of the minimum food basket between 1980 and 1992.

A low school enrolment and a high level of school absence is another factor characteristic of poor families. Of the total school-age population between 6 and 17 years (518,609 children and adolescents), only 79.3 per cent was enrolled. The adult illiteracy rate is 11 per cent nationally, 15 per cent in rural areas and 3.3 per cent in the urban areas. The population has an average of 6.7 years of formal schooling.

National educational participation rates are as follows: primary schooling 91.0 per cent, secondary schooling 44.5 per cent and higher education 25 per cent. Participation varies in relation to the degree of urbanization: in Panama City the primary school rate is 73.7 per cent, while in the San Blas Indigenous Territory (Comarca) it is 20.6 per cent.

The repetition rate in primary schools is 9.0 per cent, but in the poorer provinces it may reach 20 per cent. In secondary schools, the repetition rate is 10.2 per cent. The drop-out rate is 1.9 per cent in primary schools and 2 per cent in secondary schools. In middle schools, the repetition and drop-out rates occur in the first and second years. The socio-economic conditions of young people in middle school determine their withdrawal from school, since they drop out to look for jobs. Only one out of every four students enrolled in the first grade satisfactorily concludes the twelve years of basic education. Approximately 36,000 students fail annually and around 7,600 drop out of school.

The low-income level of the poor groups limits their access to adequate housing. The urban poor live in squatter settlements, generally in the so-called spontaneous settlements or in uninhabitable houses which are usually overcrowded. Most of these dwellings lack basic facilities such as potable water, electricity and adequate sanitation, and show signs of environmental degradation.

According to the National Population and Housing Census, in 1990 there were 524,284 privately inhabited houses of which 8.8 per cent had been officially condemned, that is, declared uninhabitable. 22.6 per cent of Panamanian families live in overcrowded accommodation. On average, public housing is less than 10m² per capita and private housing provision 16m² per person surpassing the cost of US$75,000. The housing deficit is estimated at approximately 300,000 housing units. Housing conditions are as follows: 16.3 per cent have no potable water, 27.2 per cent no electricity, 11.9 per cent no sanitary infrastructure and 18.5 per cent have dirt floors. In 1992, the Ministry of Housing recognized that between 40,000 and 50,000 families live in informal settlements.

With regard to central government social expenditure, the Panamanian government allocates approximately 35.1 per cent of its budget to the social sector, while it allocates 30.2 per cent to the servicing of debt. The most important share of social expenditure was previously on education but this is now falling. In 1989, 69 per cent of social expenditure was on education, in 1995 only 49 per cent. The social sector has maintained a stable share of approximately 25 per cent of total social expenditure, as has housing at around 5 per cent, an indication of its low priority.

The poverty in which many Panamanian families live exposes its members to multiple risks and other social problems. From 1987 to 1995, data from different non-governmental organizations reveal an increase of 75 per cent in the numbers of streets children who work to help support their homes. There has been an increase in the juvenile delinquency figures. In 1988, 8,235 juvenile detentions between the ages 10 and 24 years were registered. The figure for 1992 was 15,169. The Juvenile Court reported 2,744 court appearances by minors (10 to 17 years of age) in 1988. By 1992 this number to 3,311. In 1994, 399 deaths by violence were registered. By 1995, 91,044 cases of HIV/AIDS had been reported. An increase of alcoholism and drug abuse has also been reported; according to surveys, 4 out of every 10 youngsters use drugs.

The above are some of the characteristics exhibited by low-income Panamanian families. Many of the trends can be explained by the deterioration in the socio-economic conditions over the last few years, mainly due to neo-liberal globalizing economic policies.

In sum, we can say that poverty in Panama has a structural character. As pointed out by J. Jované: '…when poverty problems clearly acquire a persistent and reiterative form, they are known as having a structural nature. However, the poverty phenomenon not only reveals a structural characteristic in the Panamanian society, but recently it has also grown to definitely alarming levels'.[2] That is to say, it is not a simple poverty problem, but a deep structural characteristic of our society, which is characterized, among other things, by a lack of social equity, as well as by: the oblique structure of income distribution; the unemployment problem; the lack of access to land for important groups living in rural areas; and the lack of support for the development of human capital.

This condition of structural poverty is clearly revealed on the poverty map,[3] which shows that 48 per cent of the country's districts fall below the poverty line. A concerted effort is now required to deal with this problem. In 1981 the additional income needed by the poor to overcome this situation was 5.7 per cent of GDP; in the 1990s it equalled more than 8.0 per cent of this macro-economic aggregate.

Respect for Human Rights in the Face of Poverty

Human rights reveal an integral concept of human life: all are important, inviolable and for all human beings, without any distinction whatsoever. In cooperation with the United Nations, UN member states have pledged themselves to achieve the promotion of universal respect for and observance of human rights. These universal rights proclaim that everyone has the right to liberty, equality, a decent life, freedom of association, participation, work, education, health, housing, food, land and a safe environment. The neo-liberal globalizing economic policy measures have, however, impelled a scheme towards individualism, towards the restriction of state participation in the solution of social problems, and to a decrease in the participation of civil society in the decision-making process. At present, the concepts that seem to prevail in the world are 'excess population' and 'social exclusion'.

Poverty can mean more than a lack of what is necessary for material well-being. It can also mean the denial of opportunities and choices basic to human development: the right to lead a long, healthy and creative life, and to enjoy a decent standard of living, freedom, dignity, self-esteem and the respect of others.

Panama supports the 1948 Universal Declaration of Human Rights, and has ratified, *inter alia*, the International Covenant on Economic, Social and Cultural Rights.[4] Nevertheless, living conditions for 50 per cent of the population are well below the poverty line. This fact reveals a failure to fully comply with the promotion and respect of human rights. The increase in these poverty conditions has run parallel to the implementation of the economic policy measures promoted by the international financial institutions since 1979.

In April 1995, the UN Committee on Economic, Social and Cultural Rights evaluated Panama's implementation of the International Covenant on Economic, Social and Cultural Rights. Its report revealed some violations of human rights. A number of measures are therefore recommended by the committee: accelerating the studies for the approval of a national housing plan which should take into account the needs of all communities; accelerating the legislative process of delimitation of the Ngöbe-Buglé Indigenous Territory (Comarca); putting an end to the practice of forced evictions by public authorities; and proceeding to regulating of property titles. Of these, the only one achieved has been the recommendation for the demarcation of the indigenous territory (Comarca). This did not, however, meet with the approval of the claimants.

Conclusions and Recommendations

There is no doubt that the magnitude of the problem and the urgent solution it requires makes imperative a conscious and decided state action. The state is capable of mobilizing a significant number of resources which should address the problems faced by the sectors of the population living in poverty and extreme poverty conditions and promote respect for human rights in order to strengthen the sense of solidarity and equity in society.

It is vital also that we create awareness of the need for sustainable economic development, not only in the improvement of the economic aggregates that are generating social exclusion but also in terms of respect for human rights which guarantee economic and social well-being, including the right to a decent standard of living.

The strategies that have been implemented in our country to satisfy the population's basic needs have had as their sole objective the 'alleviat[ion of] basic needs', without introducing changes in the society's structure. It is necessary to modify the economic and social structure which generates this situation.

In the context of the work carried out by non-governmental organizations (NGOs), well-conceived policies addressed to the alleviation of poverty must be undertaken through the implementation of the following tasks:

• promotion and defence of human rights in all its aspects;

• promotion of the participation of the poor in all joint actions, mainly through their participation in the decision-making process;

• plans, programmes and projects must break the 'assistance approach' in which all the work is done by the government, the financing agencies, the church and, sometimes, the NGOs themselves;

• the poverty problem must be addressed without ignoring the causes that generate and reproduce it;

• concepts such as civil society must be demystified;

• spaces of community organization must be strengthened with the support of NGOs.

Let me conclude by quoting a passage from the *Human Development Report 1997*: '…a quarter of the world's people remain in severe poverty. In a global economy of US$25 trillion, this is a scandal, reflecting shameful inequalities and inexcusable failures of national and international policy' (p. 7).[5]

Notes

1. Sources: the 1990 National Population and Housing Census, Panama; FIEES (1993) *Empleo, pobreza y economia informal: informe del seminario*, Paitilla, Panama; MIPPE (1996) *Situación de Pobreza en Panamá*, Panama; United Nations Development Programme (1995 et seq.) *Human Development Reports,* New York, Oxford, Oxford University Press.
2. *Panorama Católico*, 1996.
3. UNDP (1997) *Human Development Report 1997*, New York, Oxford, Oxford University Press.
4. Ratified by Panama through Law No. 13 of 27 October, 1976.
5. UNDP (1997).

PART III
Indigenous Struggles Against Poverty

6

Indigenous Peoples and Mega-Projects
Hydroelectric dams in the land of the Pehuenches in the highlands of the Bío Bío river, Chile, utopia of development and human rights

CLAUDIO GONZÁLEZ-PARRA

In the last 500 years of occidental cultural domination, the indigenous peoples of Latin America have become the poorest sectors (in socio-economic terms) of the continent, and constitute today a large percentage of the Latin American and Chilean indigent. Despite the incessant efforts of different governments to relieve the situation of poverty and marginality of the indigenous peoples, there remain many obstacles to their autonomous social, economic and political participation.[1] In the last 20 years, however, the indigenous peoples have become better organized and capable of expressing their demands in both national and international forums and are today searching for solutions to their poverty and marginality in order to overcome the historic obstacles to their socio-economic development. At the same time, there is a greater, although limited, awareness at the international level of the need to find new ways to solve the problems of the indigenous people, especially with respect to the recognition of their legitimate ancestral rights to land.[2]

The improvements in indigenous peoples' organizations and the greater national and international awareness of their rights is, however, not sufficient. At the international level, human rights and indigenous peoples' commissions have created innumerable documents which describe the historical and daily violations of their rights by governments in particular. These violations extend from the basic right of association through to genocide and ethnocide in order to obtain access to the natural resources in the ancestral territories of indigenous people.[3]

There is also a growing pressure from the business sector on indigenous people to integrate themselves and their resources into the development process. In the case of Chile, the government and private electricity sector have built and want to continue building hydroelectric dams in the highlands of the Bío Bío river, the ancestral lands of the Pehuenche Indians.[4]

In *Mapudungún* 'Pehuenche' means 'people of the Pehuen tree'. For the Pehuenches, the Pehuen tree is holy, and in the winter their principal food is its pine nut. The Pehuenches were originally nomadic hunters who lived in the Andes mountains. With the arrival of the Spanish *conquistadores* in the seventeenth century, the Pehuenches mixed with the Mapuches. At present, the two communities are a loosely organized group held together by a shared culture, a symbolic system (including language) and their relationship to the dominant Chilean (*huinka*) society.

Dam Construction in the Highlands of the Bío Bío River

The construction of hydroelectric dams in the highlands of the Bío Bío river, hereafter sometimes referred to as the Alto Bío Bío, is a development where the recognition of the rights of the Pehuenches is presented as a prerequisite for the eradication of their poverty. Those who support the construction of the dams affirm that the dams will generate development in a needy sector and that the actions of the Pehuen Foundation (see pp. 72–3) will mitigate the Pehuenches' poverty, heralding a system of social well-being that will change the situation. Those who are against the dam argue that the dams violate the basic rights of the two communities and that their implementation will result in the destruction of the Pehuenches' way of life and the disappearance of the Pehuenche culture in a very short period.[5]

The fallacy is not, however, in the equation that the dam will create development.[6] It lies in the belief that development can be created without the active participation of the Pehuenches. Two independent researchers have evaluated the Pehuen Foundation. Both evaluations were critical, and ENDESA, the most important Chilean electricity company, and the International Financing Corporation (IFC) have striven to keep them from publication. According to the evaluation reports several issues need to be addressed in order to reduce the cultural and environmental damage wrought by the dams.

Powerful external actors are negotiating the future of the Pehuenche communities, constituting a violation of the rights of these communities freely to decide their future.[7] Innumerable meetings have been held in Santiago and Washington, without either the participation or knowledge of the group. Withholding publication of the evaluation reports prevents the Pehuenches and the general public from understanding the development plans for these communities. The following section presents a brief history of ENDESA's projects and their ramifications amongst the Pehuenche.

The Pangue Project

ENDESA's first project which directly affected the Pehuenches was the building of the Pangue hydroelectric dam, 113 metres high and 103 metres wide. The lake resulting from the dam holds 175 million m^3 and covers 500 hectares. The average annual generated energy is expected to be 2,156Wh, which is 55 per cent of full capacity. The IFC controls 2.5 per cent of the assets and contributed US$120 million of the US$450 million total cost. The president of both ENDESA and the Pangue project is the same person.

During the construction of the dam, the IFC and Pangue agreed to the establishment of the independent Pehuen Foundation, among whose objectives were to be the following:

- make the foundation into a vehicle to create sustainable development for the long-term benefit of the Pehuenche communities;

- work with those communities to mitigate the possible negative effects of the Pangue project during and after construction;

- preserve and reinforce the cultural identity of the Pehuenche;

- bring electricity to the communities.

In pursuance of these objectives, the Pangue project allocates approximately 0.3 per cent of its net gains, approximately US$130,000 per year, to the Pehuen Foundation until 2001.

According to the independent evaluations, however, the Pehuen Foundation has not pursued these objectives. ENDESA has instead used the foundation[8] to address the problems of extreme poverty in the communities as an example of the benefits to be received from the construction of the Pangue and Ralco dams.[9]

The families affected live and survive in extremely vulnerable conditions of poverty. They are below Chile's official poverty line and a third are considered to be indigent. There is little state assistance present in the area. Not surprisingly, the Pehuenches are extremely vulnerable to offers to better their living conditions, by, for example, ENDESA.

To illustrate this point, we can examine the case of the Calpan family, affected by the Ralco dam. The son, Eleuterio Calpan Quipaiñan, who works for ENDESA, wants to relocate himself to the El Barco lands. His father, Segundo Calpan Lepiman, says that if it were up to him he wouldn't move. It appears that in the majority of cases where families accept relocation, the wife or head of the household works for ENDESA and that it is that person who decides to relocate, accepting the conditions imposed by the company without the consent of the other family members.

One can also observe a lack of a sense of cultural community amongst the affected group, a product of the process of acculturation transmitted by the schools and the churches. At this time, for example, there does not exist a clear awareness that relocation is a decision that affects the community as a whole. ENDESA utilizes this weakness to its benefit in the process of convincing individual after individual to accept its proposals. One has to understand that these families perceive living areas only as places to survive in given that there are no alternatives on offer, either for living or for stable work.

The Role of the Pehuen Foundation

The two independent evaluations of the Pehuen Foundation were made by anthropologists hired by the IFC.[10] Their critical report presented evidence about the activities of the Pehuen Foundation with respect to:

- environmental damage and deforestation which remain to be corrected;

- multiple and confirmed threats of involuntary resettlement;

- practices which constitute a dramatic assault on the Pehuenche cultural customs and traditions;[11]

- cover-ups of vital information which would permit the discussion of alternatives that would mitigate the cultural, economic and environmental damage.

The fact that these are the result of actions by the Pehuen Foundation is especially important considering that the Pehuen Foundation is the institution set up to mitigate the possibly damaging cultural, social and environmental effects of ENDESA's projects, and the resettlement of approximately 1,000 Pehuenches. It is necessary to analyse the points raised by ENDESA's latest plan, while pointing out that the Chilean Environmental Protection Corporation (CONAMA) approved the plan with a few corrections. One of the changes CONAMA requested was a change in foundation membership to include the community of Ralco

Lepoy. This led to the accusation that IFC and ENDESA executives tried to organize the foundation in such a way as to hide information from its indigenous directors and the affected communities.[12]

Is it possible for ENDESA and the World Bank Group to design a resettlement plan without the advice of independent experts who would ensure that the rights of the communities are respected? Is it possible that this plan would ignore the World Bank's own standards for resettlement or that ENDESA and the World Bank would approve this plan without prior discussion with, and the participation and approval of, the communities involved? In practice, the Pehuen Foundation has not recognized the traditional leaders of the communities affected by the dams, Los Avellanos, Malla, and Quepuca Estadio.

The implementation of mega-projects and the process of resettlement without the active participation of the affected communities is a violation of these communities' rights and of indigenous law. But many argue that the development which the dam will bring will justify whatever human rights violations have occurred in the process, or is another equilibrium possible? Are there minimum conditions of resettlement which would respect the Pehuenches' human rights and facilitate sustainable development in the highlands of the Bío Bío river? Will the Pehuenches benefit from the development of the dam or will they subsidise the hydroelectric development of Chile as a whole at the expense of their local economy, natural resources and culture?

The Ralco Project

The second dam planned by ENDESA on the Bío Bío river is the Ralco, which will result in the resettlement of 88 families from the communities of Quepuca-Ralco and Ralco-Lepoy. Since the land on which the dam is to be built is indigenous land, the property cannot be sold according to Chilean Indigenous Law. The Chilean government agency of Indian development, CONADI, must approve any transfer of indigenous lands to third parties. The official position of the Chilean government is in support of dam construction.

To this end, during August 1997 a group of government functionaries together with consultants to CONADI carried out personal interviews with the Pehuenche family communities of Quepuca-Ralco and Ralco-Lepoy. The objective was to determine the number of families willing to be resettled and to identify the reasons for their decision. Amongst the families interviewed were those six families that had already requested resettlement. CONADI had access to 68 families,

Table 6.1 • Opinions with respect to resettlement

	Willing to relocate	Unwilling to relocate	Undecided	Total
Total	25	38	5	68
Percentage	37	56	7	100

Source: CONADI Regional.

Table 6.2 • Results of the interviews from home visits in Quepuca-Ralco and Ralco-Lepoy

Would relocate	Would not relocate	Undecided	Not interviewed
28.4%	43.2%	6%	22.4%

Source: Empresa Focus Limitada, 13–16 August 1997

who were visited in their homes, a significant opinion sample to compare with ENDESA's assertions about the acceptability of their scheme amongst the affected communities.[13]

This CONADI initiative constitutes a systematic effort to implement the agreement on the support policies of CONADI's Southern Region to the area affected by the flooding of the dams. The objective in this case is to make known the official position of CONADI to the families that will be directly affected by the construction of the Ralco dam. This signifies the beginning of a new mode of work for CONADI, given the difficult challenge that the Pehuenche population confronts in the Development Area of the Alto Bío Bío.

CONADI states that 37 per cent of the families favour relocation. Underlying this percentage, however, is a clear ignorance by the families of their rights and those accorded by Chile's Indigenous Law. It is also clear that the families believed that the dam will go ahead and that there are no alternatives to relocation to the El Barco lands, reflecting the policy and stance of ENDESA that no other solutions are possible.

The families that have sought relocation have been thoroughly instructed by ENDESA personnel and realize that they are under pressure to accept. The role played by the Pehuen Foundation has also directly supported ENDESA's objectives and the construction of the dam. The families believe that they will lose their lands and everything they possess below the rising water, as well as a year's benefits from the Pehuen Foundation, if they reject ENDESA's argument. In this area there is no clear difference between the functions and roles of the Pehuen Foundation and those of ENDESA.

Seven per cent of the families are undecided. These families lack knowledge of the protection which the law offers them and a belief that CONADI has little or no ability to defend their rights. There is a clear lack of confidence with respect to what CONADI can do, given ENDESA's power in this area. Against this, a small majority of 56 per cent of the Pehuenche families reject relocation, a significant number of which believe in their right to their ancestral lands and identify clearly with their traditions. In spite of everything, this important group refuses to move, convinced that it must defend its lands against the enemy.

Mapuche Claims before the UN Human Rights Commission

The Chilean government supported ENDESA's plans until August 1998, when it asked for the resignation of CONADI director Domingo Namuncura and two board members of the CONADI council. These individuals had actively intervened in the interactions between the Pehuenche community and ENDESA. At the same time, it became clear that the indigenous members of the CONADI council had become increasingly critical of ENDESA's resettlement proposals. Mapuche communities filed an official complaint to the UN Commission on Human Rights, calling attention to the severity of the human rights violation committed against the Mapuches as people of an ethnic, religious and linguistic minority.

The complaint was presented by the International Peace Bureau to the fifty-fourth session of the commission, held between 16 March and 24 April 1998, and reads as follows:

Just over 100 years ago, the Mapuche nation, spread across the present-day states of Argentina and Chile, possessed a vast territory which, on the Chilean side, stretched from the Bío Bío river down to the south. This territory was recognized first by treaties with the Spanish Crown and then by a series of treaties and parliaments held with the newly established Republic of Chile. With the military defeat of the Mapuche people in 1883, the Chileans took possession of the Mapuche territory by conquest; territory which the Mapuche communities still claim as theirs today. Despite the loss of national sovereignty and annexation to the Republic of Chile, the Mapuche have by no means renounced their claims to possession of their land and resources.

Without the recovery of these lands, and the inalienable right of property over them, the survival of the Mapuche communities and of their culture is under threat. Deprived of their lands, the Mapuche communities suffer growing social instability, with the evident danger of outbreaks of violence, which could have unforeseeable consequences for the peace and stability of the Chilean state as a whole.

We demand, therefore, the recognition of the fundamental rights of the Mapuche people, as guaranteed by legal instruments both national and international, such as the International Covenant on Economic, Social and Cultural Rights, Article 1.

With regard to the situation of its indigenous population, Chile theoretically took an important step forward with the passing of Law No. 19.253 in 1993. This law establishes norms for the protection, promotion and development of that population and recognizes a number of basic rights, such as the recognition of the Mapuche as a people. It guarantees the protection of ownership of land and water, and the introduction of multicultural and bilingual education. It also prohibits manifest and malicious discrimination. Under this law, the government must consult the indigenous peoples of Chile on all issues affecting them directly. In reality, however, this law is not implemented. With the return to democracy and the rule of law in Chile, and with the strengthening of its legal institutions and its ratification of international treaties in the field of human rights, Chile presents a normal and civilized face to the rest of the world. But if we look at recent events, it becomes clear that the treatment of the Mapuche people has not improved since the days of Pinochet's regime. Injustice, violations of human rights, usurpation of ancestral lands, inhuman and humiliating treatment, discrimination and racism are still very much the order of the day.

Between October 1997 and March 1998, 85 Mapuches, among them women and children, were detained in Temuco, Malleco, Arauco, Angol and Santiago. This was the result of the introduction of the Law of State Security and the Anti-Terrorist Law in five communes in the Mapuche region. Using these legal instruments, the Chilean police carried out a massive military operation in the entire region. Together with anti-terrorist forces, and using military vehicles and helicopters, the police patrolled the area, entering homes and threatening the inhabitants. Detentions took place at any hour of the day or night. According to the statement of one of the detained, he was held incommunicado for seven days (Chilean law stipulates five days), during which he suffered inhuman and degrading treatment.

In a confrontation between security guards from the logging company Arauco S.A. and Mapuche families from the Pichi Lonkollan and Pilin Mapu communities of the Lumaco sector of Malleco Province, who were trying to halt the exploitation of their traditionally held forest land, two trucks were burnt. These incidents can, however, hardly be considered to have constituted a 'threat to the interior security of the state'. The reaction of the Chilean state towards the Mapuche population in this case has been irresponsible and totally exaggerated.

Projects for the improvement of the country's infrastructure, such as the building of new roads and dams, are being carried out without the prior consent of the affected communities, in violation of the Indigenous Law No. 19.253 of October 1993. Not only has the Chilean government not implemented this law, due, it says, to a 'lack of economic resources' (at the very moment in which Chile is buying weapons worth hundreds of millions of dollars), it has manifestly violated it. For example, the imminent construction of a series of hydroelectric power stations on the Bío Bío river in the Mapuche Pehuenche region, without the consent of communities affected, is in direct contradiction with Article 13 of the Indigenous Law, which provides that 'indigenous lands, as national interest demands, shall enjoy the protection of this law. They shall not be alienated, seized, nor acquired by limitation, except between communities or indigenous persons belonging to the same ethnic group'.

A large number of indigenous communities are facing such situations, due to the implementation of a number of mega-projects such as the Coast Road, the Temuco By-Pass, urban expansion, exploitation of forest and privatization of coastal areas and their waters. All these projects plunge Chile's most needy ever deeper into poverty, leading to enormous social and cultural problems amongst them. The disastrous environmental consequences of the projects barely need mention.

Although the Mapuche people are not opposed to progress, they want fair, sustainable and harmonious development, with full respect for their rights and ancestral values, and a development process from which they are not absolutely excluded. Development depends, however, on the recognition of the country's cultural diversity in order to begin an historic reparation which the indigenous peoples are anxiously awaiting, and which sooner or later the Chilean state will have to consider. Only in this way will a solid base of coexistence with the country's original inhabitants be created. The demands of the Mapuches are based on full respect for the Chilean legal order, which includes the common law norms which traditionally governed them, reserving their right to self-determination as the basis for their protection and development in their ancestral territory. It is important that the Mapuche people are recognized by the Chilean Constitution and that Chile ratifies ILO Convention 169, one of the few texts, if not the only one, that recognizes the inalienable rights of indigenous peoples.

ENDESA's Quality of Life Plan

On 25 October 1998, ENDESA and all the families affected by the Ralco project signed the Resettlement Plan in support of dam construction. CONADI, the provincial government of Los Angeles and the Catholic Church participated in reaching the agreement. CONADI met with all the individuals, communities and indigenous organizations in the Quepuca-Ralco and Ralco-Lepoy areas. It carried out social surveys to determine the number of families affected by the Ralco project as well as their needs and desires. The community organizations Comunidad de Ralco-Lepoy, Organización Pehuenche Quepuca Estadio and Junta de Vecinos de Palmucho represented the 184 affected families in designing the resulting Quality of Life Improvement Plan, which reflects their concerns and aspirations.

The Quality of Life Improvement Plan will strengthen the actions contemplated in the resettlement plan and the transfer of land for the families directly affected. At the time of writing ENDESA had reached an agreement with 83 of the families. This agreement states:

- that the benefits provided by the resettlement plan for the (91) families do not generate differences or conflicts between the families of the two communities, so that the community ties remain unbroken;
- that there is full collaboration with government plans in the Development Area of the Alto Bío Bío in order to be more efficient in resource administration. It is believed that a coordinated effort will best improve the quality of life of the Pehuenches;
- that the Ralco dam is part of the solution rather than the problem of the Alto Bío Bío. The construction of the dam creates positive externalities for the Pehuenche communities that had been forgotten and isolated for years.

The Quality of Life Improvement Plan contemplates actions on several fronts to benefit the communities affected by Ralco:

- *Soil Conservation*. Collaboration in plans to achieve three forested hectares for each family. This project also includes training in plantation and soil conservation as well as temporary jobs in reforestation, conservation and soil-recovery programmes.
- *Rural Housing Subsidies*. Once land titles are established, ENDESA promises to add complementary financing to the government subsidy for rural housing as well as financing for other infrastructure projects.

- *Rural Electrification.*[14] ENDESA will provide financing for a Rural Electricity Programme whose objective is to provide electricity to all housing in the communities affected.

- *Roads.* ENDESA will construct a new road in the Alto Bío Bío to replace the one that will be flooded by the lake created by the Ralco dam. It will be 50 kilometres long, between the Pangue bridge and the El Barco Plantation (proposed resettlement location). ENDESA will also assist in the creation of paths to connect the different community farms.

- *Education.* ENDESA promises to collaborate in the development to expand and improve the existing Frontier Elementary School in Ralco to become a Technical–Professional High School.

- *Cultural Programmes and Encouragement of Tourism.* The Pehuen Foundation promises to continue supporting the development of cultural and productive activities in the two communities. ENDESA will contact the Chile Foundation to prepare a holistic design of the tourist potentials for the two communities affected as well as the proposed resettlement location, incorporating Pehuenche feedback. Additionally ENDESA promises to finance complementary studies on tourism.

- *Community Centre.* ENDESA promises to construct a community centre for the communities of Quepuca-Ralco and Ralco-Lepoy.

- *Pehuen Foundation.* ENDESA will study the reorganization of the executive committee in order to ensure Pehuenche pre-eminence.

- *Employment Opportunities.* In order to ensure employment opportunities for the Pehuenches, ENDESA guarantees important quotas for the women and men of the affected communities.

- *Implementation and Supervision of the Improvement Programme.* By express petition of the communities, this programme will be incorporated into the Long-Run Development Resettlement Plan. In this way, the programme will be implemented and supervised according to the procedures established by the government's environmental protection agency CONAMA in its approval of the Ralco project.

- *Using dialogue to continue.* Several families still refuse to transfer their lands. ENDESA has stated its desire to continue a dialogue with them in order to reach a fair agreement, rather than ask for judicial intervention to determine the situation.

Recognizing Human Rights to Achieve Development

How can power be distributed in a manner which allows the fulfilment of human rights, in this case the defence of the rights of the Pehuenches of the Alto Bío Bío?[15] How can guarantees to respect the human rights of the Pehuenche organizations be phrased? There is a general state of impunity with respect to the systematic violation of essential, basic and historic rights of the Pehuenche communities, which has placed them in a position of being forced to accept the construction of the Pangue[16] and Ralco Dams as the sole paradigm of development and the sole means of alleviating the generalized poverty of their communities.

On paper, the creation of a private foundation as an instrument for mitigating the environmental impact of the dams while at the same time ensuring that the indigenous communities share in the profits of the Pangue project and not simply suffer the harmful effects of development that hydroelectric dams generate looks promising.[17] In this case, however, good intentions and declared goals are far from the crude realities in the communities where there is no understanding of what indigenous rights are supposed to guarantee.

The construction of the dams in the highlands of the Bío Bío river need not result in the impoverishment of the Pehuenche.[18] The following proposals for the reorientation of the relationship between ENDESA, the Pehuen Foundation and the affected communities were presented by Theodore Downing, co-author of the evaluation report on the Pehuen Foundation:

- realign the Pehuen Foundation according to the agreement between the IFC and Pangue;

- reorganize Pehuen Foundation policies to satisfy the requisites about conflicts of interest, cultural information, and to promote pluralism and diversity;

- recognize the Pehuenche language, *Mapudungún*, as the second official language of the Pehuen Foundation and look for experts in indigenous issues to be independent consultants;

- make an emergency plan which would stop the indiscriminate cutting of the forests, ensure that all indigenous land is protected, and design and follow a plan to mitigate the possible social, economic and environmental effects of the present and proposed project;

- have the Pehuen Foundation prepare and implement a sustainable strategic and participatory project which emphasizes the administration of natural resources controlled by the Pehuenche, especially the virgin forests;

- ensure the full participation in a culturally adequate form of the *lonkos* (traditional leaders) who represent the affected communities;

- establish Pehuenche groups to monitor the affected communities;

- increase on-site supervision of the IFC, including assistance to the future leaders of the communities;

- have the Pehuen Foundation and the IFC publicize the independent evaluations to the affected parties.

Conclusion

A strengthening of indigenous organizations, finally culminating in the 1993 Indigenous Law, arose from the grave abuse of the rights of indigenous communities documented in Chile during the years 1973 to 1990, which resulted in political ethnocide.

With the transition to democracy in Chile, a number of indigenous peoples' demands were added to the 1993 law, but conditions were not yet ready for these demands to be recognized. The fact that the Pehuen Foundation, a private entity created by the World Bank Group, continues to exercise important influence over the Pehuenche communities in a way that is contrary to their interests and destructive of their culture has not been addressed. For example, in 1993 the Pehuen Foundation chose and donated books to the libraries of three schools in the Alto Bío Bío.[19] The donation represented 57 per cent of the funds allocated by the foundation to educational projects. The book collection was composed of a selection of great literary works of western civilization, including Homer, Shakespeare, Cervantes, and books on the history of Chile, written at a level beyond the understanding of Pehuenche students in the primary grades. Some of the books had pictures of the dismemberment of Indians at the hands of Euro-Chileans. The communities were terrorized by the books and they were hidden by the teachers. This would not have happened had the Foundation been aware of the specific needs of these communities.

The actions of external actors have broken the historic internal power equilibrium in these communities into multiple parts, as illustrated by the duplication of the various offices in the communities. It is also reinforced by the Indigenous Law.

To initiate a development process that does not result in the destruction of the Pehuenche way of life demands the harmonization of development and human rights. Any responsible person should meditate on the answers to the following questions and only then attempt to construct a new paradigm for a more just society; this is the least we can do if we are to rescue and restore a culture that will be lost due to the irreversible effects of mega-projects on the Alto Bío Bío today:[20] is it possible to speak of democratizing the concepts of human rights in a form that makes us appreciate how our decisions can generate irreversible damage in communities? What is the relationship between power and human rights? Is the answer to the last question an example of the generalized impunity of Chilean society when the basic rights of Chile's indigenous communities are violated?

Notes

1. Salomon Nahmad (ed.) (1996) 'La perspectiva de etnias y naciones: los pueblos indios de América Latina', *Colección Biblioteca Abya-Yala,* No. 33, Ediciones Abya-Yala, Quito, Ecuador.
2. José Bengoa, *Globalización, distribución de los ingresos y los derechos económicos, sociales y culturales,* paper presented to the CROP and ALOP Workshop in Santiago de Chile, 24–26 September 1997.
3. Briefing on the Pehueche Human Rights situation at the Conference of the American Anthropological Association (AAA) in Washington DC by Dr Theodore Downing, University of Arizona and Dr Claudio González-Parra, University of Concepción, 21 November 1997
4. Washington DC, 17 December 1992: 'The Board of Directors of the International Finance Corporation (IFC) today approved an investment in the Pangue hydroelectric power generation…IFC's insistence on the creation of the Pehuen Foundation, funded by the project's income to enhance the quality of life for the local indigenous population…The power generated will be clean and economically produced, for the use of 93 per cent of the Chilean population who live in Santiago and Central Chile'.
5. 'The sacrifice of human rights and the cultural survival of an indigenous group is an unacceptable cost of doing business or of economic development', Theodore Downing's letter to Tom Greaves, 1997.
6. Michael M. Cernea (1997) 'The Social Side of Hydropower: Forging a New Alliance', *Hydro Review Worldwide,* Vol. 5, Nos 1–6.
7. On 18 December 1996, Theodore Downing, in a letter to Jannik Lindbaek, Executive Vice-President of IFC, accused the 'IFC staff of joining its client in these violations, once it had been made aware of them, instituting a cover up and then, in an "in your face" response to human and indigenous rights, arrogantly forging a secret agreement with the company over the future of an ethnic group'.
8. William Ryrie, Executive Vice-President of IFC, noted IFC's 'sensitivity to the

impact of this project on the indigenous communities near the project site'. IFC Press release No. 93/32.

9. 'These steps include the establishment of an Ecological Station to monitor environmental conditions in the project area, a watershed management protection plan, development of a construction impact minimization plan, and an equitable resettlement plan including housing and land ownership for 53 people displaced by the reservoir.' Press release No. 93/32. The IFC failed to resettle the Sotomayor family (CONADI, No. 0006067) who lived in the area south of the Pangue dam.

10. Theodore Downing, Research Professor of Social Development, University of Arizona, and Jay Hair, former President of the National Wildlife Federation, made the evaluations.

11. Letter from Theodore Downing, 18 December 1996, to Jannik Lindbaek, Executive Vice-President of IFC: 'Officers of IFC responsible for the Pangue Project are involving the institution in an unacceptable, racial-discrimination practice and withholding information from certain members of the Pehuen Foundation Board of Directors on the basis on their race and ethnicity. My efforts to convince three of the officers – Martyn Riddle, Denis Koromsay, and their legal Counsel Motoko Aizawa – that IFC's actions violate Pehuenche human rights have failed.'

12. 'This racial discrimination is intended to cover up the time-sensitive findings and deprive the Pehuenche people of important knowledge which has a direct bearing on the Pehuenche economic and cultural future. The ageing interim evaluation contains evidence of on-going extensive, unmitigated environmental damage including deforestation, multiple threats of involuntary resettlement, and a misguided assault on the Pehuenche culture. Most seriously, the cover up is delaying constructive actions to mitigate on-going cultural, economic and environmental damages which had been identified' (*ibidem*).

13. The interviews were carried out by the following CONADI officials: Mr. Luis Huincache, Regional Director; Carlos Vargas, Treasurer; Juan Nanculef, Chief of Personnel, National Office; Gonzalo Toledo, Chief of Development; Manuel Namuncura, Chief of Personnel, Office of the Southern National Region; Lucy Traipe, Secretariat, Office of the Southern National Region; Cecilia Neculpan, Program for Development Fund, Office of the Southern National Region; Horacio Cheuquelaf, Programme on Lands, Office of the Southern National Region; and Luis Luszinger, Driver, National Office.

14. 'The generic lessons, however, should not distract from the tragedy in the Alto Bío Bío. I am haunted by the image of impoverished Pehuenche freezing to death in El Barco as urban Chileans are heated by the electrical power which the Pehuenches subsidized with their culture and forest.' Theodore Downing's letter to Tom Greaves, 1997.

15. Michael M. Cernea (1998) 'Impoverishment or Social Justice? A Model for Planning Resettlement', in *Development Projects and Impoverishment Risks. Resettling Project-affected People in India*, Hari Mohan Mathur and David Marsden (eds), Oxford University Press, Delhi.

16. Washington DC, 17 December 1992: 'The Board of Directors of the International Finance Corporation (IFC) today approved an investment in the Pangue hydroelectric power generation project located on the Bío Bío river in Chile. Board ratification of the proposed investment followed a comprehensive

environmental review of the project by IFC...Board members voiced strong approval of the work done by IFC in setting high environmental and social standards with respect to the Pangue project.' Press Release No. 93/32.

17. 'It is equally unacceptable that a small, indigent Indian culture must pay the tuition for the valuable lessons learned by IFC...students in the classroom, and ENDESA. Nor can I believe that an institution with such plentiful resources, and her sister institutions in the World Bank family, are helpless to act.' Theodore Downing's letter to Tom Greaves, 1997.

18. Michael M. Cernea (1997) 'The Risk and Reconstruction Model for Resettling Displaced Populations', *World Development*, Vol. 25, No. 10, October, pp. 1569–88.

19. Micheal M. Cernea (1996) 'Social Organization and Development Anthropology', the 1995 Malinowski Award Lecture, *Environmentally Sustainable Development Studies and Monographs Series No. 6*, World Bank, Washington DC.

20. For more information, see the Arizona *Daily Star* Online at: http://www.azstarnet.com/downing.

7

Human Rights, Poverty and Indigenous Peoples' Struggles in the Americas

New Directions and Case Studies from Colombia, Guatemala, Mexico and Nicaragua

CAMILO PEREZ-BUSTILLO

This chapter will seek to provide an introductory overview of: (i) the extent to which key new proposed instruments of international human rights focusing on indigenous rights issues address the link between such issues and disproportionate patterns of poverty among indigenous peoples, and (ii) the link between struggles for indigenous rights, armed revolutionary movements, and post-1986 legal reforms regarding the status of indigenous peoples in Colombia, Guatemala, Mexico and Nicaragua. Dual assumptions underlying this structuring of the issues to be addressed by this chapter are: (i) that the new instruments proposed by the United Nations (UN) and Organization of American States (OAS) systems respectively represent significant advances for tackling indigenous rights and poverty issues in the international arena, and (ii) that these new proposed mandates are best understood in the light of parallel national advances under especially difficult conditions in the countries selected for comparison.

The two newly proposed instruments under discussion here are the 1994 Draft UN Declaration on the Rights of Indigenous Peoples,[1] developed by the Working Group on Indigenous Populations of the UN Sub-Commission on the Prevention of Discrimination and Protection of Minorities, and the Draft Inter-American Declaration on the Rights of Indigenous Peoples, approved by the Inter-American Commission on Human Rights of the OAS on 18 September 1995. Both instruments are subject to further modification and ultimate approval within the UN and OAS systems respectively.

Colombia, Guatemala, Mexico and Nicaragua have been selected for comparison, to varying extents, because they are the only countries in the Americas where armed revolutionary movements have recently taken up indigenous rights demands, and where significant aspects of such demands have been successfully translated into legal mandates, or are in the process of being so. In this way they together set a kind of base-line in terms of policy standards for meeting indigenous rights demands throughout the region, independently of the kinds of formal legal norms contained in the proposed UN and OAS instruments, or of International Labour Organization (ILO) Convention 169, the most important and currently accepted set of standards for indigenous rights issues under international law (this latter convention was in fact an important point of departure for the above-mentioned reforms in each of the cited countries). Additional important examples of recent social and political mobilization among indigenous peoples in countries such as Ecuador are not included because the focus here is on the relationship between armed revolutionary movements which have incorporated indigenous rights issues into their demands, resultant reforms and their relationship with evolving international law standards.

There are important variations among a range of shared characteristics even among this sample. Only in Colombia and Mexico were the armed movements of interest here both predominantly composed of indigenous peoples and characterized by primarily indigenous leadership (Quintin Lame in Colombia, and the Ejército Zapatista de Liberación Nacional (EZLN) in Mexico). In Guatemala several predominantly non-indigenous armed movements gradually developed significant indigenous bases of support and leadership, and came to incorporate specific indigenous rights demands beyond generic demands based on class oppression. The Nicaraguan process began in a similar way with an overwhelmingly non-indigenous revolutionary movement, the Frente Sandinista de Liberación Nacional (FSLN), which, once in power (1979–90), was forced to confront specific indigenous rights demands, and gradually incorporated them into its framework for governing. Together these four countries provide a basis both for looking at legal advances at the national level in the promotion and protection of indigenous peoples' rights throughout the Americas, and for contextualizing the steps taken by the drafters of the proposed UN and Inter-American instruments. It is widely acknowledged by regional experts that both of these instruments were greatly influenced in their development and content by events in each of these countries as well, especially by the bloody conflicts in Nicaragua and Guatemala during the early and mid-1980s.

Patterns of Indigenous Poverty in the Americas

The proposed UN and OAS instruments, together with national reforms in each of the four countries cited and the underlying processes which led to them, share a consensus about the conceptual, socio-economic, juridical and political links between indigenous rights issues and disproportionate patterns of poverty among indigenous peoples. There is also a growing consensus along these lines among poverty researchers in the region. This consensus is less evident, and is given much less weight, among key policy-making institutions such as the World Bank and the Inter-American Development Bank in their general discourse, although both have begun to develop a more special-ized debate that has begun to focus on indigenous rights issues in the last few years (especially in the wake of the Zapatista uprising in the impov-erished Mexican state of Chiapas, bordering on Guatemala, in January 1994). Even the World Bank had to acknowledge the impact of the uprising in its 1995 *World Development Report*, where it noted that 'inequalities between men and women, between ethnic groups, and between geographic regions are particularly tenacious'. Interestingly, the Bank viewed Chiapas as an example not of ethnic disparities but of geographic ones, noting that in its view 'poor regions, such as the state of Chiapas in Mexico, usually stay relatively poor even when the economy as a whole expands' (ibid.), in an indirect reference to the impact of the North American Free Trade Agreement (NAFTA) and related macro-economic adjustments (pursuant to International Mone-tary Fund (IMF) strictures) on overall patterns of growth and equity in Mexico. From the Bank's perspective Chiapas reflected one of a series of lessons about why 'the longer people are left behind, the harder it becomes to break self-perpetuating inter-generational cycles of poverty' (ibid.). The stress on the supposedly 'self-perpetuating' nature of such patterns deflects, of course, a deeper structural analysis of the causes of indigenous deprivation in Chiapas or in dozens of similar enclaves of indigenous poverty throughout the continent, and elegantly ignores the role of the IMF and the Bank itself, and the neo-liberal policies promoted by them and their domestic allies in fomenting such tragedies.

The World Bank's apparent lack of interest in the impact of its policies on indigenous peoples is also evidenced in the scant references to this subject in Sebastian Edwards' book, *Crisis and Reform in Latin America: From Despair to Hope*, published by the Bank in 1995 as its authoritative overview of the implementation of neo-liberal policies in the region. At the time of the book's publication, Edwards was the

Bank's economist for Latin America and the Caribbean. Only two of the book's 330 pages contain specific references to the region's indigenous peoples and their living conditions. The first reference – on page 266, notes that in Bolivia 'infant mortality also varies according to ethnicity, with the indigenous non-Spanish-speaking population having a 35 per cent higher rate than the Spanish-speaking population'. In a closing chapter on the Mexican crisis of 1994, there is an additional reference, this time to the need to 'incorporate traditionally neglected groups into the modern economic sectors' and that therefore 'the education of the indigenous population has to be upgraded through bilingual programs' (p. 310). Interestingly enough, however, the book contains five different references to the Zapatista uprising in Chiapas as a matter of some evident concern to the Bank. Apparently a few thousand indigenous peoples in arms in South-East Mexico are of significantly greater concern to Edwards, and to the Bank which employs him for his expertise, than millions of unarmed others who end up relegated to his passing references to indigenous health and education issues.

Recent reports issued by the United Nations Development Programme (UNDP) take a much less superficial and more nuanced view of the impact of ethnic disparities on the overall level of well-being in countries around the world. The 1994–98 annually published *Human Development Reports* stress the importance of disaggregating the UNDP's human development indicators on the basis of factors such as gender, race and ethnicity, and geography in order to portray more accurately and act appropriately with respect to a country's true status in terms of these indicators.

The results of such disaggregation for Mexico are especially illustrative for our purposes. For example, Mexico overall ranks forty-eighth amongst the 120 countries surveyed in the 1996 report. When the country's indigenous population is excluded from the results, Mexico ends up ranking twenty-ninth, just above South Korea and Argentina (the highest-ranking Latin American country in the study). If Mexico were ranked according to the *Human Development Index* (HDI) prevalent among its indigenous peoples, its ranking would fall to somewhere between the Dominican Republic (eighty-seventh) and the former Soviet Central Asian Republic of Kyrgyzstan (101).[2] The only other Latin American country in this grouping is a non-disaggregated Peru (91). The lowest-ranking countries in the region then follow: Bolivia (111), Guatemala (112), Honduras (114), El Salvador (115), Nicaragua (117), and Haiti, the lowest ranked (145). It is worth noting that Peru, Bolivia and Guatemala, the three countries in the region with the highest relative concentration (if not total absolute number) of indigenous peoples, are also three of the seven most limited in UNDP human development terms, even without disaggregation. It is likely that the disaggregated ranking of these countries' greatly impoverished indigenous populations would thus place them somewhere between Nicaragua and Haiti at the bottom of the region's HDI rankings. Something similar but somewhat less drastic would happen with the ranking of Ecuador's disaggregated indigenous population, although the country ranks significantly higher overall than any of the other low-ranking countries mentioned (64). Colombia ranks still better (48, just above non-disaggregated Mexico), but the impact of the disaggregation of its indigenous population would be minimal because of the very small percentage of its total population which is so identified (approximately 2 per cent). Further attention is directed by the UNDP to the 'bleak future' for indigenous peoples in Latin America in its 1997 report, with specific references to persistent, deepening patterns of indigenous poverty in Mexico, Guatemala and Bolivia.[3]

Additional sources on the socio-economic status of the region's indigenous peoples include a 1995 Brookings Institution publication, *Coping with Austerity: Poverty and Inequality in Latin America*, edited by Nora Lustig. Lustig is currently a senior official at the Inter-American Development Bank (IADB), in charge of the Bank's anti-poverty policy research. In citing research by Abel Fiszbein, George Psacharopoulos and others, Lustig notes, in her introduction to the book, the role played by gender and ethnic discrimination in the region 'in determining who is poor' (p. 28). An example cited by her is that 'indigenous people in Bolivia and Guatemala have more than a 20 per cent probability of belonging to the bottom quintile, as do mulattos and blacks in Brazil'. But she stresses that 'discrimination, in particular ethnic discrimination, has not usually been a serious matter of study or significant policy in Latin America', and concludes that 'in light of these results, the eradication of discriminatory practices in the labor market should become a primary concern for governments and international lending institutions'. Later in the introduction she notes the specific need, as well, for anti-discrimination legislation wherever such patterns are present (p. 28).

Country-specific studies of the socio-economic status of the region's indigenous peoples, surveyed briefly below, shed greater light on this issue than do the kinds of generalities indulged in by institutions such as the World Bank. This section of the chapter is perhaps unduly weighted by references to the situation in Mexico, but will attempt to provide a necessarily brief but hopefully useful overview.

Colombia

The importance of recent legal reforms regarding the status of Colombia's indigenous population outweighs the relatively small absolute size of this population in comparison to the much greater relative and absolute demographic presence of indigenous groups in countries such as Guatemala, Bolivia, Peru and Mexico. The importance of indigenous demands for justice as a political factor in recent Colombian history – such as in the process leading to the new 1991 Constitution and in the overall, and still incomplete, 'peace process' of the mid-1980s through the early 1990s which led to the demobilization of the indigenous armed group known as *Quintin Lame*, which were closely intertwined – has also been reflected in academic studies of the status of this population (See ONIC 1995 and Gros 1991).

Data summarized in an extensive introductory overview chapter to ONIC (1995) indicate sharp inter-ethnic disparities in terms of access to education and health services. For example the 1985 census reported a 44 per cent illiteracy rate among the country's 64 different indigenous linguistic groups, compared to a 30.6 per cent overall average of illiteracy among the rural population as a whole (ONIC 1995: 14). Similarly an overall enrolment rate of 84 per cent of eligible primary-school age children compares with only 11.3 per cent enrolment amongst indigenous children. This results in extremes of academic achievement, for example: in 1995 a total of 176 indigenous students were enrolled at the National University, with eight graduated as of that year. The government's principal response to this has been the systematic provision of bilingual educational programmes to indigenous communities since 1978 and the adoption of a national law known as Decree 1142. By 1995 official data reported 80 per cent coverage by these progammes, known as *etno-educación*, up from 60 per cent in 1991. The sources available do not indicate or discuss whether there might be a certain cause and effect relationship between this degree of increase in coverage and the fact that Article 10 of the 1991 Constitution mandates bilingual educational progammes for the country's indigenous peoples and also grants indigenous languages official status in the regions where they are spoken. Further analysis of the extent to which these officially promoted bilingual progammes in fact reflect the demands of indigenous groups independent of government control is essential in order to understand this data.

Gros (1991) stresses the role played by the traditional Colombian legal system of land tenure in regions heavily populated by indigenous peoples (especially peripheral tropical-forest regions such as those bordering on Amazonia, and temperate highlands) in marginalizing their claims to legitimate title. His argument, in sum, is that it is this legal system itself which is a barrier to indigenous advancement, and a cause of indigenous peoples' disproportionate poverty and 'social and cultural disintegration' (p. 279). He notes that in 1991 47 per cent of the country's indigenous population lacked legal title to the land upon which they resided and upon which their sustenance depended (p. 269). More current figures would be necessary to analyse whether, and to what extent, reforms in the 1991 Constitution intended to stabilize indigenous land ownership (e.g., Articles 286, 287, 329 and 330), building on Law 89 of 1890 (one of the first laws adopted in Latin America intended to protect indigenous rights), have in fact resulted in greater equity, and ultimately greater self-sufficiency.

Regardless of any of the above-described legal reforms, endemic political violence in rural Colombia has deepened, rather than abated, since the adoption of the 1991 Constitution and the halting of the abortive peace process which accompanied it. Indigenous people in general, and independent indigenous political activists in particular, continue to be disproportionate victims of political violence in which the armed forces and so-called paramilitary sectors are either protagonists or systematically complicit, until recently with extensive US training, material, and financing (ONIC 1995: 16). Meanwhile the continent's oldest armed revolutionary movements, the Fuerzas Armadas Revolucionarias Colombianas (FARC), and the Ejército de Liberación Nacional (ELN), continue to grow in strength, with the country's indigenous rural peoples often caught in the cross-fire between these forces and an increasingly desperate ruling élite. Efforts to rekindle a peace process with both FARC and the ELN were under way in early 2001, but it is not at all clear to what extent a new round of negotiations will actually result in reforms specifically addressing indigenous rights issues, much less whether peace agreements as a whole will ever be reached. Meanwhile, violence by paramilitary forces acting with impunity and apparently complicit with sectors of the government and armed forces persists and has resulted in the assassination of several indigenous rights advocates and activists. (The March 1999 murders, at the hands of FARC guerrillas apparently acting without authorization from the movement's central command, of three foreign indigenous-rights activists in the international movement acting in solidarity with the struggle of Colombia's U'wa indigenous people against displacement from their land due to a World Bank-style mega-project, compounds this tragic situation.) Many observers and analysts of the human rights struggle in Latin America note increasingly disturbing parallels between current experiences of militarization and increasing paramilitary terrorist violence with state complicity in the most heavily indigenous regions of both Colombia and Mexico (and emulating, in part, earlier patterns of repression in Guatemala).

Colombia, ironically, marks therefore both a high-water mark for the translation of indigenous demands into constitutional legal mandates (see also Articles 7, 63, 72, 80 and 171 of the 1991 Constitution) and a low point as to the relative meaninglessness of such reforms in the absence of more fundamental social and economic transformations. Uniquely in the region, two senators elected by the country's indigenous communities via a national list (*circunscripción nacional*) from these groups' traditional authorities sit in the national congress, pursuant to Article 171 of the 1991 Constitution. But this unprecedented formal and nationally recognized political power has not yet been reflected in the kind of socio-economic progress that might have been anticipated. This may well reflect the kind of critique made by Hector Diaz Polanco (1991, 1997) of the hollowness of majoritarian-type legal and political reforms intended to benefit indigenous peoples in the region, which fail to provide for a real transformation in the political relationship between mestizo-dominated states and indigenous peoples. From his perspective, only a regime of indigenous autonomy in which the state is redefined as multicultural in terms of the redistribution of power among its constituent ethnic communities creates the basis for both full democracy and socio-economic equity rooted in self-determination. The demand for autonomy is the most effective anti-poverty progamme of all in terms of creating the necessary conditions for transcending both political and economic inequities inherent in current structures and relations of power. Diaz Polanco was a key adviser to the EZLN during the 1995–96 peace talks with the Mexican government.

Guatemala

Scholarly treatment of issues of indigenous poverty in Guatemala is surprisingly scarce, according to an initial review of the available literature. Guatemala is one of the poorest countries overall in Latin America and specifically in Central America, but it is also clear that its poverty is disproportionately concentrated among the indigenous majority of its population. In Susanne Jona's now classic *The Battle for Guatemala: Rebels, Death Squads, and U.S. Power*, she noted that the life expectancy for the country's Mayan indigenous peoples was 16 years lower than for the non-indigenous (*Ladino*) population. The indigenous literacy rate was

39 per cent compared to 61 per cent for *Ladinos*, and the infant mortality rate 160 per thousand in the country's predominantly indigenous highlands regions compared to an overall rate of 80 per thousand (p. 179).

According to Cultural Survival (1993) ethnic disparities in terms of access to educational services are especially stark. Mayan students represented 25 per cent of all primary-level students (less than half of their actual proportion of the population of that age group), 10 per cent of secondary-level students and 5 per cent of university enrolment (p. 230).

Further conclusions on the position of the country's indigenous communities can be drawn in terms of patterns of malnutrition in Guatemala from Brown and Pollitt's (1996) widely noted study. The authors summarize results of one of the most concerted longitudinal studies on patterns of malnutrition ever conducted, analysing data collected by the Institute of Nutrition of Central America and Panama in four different rural Guatemalan villages (almost certainly indigenous although not explicitly identified as such). Their results indicate the powerful effects on (relative) infant mortality and growth rates, motor skills, intellectual and emotional development, and enhanced educational and social opportunities of the more nutritious of two different dietary supplements given to children among the two sets of villages studied. Interestingly, the most beneficial of the two supplements given was Atole, apparently an enhanced variant of a traditional Meso-American indigenous corn gruel, while the much less beneficial supplement Fresco is described as a Kool-Aid type of 'sweet, fruit-flavoured drink, which contained no protein' (p. 29).

Brown and Pollitt noted (p. 29) that

> [the] strongest effects of Atole were observed among those at the low end of the social and economic ladder: these children performed as well as the more privileged children in their villages…Atole thus served as a kind of social equaliser…But the children of this study all lived in extreme poverty and did not perform at the same level as, say, a child from a middle-income household in a more prosperous area of Guatemala. Hence, adequate nutrition by itself could not fully compensate for the negative effects of poverty on intellectual growth.

In other words: adequate nutrition helps, but is only a necessary and not a sufficient condition to redress the structural inequities. As Brown and Pollitt (p. 30) concluded, the results in Guatemala are also 'consistent with the prevailing understanding of the interactions between poor nutrition, poverty and education. Nutritional supplements combat the effects of poverty, but only somewhat. A well-nourished child may be better able to explore the environment, but an impoverished community may offer little to investigate'. Amongst other measures, enriched educational progammes for these children are also required because 'most undernourished children face persistent challenges that can exacerbate the effects of underfeeding. They frequently live in areas with substandard schools and little or no medical care. Their parents are often unemployed or work for very low wages. And the children may suffer from illnesses that sap energy needed for the tasks of learning' (p.31).

Recent legal reforms in the status of Guatemala's indigenous minority resulting from its own peace process, apparently ending 34 years of armed conflict which have left over 100,000 dead (primarily indigenous), do not fully address the kind of concerted socio-economic reform agenda implicit in Brown and Pollitt's conclusions, much less the more fundamental approach suggested by Diaz Polanco (1991, 1997). The current package of proposed reforms, which ranges from constitutional changes to a detailed accord on indigenous rights, and which was part of the overall peace agreement ending the conflict,[4] has not yet been fully reflected in national legislation. Compliance with the terms of the indigenous rights accord is, however, specifically subject to verification by the United Nations MINUGUA peace mission in the country and by the UN Secretary-General.

The Accord itself is quite detailed. (For the text of the Accord see Sanchez 1996: 343 et seq.) The fifth paragraph of its preamble stresses the link between discriminatory patterns of socio-economic deprivation, exploitation and injustice borne by Guatemala's indigenous peoples and the overall socio-economic conditions of the majority of the country's population. The seventh paragraph in effect argues that until the particularized discrimination against the country's indigenous majority is eliminated, Guatamala will never be able to develop its full economic, political, social and cultural potential, nor take the place in the world that is its due (p. 344). The body of the Accord is divided into seven substantive sections.[5]

Article IIa of the Accord stipulates that discrimination against indigenous peoples is to be treated as a criminal offence, and that all hitherto existing laws that have a discriminatory effect shall be abolished. This process of eliminating discrimination from Guatemalan society is to be facilitated by the 'widespread diffusion' of the nature of indigenous rights in the mass media and educational system, and by the establishment of national networks of indigenous rights' defenders providing free legal assistance (pp. 345–6). Article IIb focuses specifically on the double burden of discrimination borne by the country's indigenous women and on how this is aggravated by profound conditions of poverty and exploitation (p. 346). Article IIIf addresses issues related to science and technology and of the recognition of intellectual property rights related to spheres of traditional indigenous knowledge. The legally enforceable 'value' of such knowledge is affirmed, but no explicit right to compensation for its use is indicated (p. 351). This is a key issue in terms of the increasing expropriation of traditional indigenous knowledge in fields such as agriculture, botany, forest maintenance, nutrition and the use of medicinal plants, among others, by transnational corporations without adequate compensation.

Article IVb, dealing with civil, political, economic, social and cultural rights recognized under international law recognizes the importance of indigenous community authorities and their role in enabling national development and social progress, including measures to ensure the equitable distribution of public funds (pp. 354–5). Articles IVc and IVe focus respectively on the regionalization of social services and on the need for formal recognition within Guatemala's hitherto dominant legal system of traditional systems and norms of indigenous customary law, a crucial issue throughout the region (pp. 355–7). Interestingly in this respect the Guatemalan accord is a more advanced statement of indigenous rights than the San Andres Accords in Mexico, discussed below, in that the latter failed to incorporate a specific recognition of indigenous customary law and of the principle of what has come to be called legal pluralism.

Article IVf addresses issues related to indigenous land rights, including the recognition of indigenous community rights to the enjoyment of natural resources for community benefit, restitution of lost community rights and a right to compensation for dispossession (pp. 357–61). Article VI, regarding issues of resources for compliance with the Accord, incorporates a governmental commitment to 'undertake all necessary efforts' to ensure the generation and channelling of financial resources required to obtain compliance with its terms, in conjunction with available sources of international aid (pp. 361–2).

A detailed analysis of the steps taken so far to translate the Accord's terms into binding national law and to comply with its substantive aspects is a prerequisite for any fuller assessment of its impact. It was assumed that those aspects of the Accord requiring incorporation into Guatemala's Constitution would be part of the constitutional reform package to be approved in a national referendum scheduled for May 1999. The proposed reforms, which included indigenous rights, were, however, overwhelmingly defeated in a very low voter turnout. The referendum process has been criticized by many independent analysts for its failure to undertake vigorous efforts to promote voter participation in general and specifically by the country's previously disenfranchized indigenous majority (including the absence of targeted efforts among both the large numbers of illiterate potential voters and tens of thousands of monolingual speakers of indigenous languages). The effort to secure the constitutional reforms necessary to translate the general terms of the various aspects of the Peace Accords into binding national law continues, but the situation continues unresolved at the time of writing. It is clear however that (i) in Guatemala as in every country in the region, issues of equity for indigenous peoples cannot be addressed effectively outside the context of dealing with overall patterns of socioeconomic deprivation; and (ii) that international and national legal norms related to these questions have become inextricably intertwined. There is a direct relationship between the evolving character of indigenous rights standards in Guatemala and the overall process which led to the adoption of the proposed UN instrument.

Mexico

According to government census data, some 7.9 per cent of the country's population over 5 years old is identified as of indigenous origin (some 6.4 million in 1990). Indigenous scholars and activists generally reject this as inaccurate and methodologically flawed, because it defines as indigenous only those who identify themselves as speakers of indigenous languages. More generally accepted estimates range between 10 and 20 million, with broader criteria applied including self-identification and cultural indicators, raising the indigenous percentage of the total population (approximately 95 million at present) to between 10 and 20 per cent. Regardless of the total figure, however, all sources agree that Mexico's indigenous peoples are disproportionately over-represented among the country's poorest and most marginalized sectors according to multiple convergent criteria. Since its emergence on 1 January 1994, the Zapatista National Liberation Army (EZLN) has stressed the link between indigenous marginalization, poverty and the lack of democracy in Mexico as the heart of its critique of neo-liberalism, and the guiding thread of its vision for a fundamental transformation of Mexican society.

The recently released Enal '96 official data confirm the longstanding relationship between indigenous status and poverty in Mexico.[6] The data were compiled with unprecedented inter-institutional co-ordination by all the key national providers of basic social services (health, housing, social development, etc) to the country's rural sectors through their decentralized regional and local branches.

Overall, the survey concludes that malnutrition is most pronounced (58.3 per cent of the total population under age 5) in the Mexican rural communities with the highest concentration (70 per cent or more) of indigenous people, when measured by the ratio between height and weight. This compares with a still serious but less spectacular rate of 38 per cent among children below age 5 in predominantly non-indigenous (less than 10 per cent) communities, and reaches a devastating 73.6 per cent among all indigenous youth (ages 0–16) in predominantly indigenous communities. This compares with a 50.9 per cent malnutrition rate in predominantly non-indigenous communities, when measured by the ratio between age and height (Montemayor 1997: 1). Guerrero, the poorest-ranking state and site of the recent emergence of the new armed insurgent movement *Ejército Popular Revolucionario* (People's Revolutionary Army, EPR), has a 71.3 per cent malnutrition rate among children under 5 in predominantly indigenous rural communities when measured by the age and height ratio (Blanco 1997: 1 and 6). Overall malnutrition rates of between 55 and 62 per cent (the highest-ranking) prevail in heavily indigenous regions such as the Huasteca, Northern sierra of Puebla, the Mixteca, the isthmus of Tehuantepec and southern Chiapas. The lowest per capita expenditures on food (less than an average of 3 pesos a day, where the average national minimum wage is supposed to be 30 pesos a day (US$1 = 8 pesos) prevail in Chiapas, Guerrero, Hidalgo and Puebla, all among the ten states with the largest total indigenous populations.

The worst overall housing conditions (lack of sewerage and potable water, dirt floors, overcrowding) are found in the five states of Guerrero, Veracruz, Oaxaca, Puebla and Chiapas, in order of severity, the latter four constituting four of the five states with the largest indigenous populations (Blanco 1997). The highest rate of parents without schooling is also found in Guerrero (55 per cent), with rates of over 40 per cent in Chiapas, Hidalgo, Oaxaca, Puebla and Veracruz, virtually the same line-up as for housing.

On a national level the country's indigenous population lives, of course, primarily in rural communities (concentrating 28.7 per cent of the country's total population), where according to Blanco 70 per cent of Mexico's most extreme poverty is concentrated, with an average schooling level of 3.1 years. According to official figures, at the same time that the poverty rate was declining in urban areas between 1989 and 1992, it rose in the countryside (Pazos M. 1994: 10). By 1993, on the eve of the Zapatista uprising, governmental data estimated that 341 (approximately 14 per cent) of the 2,403 municipalities in the country had high levels of marginalization (defined using an index weighting a series of characteristics in terms of housing, health, nutrition, access to electricity, educational levels, illiteracy, unemployment rates and low wages), with such conditions also prevailing in 281 (approximately 35 per cent) out of 803 communities with indigenous populations of over 30 per cent. Put another way, 281 (more than 80 per cent) of the 341 most marginalized communities in the country had indigenous populations of at least 30 per cent at this time (Cano 1994: 3 and 5).[7]

Two major sets of legal reforms have been proposed to address the inequitable status of Mexico's indigenous peoples in the last decade. These provide a unique kind of controlled social experiment in the realm of indigenous rights because of their unusually contrasting characteristics. The first is that of a top-down governmental initiative by President Carlos Salinas de Gortari (1988–94) between 1989 and 1992. This resulted in an amendment to Article 4 of the Mexican Constitution in January 1992. This explicitly recognized the existence of the country's indigenous peoples in its national charter for the first time, but in purely rhetorical terms. The translated text of the revised version of Article 4 reads:

> The Mexican nation has a multicultural composition which has its origin among the country's indigenous peoples. The development of their languages, cultures, traditional customs and practices, resources and specific forms of social organization, shall be legally protected and promoted in a way which guarantees their access to the national legal system. Their legal customs and practices shall be taken into account in agrarian legal proceedings in which they are parties, in terms to be established by law.

This amendment followed a pattern previously exhibited in Guatemala in 1985 where a series of constitutional reforms supposedly recognizing indigenous rights (articles 59, 66–70) were adopted amid that country's bloody civil war in which tens of thousands of indigenous people were massacred. These reforms remained a dead letter until the indigenous rights Accord which helped pave the way for the end of the armed conflict was signed ten years later. Similarly, in Mexico the 1992 constitutional reform has had no legal impact at all on the status of the country's indigenous peoples for technical, legal, and political reasons. In technical legal terms, the language of the amendment is cramped and empty of substance, falling both far short of international legal minimums contained in varying terms in instruments such as ILO Convention No. 169 (itself ratified by Mexico in January 1991, prior to the enactment of the changes in Article 4), and of the proposed UN and OAS declarations discussed below, and of the increasingly influential demand by indigenous rights scholars and activists for territorial autonomy. Under Mexican law constitutional mandates of this type have no practical effect in the absence of a congressionally adopted implementing law (*ley reglamentaria*). Amendments to the Mexican Constitution are in this sense not self-executing (a parallel debate exists in the context of international agreements). Due to governmental opposition no such implementing law has yet been passed, nor is any such law on the horizon. The current impasse on this issue is similar to that which has recently emerged in Guatemala.

In Mexico the stunted reform of Article 4 of the country's Constitution clearly served a governmental purpose of symbolically addressing the demands of an increasingly powerful grassroots indigenous movement ultimately capable of undermining the ruling Institutional Revolutionary Party's (PRI) lock on the rural vote in the aftermath of a closely contested, probably fraudulent victory in the 1988 presidential elections. The high-profile public debate on the proposed changes to Article 4 helped feed the fire of the activist indigenous sectors which the government had sought to coopt. This spiral was only reinforced by the impact of the Zapatista uprising in January 1994.

The so-called San Andres Accords, signed on 16 February 1996 in the highland Mayan town after which they are named, were the outcome of an on-again/off-again negotiation process between the Zapatistas and the Mexican government which began in late February 1994. The first round of talks resulted from the political pressure generated by the peaceful mobilization of hundreds of thousands of Mexican citizens for a negotiated resolution to the demands of the primarily indigenous Zapatista rebels in the immediate aftermath of the January uprising.

From the beginning, the Zapatistas stressed the national character of their demands for 'freedom, justice and democracy', as well as of their call for a fundamental transformation in the living conditions of Mexico's indigenous peoples (Collier 1994). In a parallel way the governments of first Carlos Salinas and then Ernesto Zedillo sought to relegate the revolt to a localized status in Chiapas and to extricate its indigenous character from broader demands for the overall democratization of the country. In effect, both the Salinas and Zedillo administrations and their intellectual allies have ended up arguing that the indigenous question in Mexico is somehow both national and local, but divorced from other fundamental issues on the national political agenda.

Meanwhile the Zapatistas have increasingly stressed the globalized character of the neo-liberal policies which they argue have contributed powerfully to the immiseration not only of Mexico's indigenous peoples, but of those throughout the Americas and the world. The relationship between the imposition of transnational neo-liberal policies by the IMF and the World Bank, the erosion of national economic sovereignty, and the increasing poverty and violation of the rights of indigenous peoples in Mexico and Latin America has been explored by Gilberto Lopez y Rivas (1995: 105–25). A much less critical approach is taken by a privately circulated study undertaken for ECLAC , the UN Economic Commission on Latin America and the Caribbean.[8] All of these currents helped shape the process which led to the San Andres Accords, the only accords arrived at thus far between the Zapatistas and the government, and help explain the current impasse occasioned by the government's refusal to adopt the constitutional and legislative reforms necessary to implement them.

The link between disproportionate patterns of marginalization and poverty among Mexico's indigenous peoples and the need for vindication of their basic human rights is explicit in, and central to, the San Andres Accords, as it is to the Zapatista rebellion itself. According to the joint declaration by the government and the EZLN which serves as an introduction to the Accords, 'the conditions of poverty and marginalization which affect indigenous peoples demonstrate the unequal character of the development of Mexican society, and define the reach of the demands for social justice which the State must attend to' (point 2 of the declaration). There are deliberate echoes here of the Guatemalan accord on indigenous rights discussed above, signed on 31 March 1995 in Mexico City, just a few weeks before the San Andres talks began. A key human link between the two parallel peace processes is renowned Mexican anthropologist and activist Gilberto Lopez y Rivas, who served as an adviser to the Guatemalan guerrillas regarding indigenous rights issues during the talks which led to that country's peace accords, and who served in the same capacity with the EZLN at San Andres. He was also involved, together with Hector Diaz Polanco, another key adviser to the EZLN at San Andres, in the process which led to the adoption of the Sandinista autonomy law for the Atlantic Coast region in Nicaragua.

In essence the San Andres accords commit the Mexican government to promote a series of constitutional and legislative reforms which would: (i) broaden opportunities for indigenous peoples' political representation and independent, non-partisan participation; (ii) guarantee their access to the national legal system; (iii) promote and protect their cultural, linguistic, educational, productive and employment-related rights; (iv) satisfy their basic socio-economic needs; and (v) defend the rights of indigenous migratory workers. The Accords open the door to constitutional recognition and legislative enactment of indigenous rights to autonomy at the municipal or community level.

But Diaz Polanco and other originators and supporters of the demand for autonomy as a central aspect of a contemporary indigenous rights platform are critical of the Accords on account of their failure explicitly to recognize the need for regional levels of autonomy as a kind of inter-mediary step between state authorities (e.g., Chiapas, Guerrero) and municipalities in the Mexican federal system. The *autonomista* critique of the existing power structures is precisely that they have served primarily to protect non-indigenous interests in predominantly indigenous regions, taking advantage of the atomization of indigenous identity in fragmented communities lacking formal political power and legitimacy. But advocates of a combined system of regional, municipal or community-level autonomy argue that what is needed is reforms that confer such power and legitimacy on the exercise of indigenous self-determination at all three levels, with coordination encouraged among them. At the heart of this vision is the need to create spaces for the exercise of indigenous self-determination within existing state structures that would enable the planning and implementation of progammes for sustainable local development (Diaz Polanco 1997: 30–31). Models from Nicaragua to Greenland and Spain are invoked in support of this argument (ibid.: 15–31, 55, n. 3). Grassroots indigenous groups which mobilized nationally around the San Andres negotiation process vary in their insistence on autonomy as a central demand and in their definition of what it should entail. The government and its allies among the con-servative legal community have been emphatic about their rejection of any but the mildest, most watered-down versions of indigenous autonomy, and have insisted on the separatist dangers posed by anything like the model urged by Diaz Polanco. Many references have been made in the press to the implications posed by recognizing indigenous rights to natural resources such as the extensive oil and uranium reserves, tropical forests and vast biodiversity in the Chiapas region. Critics who invoke this kind of example seem to have greater fear of indigenous control of such resources than of their exploitation by foreign transna-tional corporations.

The bottom line at present is that, regardless of their limitations, the San Andres Accords have no independent legal weight at all, and not even the advantage of the Guatemalan Accords of being expressly subject to international verification. The next step is in the hands of the Mexican Congress, which is more pluralistic than previously, for the first time without a ruling PRI majority. Elected members of the current congress include Lopez y Rivas, the former commander of the Seventh Military Region in Chiapas, and the former chief governmental nego-tiator in the San Andres talks, which have been suspended since September 1996. It is likely that many of the above-described arguments will be reprised in the continuing debate over what to do with the San Andres Accords and how to get the peace talks with the EZLN back on track. At the time of writing no further steps towards the adoption of new national legislation on indigenous rights have been taken, nor are likely to be taken due to political deadlock until after presidential elections in July 2000.

In August 1998, the United Nations Sub-Commission on Preven-tion of Discrimination and Protection of Minorities became the first UN body to adopt a resolution critical of the Mexican government's record of compliance with international human rights standards. The historic resolution, 'Developments in the Situation in Mexico',[9] focused on persistent violations of the rights of the country's indigenous peoples, and specifically called for the signatories of the San Andres Accords to re-initiate the still-suspended peace process. (The full text of the resolu-tion can be found as an Appendix to this chapter.) Two distinguished participants of the CROP research network, Asbjørn Eide of Norway and José Bengoa of Chile, who are members of the Sub-Commission, were among the most active proponents of the resolution. A major factor spurring the Sub-Commission's action was the massacre on 22 December 1997 of 45 indigenous supporters of the EZLN (36 of them women and children) in the community of Acteal in Chiapas, by one of the region's increasingly active paramilitary groups reminiscent of those involved in many similar massacres in Colombia, and in the past in Guatemala. Recent evidence substantiates charges of complicity by sectors of the Mexican government and armed forces in this kind of sys-tematic low-intensity violence and psychological terror targeting indigenous communities, especially in Chiapas and Guerrero. The concerns expressed in this resolution were re-examined during the August 1999 session of the Sub-Commission and also as part of the UN Human Rights Committee's July 1999 review of the Mexican govern-ment's report on state compliance with the relevant provisions of the International Covenant on Civil and Political Rights.

Meanwhile the EZLN has called for an unofficial national refer-endum on indigenous rights issues based both on the San Andres Accords themselves and on their reflection in the legislative proposal to enact the Accords submitted by the congressional peace commission,

COCOPA, on 21 March 1999. The vote, which drew some three million participants throughout the country, was accompanied by a mass peaceful exodus of some 5,000 unarmed Zapatista delegates from Chiapas who travelled in delegations of two (one woman and one man) to each of the country's 2,433 municipalities to promote support for the San Andres/ COCOPA initiatives. This referendum initiative was intended to re-inject indigenous rights issues into the arena of national debate and national public opinion in time for the forthcoming presidential elections.

Nicaragua

The Nicaraguan experience raises fundamental questions relevant to each of the other case studies considered in this paper (Rodolfo Stavenhagen in Jenkins Molieri, 1986: XII):

> What should and can be the relationship between an indigenous group with its own culture and identity, and which wishes to preserve its identity, and a democratic and revolutionary movement which has known how to mobilize the resources and grassroots forces of a whole nation in the struggle for its emancipation? And when a movement such as this is able to take power in a poor and dependent country, after enormous sacrifices, and is then subjected to aggression by the most powerful imperialism in the world that daily imperils its survival, what could and should be the forms of political coexistence between this revolutionary state and this indigenous group?

The Nicaraguan autonomy law could never have been adopted without two different phases of armed struggle which, as in Colombia, Guatemala and Mexico, brought the issue of indigenous rights to the fore of national debate, and to the negotiation table, for the first time. The first phase of armed struggle which created a new revolutionary state dominated by the Sandinista National Liberation Front was the violent overthrow of the long-standing Somoza family dictatorship in July 1979. The second phase was an armed revolt by the Atlantic Coast's indigenous Miskito, Sumu and Rama peoples against Sandinista rule, instigated and financed by the US as part of its low-intensity war against the Sandinista revolution throughout the 1980s. Legitimate sentiments of indigenous resistance against historic domination and exploitation of the Atlantic Coast region by outsiders was used and twisted to serve US foreign-policy aims in ways similar to those of the British in the Arab revolt against Ottoman rule during the First World War, or in US promotion of the separation of Panama from Colombia in 1902. But in Nicaragua the tool became indigenous rights against supposed Marxist-Leninist dictatorship.

The roots of the conflict lay in the history and characteristics of the relationship between the Atlantic Coast region and the rest of Nicaragua. As Jenkins Molieri (1986: 2) notes:

> With the advent of the revolutionary triumph in Nicaragua on July 19, 1979 the situation of indigenous peoples in the region could not be worse. Representing less than 4 per cent of the total population of the country and located in the least densely populated zone (amounting to almost half the national territory), and that which was most backward and least accessible in terms of transportation…Exploited brutally by foreign corporations which owned virtually all of the territory known as the Atlantic Coast…

The prevailing conditions in the region were the 'irrational sacking of natural resources and destruction of the environment' (ibid: 7). Amidst all this, a unique syncretic regional culture had developed, distinct from that of the rest of the country and drawing both on indigenous roots and heavy influence from Afro-Caribbean, US and European sources (for example, Moravian missionaries). The Sandinista problem became how to manage the reincorporation of the region into a revolutionary project applicable to the whole country, and yet how to do so without pursuing an assimilationist model. The region was also crucial to the regime's national security in the face of US aggression.

The Sandinistas' response was, in their own words, to 'retrieve the national sovereignty which had been lost for so long in the region, recover for their rightful owners the natural resources which had been alienated to foreign interests, move the region's peoples out of backwardness and marginalization, rescue their forgotten and distorted cultural values, in sum, place them on the road to a new history of redemption and progress' (ibid: 9). This kind of revolutionary paternalism is characteristic of the *indigenista* policies pursued by the Mexican revolution during its earlier, especially 1920s and 1930s phases. It was ironically this approach that led to constitutional and legislative reforms instituting a new autonomy regime which revolutionized Latin American practice regarding indigenous rights. The 1986 reforms (see Articles 5, 8, 27, 89, 90, 121 and 180 of the new constitution, and the text of the Autonomy Law) mark a turning point in this field which the subsequent Colombian, Guatemalan and Mexican processes have drawn upon heavily. At the same time, as has been noted above, these processes cross-fertilized. The Nicaraguan reforms are key not just in terms of the implementation of the concept of territorial autonomy later drawn upon by Diaz Polanco at San Andres, but also in terms of the recognition under national law of internationally recognized socio-economic, cultural, linguistic and educational rights for indigenous peoples. This resulted concretely, for example, in the Sandinista literacy campaign being conducted in a multilingual manner, and in the widespread implementation throughout the Atlantic Coast region of bilingual education programmes for the first time. Many of these reforms were undermined by the counter-revolutionary war of the 1980s, and by the shift towards a neo-liberal model after the Sandinista electoral defeat in 1990, but remain as points of departure for both reconceptualization and implementation in other settings.

The New UN and OAS Instruments

The need for a new UN instrument on indigenous rights stems from recognition of the limitations of the principal current source of international obligations, ILO Convention No. 169 which, according to Henry J. Steiner and Philip Alston (1996: 1008), 'takes an important step but a short one. The few duties imposed on governments include duties of consultation rather than, say, duties to obtain consent of indigenous peoples before enacting certain measures. The Convention does not indicate the means or forms of participation by indigenous peoples in national decision-making. It gives no effective rights of autonomy'.

The current UN draft declaration on indigenous rights has grown out of a process beginning with informal working groups organized by indigenous leaders, scholars, and activists from throughout the Americas in 1977, and the creation of a formal UN working group on Indigenous Populations of the UN Sub-Commission on Prevention of Discrimination and Protection of Minorities in 1982. Drafting by the working group began in 1985, and was finally brought before the UN Human Rights Commission for consideration in 1995 (ibid). This decade-long drafting process coincides of course with the period of the sharpest conflicts in Nicaragua, Guatemala, Colombia and Mexico noted in this chapter. According to Steiner and Alston, a key factor which has influenced the drafting process is that between the UN Human Rights Commission as a body composed of representatives of UN member states, and the sub-commission on minorities, which is composed of independent experts and oversees the working group directly. The annual sessions of both entities have become critical organizing forums for the international indigenous rights movement, leading among other things to Rigoberta Menchù's Nobel Peace Prize in October 1992 and to the declaration by the UN of a Decade of Indigenous Peoples during 1993–2004. Steiner and Alston suggest that the annual meetings of the working group are 'considered among the most broadly participatory in the entire UN system' (ibid.: 1009). Participation at the sessions increased from some 600 international indigenous rights activists and observers in 1993 (ibid.), to some 900 in 1997.[10]

The Draft Declaration continues to be on the agenda of the annual sessions and most observers agree that it is unlikely to move quickly into the next phases of adoption by the General Assembly. The proposed Interamerican Declaration has had a parallel history within the OAS system. From the Preamble onwards, the current UN draft stresses the link between indigenous poverty and the violation of indigenous rights: 'Concerned about the fact that indigenous peoples have frequently been deprived of their fundamental human rights and liberties, which has resulted in the dispossession of their lands, territories, and resources, as well as in poverty and marginalization' (fourth paragraph of the Preamble). The proposed Interamerican Declaration is even more emphatic in this regard:

> Recognising the severe poverty suffered by indigenous populations in many regions of the Americas, and that their living conditions are generally deplorable; and concerned by the deprivation…of their human rights and fundamental freedoms, which have resulted…in their colonization and in the dispossession of their lands, territories, and resources, thereby depriving them of their right to develop in a manner consistent with their own needs and interests…[11]

Paragraph 1 of the UN Draft Declaration recognizes the right to free pursuit by indigenous peoples 'of their own economic, social, cultural, and spiritual development in conditions of freedom and dignity'. Paragraph 6 recognizes their right to protection against acts of 'cultural genocide' and to the prevention and appropriate compensation for the 'dispossession of their lands, territories, and resources', laying the basis for a right to restitution later spelled out in Paragraph 16, which is also recognized in Article VII, Paragraph 2 of the Draft Interamerican Declaration, and also in Articles XVIII, Paragraph 4, and Article XXI, Paragraph 2.

Paragraphs 9 and 10 recognize indigenous educational and cultural rights including the right to state funding of 'their own' educational systems and institutions, and to interpretation services. Similar rights are recognized in Article IX, Paragraph 4 and in Article VIII, Paragraph 3 of the Draft Interamerican Declaration. Paragraph 12 concerns rights of access and the use of mass media and commits signatory states to take 'effective measures' in this regard. Paragraph 13 establishes a right to 'adequate financial and technical assistance' on the part of states and the broader international community, in order to enable 'their own economic, social, and cultural development'. Paragraphs 14 and 15 recognize indigenous rights to maintain their 'distinctive' relationships with their natural environments, and individual and collective rights to 'possess, control, and use' their lands and territories, including 'full recognition of their own laws and customs, land tenure systems, institutions for the management of their resources, and the right to have effective state measures taken to avoid all intervention with or usurpation of these rights'. Similar recognition is accorded in Articles XVI and XVII of the Draft Interamerican instrument.

Paragraph 17 of the UN draft focuses on the protection of indigenous environmental rights and recognizes a right to receive necessary state funding toward this end as well as support from the international community. A parallel recognition is undertaken by articles XIII, Paragraph 5, and XVIII, Paragraph 4, of the Draft Interamerican Declaration. Article XXI of this proposed instrument goes further than the UN version, and recognizes a right to take measures 'to mitigate the effects of adverse ecological, economic, social, cultural, or spiritual impacts' on indigenous peoples' way of life.

Paragraph 18 of the proposed UN Declaration recognizes a right to economic autonomy, and for indigenous peoples not to be deprived of their 'means of sustenance'. This is further specified in Paragraph 19 in terms of indigenous rights to 'special state measures' with prior consent, which reflect self-determined priorities and which are aimed towards the immediate, effective and constant betterment of social and economic conditions. A similar recognition is contained in Article XXI of the proposed Interamerican Declaration. Paragraph 20 focuses on indigenous peoples' rights to determine, plan and implement economic and social programmes which affect them, preferably through their own institutional structures.

The advances and limitations of the processes at the national level summarized above are reflected in both draft declarations. Each declaration in fact is made necessary by the unevenness of these processes, and by the lack of parallel processes of any significant uniformity or depth elsewhere in the region. Even if each of the declarations is in fact adopted as drafted, the struggles for their meaningful implementation will be, primarily, national processes. But never again will such processes be disconnected or isolated from each other, and a significant measure of their success or failure will be in the capability of indigenous movements to mobilize the attention and support of international civil society, international public opinion and international law.

Conclusion

Few international human rights issues are as intertwined with basic issues of transnational socio-economic equity as are those related to indigenous rights. As Barnet and Cavanagh (1994: 22) suggest:

> As traditional communities disappear and ancient cultures are overwhelmed, billions of human beings are losing the sense of place and sense of self that give life meaning. The fundamental political conflict in the opening decades of the new century, we believe, will not be between nations or even between trading blocs but between the forces of globalization and the territorially based forces of local survival seeking to preserve and to redefine community.

In this sense the struggle immediately to reduce and ultimately eradicate poverty is of itself necessarily transnational and must include as effective measures the redistribution of wealth and power. This effort must in turn incorporate at its heart the kind of commitment to a radical, multiculturalist democracy as proposed by the renowned Mexican philosopher Luis Villoro (1997: 345) in a series of writings reflecting upon the significance of the Zapatista revolt in the context of Mexico's troubled dual process of transition towards both greater democracy and social justice:

> A radical democracy would be one which would return to the people the ability to participate actively in the process of deciding with respect to all the collective affairs which affect their life, and which would finally succeed in achieving that the people not obey any other master but their own will. But the people in reality are not the sum of undifferentiated individuals that are supposed to compose a homogeneous nation-state. The people in reality are heterogeneous, formed by a multiplicity of communities, villages, social organizations, sectors, ethnicities and nationalities, regions, strata, interest groups, associations of workers, employees, employers and professionals, religions, sects, etc, distinct, sometimes in confrontation, and other times in intermixture. The individual human beings who make up these communities are not abstract citizens, 'somebody' equal to anybody else. Each is a person affiliated to various social entities, belonging to various different specific groups and cultures, each with its own characteristics and with an identity which differentiates it from others…For that person to exercise their autonomy would mean the ability to make decisions about their own life, in a concrete setting, and therefore to participate in collective decisions to the extent that they affect his or her personal situation. And that situation includes that person's roots in a singular place, where they work, where they

live…A radical democracy would be one in which all power rests in fact upon that concrete basis of a real community.

This is where the increasing convergence between international and domestic legal standards regarding indigenous rights must increasingly take us, as is reflected in the achievements and contradictions of the initial case studies outlined in this chapter regarding the evolving relationship between indigenous human rights issues and the struggle against poverty.

Appendix

Developments in the situation in Mexico

(SUB-COMMISSION RESOLUTION 1998/4)

The Sub-Commission on Prevention of Discrimination and Protection of Minorities,

Guided by the principles of the Charter of the United Nations, the Universal Declaration of Human Rights and the international conventions relating to the promotion and protection of human rights,

Taking note of information from corroborative sources indicating that developments in the human rights situation in Mexico are becoming more and more disturbing, particularly as far as the indigenous populations are concerned,

Considering the information and recommendations by the Special Rapporteur of the Commission on Human Rights on the question of torture (E/CN.4/1998/38/Add.2) and the Special Rapporteur on the sale of children, child prostitution and child pornography (E/CN.4/1998/101/Add.2) following their visit to that country,

Noting with satisfaction the importance of the announcement made to the Sub-Commission by the Mexican Government of its support for the adoption by the General Assembly of the draft Declaration on the Right and Responsibility of Individuals, Groups and Organs of Society to Promote and Protect Universally Recognized Human Rights and Fundamental Freedoms, approved by the Commission on Human Rights in its resolution 1998/7 of 3 April 1998 and by the Economic and Social Council in its resolution 1998/33,

Regarding as an encouraging sign and a positive development the statement made to the Sub-Commission by the Mexican delegation on the general strategy decided by the Government to resolve the question of Chiapas with the help of dialogue and without first requiring the Zapatista National Liberation Army to hand over its weapons, by reconciliation and peace in dignity and in justice, by re-establishing and maintaining the rule of law, including the disarming of armed groups and the resumption of dialogue with the Zapatista National Liberation Army, and by tackling the structural causes of marginalization and extreme poverty connected with the underdevelopment of that region,

Reaffirming its conviction that preventive action by the Commission on Human Rights and other protection mechanisms is the surest way, while there is still time, to prevent violence and impunity from irreparably impairing the rule of law,

1. *Requests* the Mexican authorities to ensure full respect for the international instruments to which Mexico is party and, to this end, to attach the highest priority:

   (a) On the one hand, to combating the impunity of perpetrators of serious human rights violations, especially those suffered by numerous members of the indigenous populations;

   (b) On the other hand, to promoting the action of human rights defenders and guaranteeing their safety;

2. *Appeals* to the signatories of the San Andres accords to resume the process favouring dialogue;

3. *Requests* the Commission on Human Rights, in the interest of prevention, to consider at its next session the developments in the human rights situation in Mexico and decides, should the Commission be unable to do so, to continue the consideration of these developments at its fifty-first session, under the same agenda item.

26th meeting
20 August 1998
(Adopted by secret ballot by 12 votes to 6, with 6 abstentions.)

Notes

1. UN Doc. E/CN.4/Sub.2/1994/2/Add.1, 20 April 1994.
2. UNDP, *Human Development Report 1996*, 33–6; see also Table 1.7.
3. UNDP, *Human Development Report 1997*; see the boxes at pp. 43 and 88.
4. *Acuerdo sobre identidad y derechos de los pueblos indígenas en Guatemala*, signed 31 March 1995.
5. Indigenous Peoples' Identity, The Struggle Against Discrimination; Cultural Rights; Civil, Political, Social, and Economic Rights; Implementing Bodies; Resources; and Final Conclusions.
6. The fourth *Encuesta Nacional de Alimentación en el Medio Rural Mexicano* (National

Survey of Nutrition in Rural Mexico; Enal '96).

7. Chart compiled from multiple official sources.

8. *Libre Comercio Integración Económica, y Los Pueblos Indígenas Surandinos*, Document No. LC/R. 1480, no author, 29 December 1994.

9. E/CN.4/Sub.2/1998/L.18, 14 August 1998.

10. *La Jornada*, 5 August 1997.

11. All quotes from the UN draft are taken either from the edited English version in Steiner and Alston (1996), pp. 1011–16, or translated from the complete Spanish version in: *Manual de Documentos Para la Defensa de los Derechos Indígenas*, Academia Mexicana de Derechos Humanos (1989), pp. 119–24. Quotes from the Draft Interamerican Declaration are taken from the full Spanish version in: *Derechos de Los Pueblos Indígenas en las Constituciones de América Latina*, Enrique Sanchez (ed.), Disloque Editores, 1996, pp. 329–41.

Bibliography

Barnet, Richard J., and John Cavanagh (1994) *Global Dreams: Imperial Corporations and the New World Order*, Simon and Schuster, New York.

Blanco, José (1997) 'Hambre Inaceptable', *Perfil de La Jornada*, 22 July.

Brown, J. Larry, and Ernesto Pollitt (1996) 'Malnutrition, Poverty and Intellectual Development', *Scientific American*, February.

Cano, Arturo (1994) 'Reclaman, No Se Extinguen', *Revista Enfoque*, Reforma newspaper, October 9.

Collier, George A., with Elizabeth Lowery Quaratiello (1994) *Basta: Land and the Zapatista Rebellion in Chiapas*, Food First Books, San Francisco.

Cultural Survival (1993) *State of the Peoples: A Global Human Rights Report on Societies in Danger*, Beacon Press, Boston.

Diaz Polanco, Hector (1991) *Autonomía Regional: La autodeterminación de los pueblos indios*, Siglo XXI, Mexico, DF.

Diaz Polanco, Hector (1997) *La Rebelión Zapatista y la Autonomía*, Siglo XXI, Mexico, DF.

Edwards, Sebastian (1995) *Crisis and Reform in Latin America: From Despair to Hope*, World Bank, New York.

Gros, Christian (1991) *Colombia Indígena: Identidad Cultural y Cambio Social*, CREC, Santa Fé de Bogotá.

Jenkins Molieri, Jorge (1986) *El Desafío Indígena: El Caso de los Miskitos*, Katun, Mexico, DF.

Jonas, Susanne (1991) *The Battle for Guatemala: Rebels, Death Squads, and US Power*, Westview Press, Oxford.

Lopez y Rivas, Gilberto (1995) *Nación y Pueblos Indios en el Neoliberalismo*, Plaza y Valdes/Universidad Iberoamericana, Mexico, DF.

Lustig, Nora (ed.) (1995) *Coping with Austerity: Poverty and Inequality in Latin America*, Brookings Institution, Washington DC.

Montemayor, Carlos (1997) 'Desnutrición y Violencia Social', *Perfil de La Jornada*, 22 July.

ONIC (Organización Nacional Indígena de Colombia) (ed.) (1995) *Tierra Profanada: Grandes Proyectos en Territorios Indígenas de Colombia*, Disloque Editores, Santa Fé de Bogotá.

Pazos M., Cesar (1994) *Estudio sobre la pobreza en México: Bases para la elaboración del Marco Programático del Sistema de Naciones Unidas para el próximo período de cooperación con el gobierno de México*, unpublished manuscript prepared for the InterAmerican Development Bank.

Sanchez, Enrique (ed.) (1996) *Derechos de los Pueblos Indígenas en las Constituciones de América Latina*, Disloque Editores, Santa Fé de Bogotá.

Steiner, Henry J. and Philip Alston (1996) *International Human Rights in Context: Law, Politics, Morals*, Oxford University Press, New York, Oxford.

United Nations Development Programme (1994 et seq.) *Human Development Reports*, Oxford University Press, New York, Oxford.

Villoro, Luis (1997), *El Podor y El Valor: Fundamentos de una ética política*, Fondo de Cultura Económica, Mexico, DF.

World Bank (1995) *World Development Report*, World Bank, Washington, DC.

8

Indigenous Poverty
and Social Mobilization

LUIS HERNANDEZ NAVARRO

The Souls of Indigenous Folk

If during the Spanish colonization of Mexico the debate was over
whether indigenous people had souls or not, and if since the presidency
of Lazaro Cardenas (1934–40) Mexican state policies directed at the
country's indigenous peoples have stressed the need for the disappearance
of their particular identities into a supposedly common Mexican identity,
since the Zapatista rebellion in January 1994 and the signing of the 1996
San Andres Accords regarding Indigenous Rights and Culture, the
debate has been as to whether or not indigenous peoples should be
accorded 'special' rights. The refusal to recognize the existence of their
souls, of their own identities or of their rights is part of the same way of
thinking: that which is based on notions of racial superiority or of racial
mixture (*mestizaje*) as destiny, and which refuses to accept the idea of a
right to be different, a right to 'otherness', on the part of those who are
culturally distinct.

Over the past three years Mexico's indigenous 'question' has been
debated with an intensity, passion and virulence unprecedented in our
country's recent history. In the heat of the discussion both prejudices
and idealizations have emerged. Well-informed and empirically based
opinions have been lumped together with judgements that are at best
unfortunate in character and often rooted in ignorance. Reflections
regarding these issues seem to become a kind of labyrinth of errors from
which there is no exit.

In the Deepest Part of the Pit

At least one out of every ten Mexicans is officially considered to be of
indigenous origin. According to a recent study by Mexico's national

115

institute of indigenous affairs, *Instituto Nacional Indigenista* (INI), their number is over 8.7 million people, belonging to 59 different ethnic groups. The definition of indigenous status employed in this chapter is that of the 1989 International Labour Organization (ILO) Convention No. 169 concerning Indigenous and Tribal Peoples in Independent Countries. (Mexico was one of the first three countries to ratify the convention.) According to Article 1, Section (b) of that instrument, indigenous peoples are those

> who are regarded as indigenous on account of their descent from the populations which inhabited the country, or from a geographical region to which the country belongs, at the time of conquest or colonization or the establishment of present State boundaries and who, irrespective of their legal status, retain some or all of their own social, economic, cultural and political institutions.

Article 2 further provides that 'self-identification as indigenous or tribal shall be regarded as a fundamental criterion for determining the groups to which the provisions of this Convention apply'.

Mexican government data must be handled with caution. According to anthropologist Pierre Becaucage, a comparison of official census figures from 1950 and 1980 indicates an increase in the numbers of indigenous people reported, which is not explainable by reference to increases in birth rates but which instead reflects a process of redefinition of ethnic identity: for the first time indigenous peoples were willing to confess their true identity to census takers and the latter, who are often indigenous people with higher education than average, were not precluded by shame from counting the real number of indigenous people in their own communities.

Some indigenous peoples are concentrated in a relatively compact territory (for example the Mixes in the Pacific coast state of Oaxaca), while others are distributed throughout several different states (for example the Nahuas, speakers of contemporary variants of the language Náhuatl, spoken by the Mexicans at the time of the Spanish conquest). At the same time some of these groups are quite numerous (from hundreds of thousands, such as Zapotecs and Mixtecs, to more than a million each in the case of Nahuas and Mayas), while others amount to just a few families.

As a whole Mexico's indigenous peoples live in alarming conditions of extreme poverty and marginality. It is virtually synonymous in our country to be indigenous and to be poor. Virtually all of the indigenous people living in municipalities with 90 per cent or more indigenous population are catalogued as extremely poor. According to a CONAPO (National Population Council) study based on 1984 census data, more than three-quarters of all indigenous people in the country live in 281 municipalities (out of a national total of 1,234) classified as 'extremely marginal' by government criteria. Indigenous illiteracy is almost 50 per cent, while the national average is 12 per cent. About half of all municipalities with high concentrations of indigenous people lack electricity and potable water, while the national average of those without such services is 13 and 21 per cent respectively. In almost 60 per cent of these predominantly indigenous municipalities, migration in search of work is a structural necessity, and those who migrate live in generally poor conditions. The Valley of Mexico around Mexico City, the agricultural fields of Sinaloa and cities such as Los Angeles or Chicago in the US concentrate large numbers of Mexican indigenous migrant workers. Between 70 and 84 per cent of indigenous children below age 5 present elevated levels of malnutrition according to the national survey of nutrition, *Informe Nacional sobre Seguridad Alimenticia*. The index of mortality of these same children is 26 per thousand compared to a national average of 20 per thousand. Some 80 per cent of the illnesses they suffer are of infectious origin and attributable to nutritional deficiencies, anemia, and lack of adequate sanitation. Their life expectancy is an average of 69.5 years while the national average is 73.7.

Their economic marginalization is compounded irremediably by injustice. In 1993, the year before the Zapatista uprising, 170 political murders, 18 disappearances, 367 cases of illegal arrest, 3,620 cases of harassment, 21 detentions incommunicado, 410 injuries, 7 political kidnappings and 37 cases of torture were inflicted upon indigenous people throughout the country. The principal origins of these human rights violations include, in order of importance, political repression, agrarian conflicts and problems in the administration and ineffective prosecution of justice. According to Jorge Madrazo Cuellar, currently national Attorney-General, the country's courts are unable to provide justice for Mexico's indigenous peoples: 'The procedural reforms promoted by the CNDH [the National Human Rights Commission, the governmental body which he headed before becoming Attorney-General] for ensuring the provision of translators and interpreters, and infusing knowledge on the part of judges regarding indigenous customary law, cannot be complied with even in modest ways'.

This situation is attributable in part to the lack of recognition of indigenous political institutions and to their lack of political representation in institutions which wield power at the municipal, state and federal levels. There is no relationship between the demographics of the distribution of the indigenous population and their political representation at various levels of government. There are very few indigenous deputies or senators at the state or federal level. In addition, much of the existing political structure of the country is alien to indigenous traditions of governance.

A similar pattern of disempowerment exists at the municipal level, even where these are predominantly indigenous in population, since political offices tend to be monopolized by mestizos living in the seats of municipal government (indigenous people tend to live in outlying communities). This lack of formal political representation has serious consequences for indigenous communities.

Another obstacle to indigenous political mobilization and participation is the insistence in every state but Oaxaca on electing municipal governments through a system based on political party affiliation and organization. In most indigenous communities traditional forms of participation and organization prevail, based on decision-making in community assemblies, by plebiscite or consensus, and according to systems of rotation of responsibilities. As a result, political participation becomes monopolized by officially recognized political parties. Indigenous norms of customary law regarding ways of exercising and structuring power, lengths of time in office, the handling of public works or the removal of authorities are not recognized as having full legal standing. In addition, indigenous communities do not have any formal juridical status or standing as such except in some matters related to land tenure and resource management pursuant to agrarian law.

In the same way governmental design, administration and delivery of services to indigenous communities are all carried out without participation by indigenous people. These problems are further complicated both by the evolving electoral system based exclusively on political parties and by the one-party state which has prevailed in the country since 1929, neither of which corresponds to the realities and needs of the country's indigenous peoples. They also result from a process of vertical, authoritarian modernization which has marginalized and impoverished vast segments of the population. In this way, the poverty in which indigenous populations are immersed is not the result of indigenous culture, as some claim, but rather systemic in origin. All of this is further contributed to by disproportionate concentration of land in the hands of a small number of owners and by corruption in the agrarian reform process.

The De-Indianization of the Indians

Spanish conquest and colonization delivered a fierce blow to the original inhabitants of Mexico. Their ways of living and cultures underwent vast transformations. Once their best lands were taken away from them, many were forced to take refuge in isolated mountain regions. The living conditions and lack of political representation of indigenous peoples are to a great extent the product of their colonization, as well as of the policies (*indigenismo*) pursued by the Mexican state allegedly to address their needs.

Indigenismo is simultaneously a theory, an ideology and a government policy. Theoretically it is the product of the efforts of a group of intellectuals among which stand out Manuel Gamio, Moises Saenz, Alfonso Caso and Gonzalo Aguirre Beltran. Their shared emphasis was on the need to undertake careful studies of the actual conditions in which indigenous people live, the nature of their community life, the patterns of intercultural relationships between these communities and others in their surrounding regions, and the possibilities of indigenous community survival. In terms of government policy, *indigenismo* followed from President Lazaro Cardenas' statement to the first Inter-American Indigenous Congress in Patzcuaro, Michoacan in 1938 where he stated that:

> our indigenous problem lies not in keeping Indians Indian, nor in making Mexico Indian, but rather in Mexicanising the country's indigenous people. And to do so respecting their blood, capturing the strength of their emotion and love for the land and their unbreakable tenacity. In this way their attachment to the Mexican nation will be strengthened, and the nation will be enriched by moral virtues which will deepen the patriotic spirit and affirm Mexico's distinct character.

With the passage of time, the integrationist tendencies in the Cardenista discourse would become more marginal. In this context, almost 30 years ago, the then Mexican Ambassador to the US, Hugo B. Margain (also a high level Treasury official for many years, as well as Ambassador to the United Kingdom) noted:

> The tendency is towards accelerating the shift from the isolation which geographical patterns have imposed upon predominantly aboriginal communities, in a fertile process of national incorporation by means of vehicles such as language and culture. The goal is to arrive at a point where a broader conception prevails about our culture, with the aspiration of affirming our national identity within, and the affirmation of that which is Mexican in the world at large, thereby responding to the impoverished and reductionist

identification of who we are with a tribal landscape, confined to some isolated hut that is cut off from the rest of the world. In this way we can arrive at an idea of the nation where all our aspirations come together, in such a way that indigenous people cease to exist and become simply Mexicans.

Indigenismo as a government policy is then a framework designed and implemented by non-indigenous people whose centre of gravity lies in the cultural and national assimilation of indigenous peoples in the name of development, universal civilization and values, and indigenous peoples' own good. In the words of Gonzalo Aguirre Beltran: '*Indigenismo* is not a policy formulated by indigenous people for the solution of their problems but rather that developed by non-indigenous people for those heterogeneous groups that are in general labelled as indigenous'. Its principal instruments were agrarian reform, public education, agricultural extension programmes, specialized programmes, anti-poverty programmes and a process of corporatist integration into the ruling Institutional Revolutionary Party (PRI) by means of the government-controlled CNC (National Peasants' Confederation) or the government-controlled indigenous governing councils (*Consejos Supremos Indígenas*). Among these policies' principal operators were indigenous people with higher levels of education than the norm who often evolved into regional *caciques* (political bosses). With time, some of these features of *indigenismo* became transformed, but in any case the new indigenous struggles in Mexico have emerged to a great extent from critiques of and battles against *indigenismo* both at the institutional and ideological levels. Repeated criticisms of the INI as an institution emerge in this context.

The contemporary stress on demands for autonomy is in this sense an initiative which seeks to redefine the terrain of indigenous social struggles. The intensified pace of such struggles in the aftermath of the 1994 revolt buried the moribund corpse of *indigenismo*. With the signing of the San Andres Accords between the Mexican government and the EZLN on 16 February 1996 the funeral rite was completed. The Mexican state was compelled to recognize its theoretical orphanhood regarding the indigenous question and the failure of its attempts to 'mexicanise indigenous people by de-indianizing them' as a matter of government policy. But the struggle continues. In place of the old approach new ways of indigenous thinking have emerged which are vigorous and deeply rooted, and which will transform Mexican culture and national politics. This is a kind of thinking which emerges from years of resistance and reflection about what is characteristic of each group, and what is alien to it. It is the result of the gestation process of a new indigenous intelligentsia which is characterized by high levels of western-type education and which is deeply rooted in its home communities, and of the formation of hundreds of local and regional organizations with authentic leadership and understanding of indigenous struggles throughout Latin America.

Social Exclusion and the Construction of Citizenship

Like an explosive wave growing in intensity and regularity, indigenous people have since January 1994 become central protagonists, who have transformed Mexico's political map. Their struggles do not have a single organizational centre and their demands are diverse. They can be differentiated from traditional mobilizations for land or against poverty, which were especially significant during the 1970s and 1980s, in that they now have ethnically based demands as their central axis. Their key actors assume themselves to be not *campesinos* (peasants) but indigenous people. Their organizations, which have played a critical role in this whole process, have undergone a transformation from being agrarian or production-oriented in character to becoming ethno-political. Some of their mobilizations are evidently defensive and in response to the aggressions of landowners and rural death squads (*guardias blancas*). Others are decidedly offensive and seek the reconfiguration of power relations. Together they all reflect an irreversible trend which has to do with demands for inclusion in a broader conception of citizenship and access to greater social equality. They push for their recognition as differentiated political actors, as collective subjects, and not only for individual access to rights of citizenship, and act on the basis of redefinitions of identity based on membership in groups of indigenous peoples (e.g., as Mixes, Mayas, Zapotecs and Mixtecs) rather than on the basis of origin in a particular community or village.

They are also the protagonists of a new kind of insertion into public spaces through a complex and uneven process, which flows from their transcendence of a status as the excluded promoted by integrationist policies that sought to annihilate their status as belonging to different cultures. From an initial stage, in which their demand is for equality, there is a transition to a second stage, in which the emphasis is on the affirmation of difference. There is a parallel here to the process undergone by workers' struggles in the past, and which is currently being experienced by the struggle of women.

The struggle for full citizenship assumes equality with others and the possession and effective exercise of equal rights and obligations. It is at the same time, then, a struggle for dignity and against racism. It is a process characterized by the construction of equalities, against exclusion, in which concrete demands transcend clientelistic concerns so as to insert themselves into a framework of rights. It also involves a recognition of the interdependency of rights, where the struggle for collective rights is a vehicle for making individual rights a reality.

The struggle for the recognition of difference stems from the acceptance of different legitimate ways to exercise authority and to constitute a collectivity with rights of its own. It takes up a struggle for the right to equality and for a differentiated exercise of this right. It also flows from international law and from the Mexican government's incorporation of standards such as ILO Convention No. 169 into its own domestic law. Such legal reforms are understood to be part of a process whereby the full equality of rights which is formally conceded but constantly negated in practice can finally be fulfilled. But this struggle does not seek, as some analysts would have it, to lay the basis for the reproduction of a *cacique*-like traditional leadership threatened by demographic growth, pressure on the land and modernization, but, to the contrary, is the means by which organized indigenous communities can free themselves from the undue influence of mestizo landowners and middlemen. At the heart of this movement is the struggle for self-determination based in both the International Covenant on Civil and Political Rights and the Covenant on Economic, Social and Cultural Rights, which together with the Universal Declaration of Human Rights make up the International Bill of Human Rights. Autonomy is the internal expression and reflection of the exercise of this right.

Indigenous peoples have become an autonomous political subject with their own proposals for change. This is a process which is in the ascendant and is irreversible. Their demand is for a new political and institutional order capable of enabling them to overcome the conditions of exclusion to which they have been relegated. In doing so they nourish the emergence of the pluralism which the current centralized state denies. All of this is possible, despite what government spokespersons say, because their identities have been profoundly transformed and because today they assume their character increasingly as peoples and not merely as insular communities.

In this way the struggle for the self-determination and autonomy of indigenous peoples and for the construction of a differentiated citizenship are elements which favour the democratization of the whole nation. They do not have the intention of ghettoizing indigenous peoples' struggles but rather of making them part of the overall struggle to dismantle Mexico's one-party state. The torrent of indigenous mobilizations in the last few months will intensify and diversify in the immediate future.

From the Deepest Roots

The Zapatista insurrection of January 1994 served as catalyst for the emergence of a new indigenous rights movement in Mexico, but this movement already had deep roots. In its modern expression, as a series of ethno-political, agrarian, productive or civic organizations, the indigenous movement is more than 20 years old, part of which can be traced back to the Indigenous Congress organized in San Cristóbal de Las Casas, Chiapas in 1974 (during the 400th anniversary year of the death of Chiapas' first bishop, indigenous rights pioneer Bartolome de Las Casas, after whom San Cristóbal is named) by Bishop Samuel Ruiz. But a more recent key phase in this process is from September 1989 to October 1992, when the new indigenous movement as we know it began to yell throughout Latin America in preparation for the commemoration of 500 years of indigenous resistance.

The symbolic and historical importance of the 500-years anniversary in 1992 helped systematize lines of thought and reflection and to articulate continental, regional and national platforms of struggle regarding the indigenous question. In the heat of this intensive process of mobilization new organizations emerged with new indigenous leaderships. Many of these leaders were educated in western ideas but returned to their communities of origin with renewed commitments to struggle. There is an increasing, albeit unevenly distributed, tendency for higher levels of education among indigenous people to fail to produce expected levels of social mobility, especially in the cities. The open path towards social ascent that education is traditionally assumed to be has become a congested tunnel. The reality is about social exclusion and the incapacity of the labour market and social system to absorb indigenous people educated according to western norms, in the context of intensifying community-based struggles towards the revaluation of indigenous identity. Some of these leaders are graduates of public institutions of higher education, including lawyers, engineers and teachers.

Many others are transient migrants in the big cities, in the agricultural workplaces of Mexico's north-east or in the US who at some point return to their communities of origin. The social webs and networks of solidarity and mutual aid generated around the migrant experience have also precipitated a kind of revaluation of ethnic identities. Organizations of indigenous migrant workers have become a kind of identity school.

Others who have played key roles in these movements were educated through the evangelical work of various different religious groups, especially by those close to progressive sectors of the Catholic Church. This has resulted in many of these activists becoming promoters of organizing efforts and of ethno-political movements. Over time, however, groups originally rooted in such origins have become increasingly lay-oriented. Other organizations resulted from grassroots development projects promoted by various different kinds of non-governmental organizations (NGOs), which were often also linked to religious networks and organizations. Such leaders then, in addition to playing a leadership role in their communities, have also participated in political parties, NGOs, religious organizations or *indigenista* programmes. Many of these leaders, and in some instances entire communities, are linked in various different ways to international networks of organizations involved in the defence and promotion of indigenous rights and development with which they are able to exchange experiences and reflections. Together the diverse vision and experience of the world which these kinds of change agents have acquired has little to do with Margain's vision of isolated indigenous community lives.

Nonetheless the shift towards new forms of indigenous actions and actors cannot be explained exclusively in terms of the generation and availability of new leadership groups. It also results from the formation and growth of a large number of socio-political organizations committed to indigenous rights and demands, which reflect the restructuring and redefinition of indigenous communities and regions. In the majority of cases, these organizations began as *campesino*-based groups fighting for land, services or for the appropriation of production processes in their own interests, and in many cases have transformed themselves into ethno-political forces. Many of the regional expressions of this tendency have reconstructed themselves in the heat of the impact of the Zapatista movement and have begun to take up ethnic demands. Many of these organizations, which were originally focused on issues of development and improvement in social conditions, have become schools of political and social participation and begun to transform the power relations between these communities and regional power-brokers.

In similar ways many indigenous communities have undertaken a recovery of their traditions as a vehicle for resistance. In dozens of indigenous municipalities in Oaxaca, and in hundreds of indigenous communities in other states, but also in many parts of Mexico City, the San Quintin valley or in the US, tradition has been reinvented or reconstructed as a path to struggle against *caciquismo*, to reaffirm identity or to confront supposed modernization. This process of developing new forms of leadership, of building regional organizations and of recovering community identities has profound origins. A central role has been played in all of this by a new indigenous intelligentsia and by the revaluation of indigenous culture in general, and of literature in indigenous languages in particular, in ways very distant from the folkloric exoticism of the 1970s.

The Zapatistas did not invent Mexico's contemporary indigenous peoples' struggles but gave them a national dimension, stimulated their growth, unified many of its currents, helped systematise their experiences and programmatic concerns, wrested from the state the commitment to undertake necessary constitutional reforms regarding indigenous rights, transformed the terms of the relationship between indigenous peoples and the rest of Mexican society and helped the indigenous movement to build a more stable organizational platform. The Zapatista insurrection provoked an overflow of indigenous movements throughout the country. The national debate over indigenous rights and their consequences for national political life and the emergence of a new national political actor – the autonomous indigenous movement grouped together in the *Congreso Nacional Indígena* (National Indigenous Peoples' Congress, CNI) – stemmed directly from the signing of the San Andres Accords.

The indigenous question has been placed at the centre of the national political agenda. Discourse about the boundaries of national identity, anti-poverty policies, the country's process of democratic transition and democratization, the nature of the new regime needed and the relationship between morals and politics have all been transformed. There can be no reform of the state without a just solution to the indigenous question. There can be no peace in Chiapas in the absence of a thoroughgoing process of constitutional reform which duly recognizes the rights of this country's original inhabitants.

The new indigenous rights struggle, articulated and promoted by the Zapatistas, has profound implications for the development of a new kind of nation. As promoter of a democratic multiculturalism, this struggle is a central force in the resistance to a process of globalization that serves the interests of the most powerful, and is also a force in the struggle in defence of minority rights and against social exclusion. It is the midwife of a new national pact based not only on individuals but also on the country's constituent peoples, thereby stimulating the reinvention of the kind of state and nation that we really want to be.

The 1996 San Andres Accords are a manifestation of the fact that Mexico's indigenous peoples exist, are alive and are committed to struggle. They are proof of the fact that both old and new integrationisms, dressed up as supposed nationalisms or universalisms, have not been able to destroy them, and that a part of the governing élite and intellectuals continue to profess a distilled version of nineteenth-century liberalism. All of this bears witness to the fact that Mexico's indigenous peoples are not living relics but living political actors endowed with a vision for the future. Cultures are under siege, but possessed with an extraordinary vitality.

Without doubt the reflections of the poet and leader of Czechoslovakia's anti-authoritarian revolution, Vaclav Havel, made for other lands and circumstances, can be applied to the new indigenous rights struggle addressed here:

> Yes, the politics of anti-politics is possible. Politics from below. Politics of the people, not of the apparatuses. A politics that emerges from the heart, not from a thesis. It is no accident that this hope-inspiring experience has to be lived here on this terrible field of battle. When the daily conditions which prevail are tedious, it is then that it is necessary to descend to the bottom of the pit before we can rise up again to see the stars.

References

Beaucage, Pierre (1988) 'La condición indígena en México', *Revista Mexicana de Sociología*, vol. L, no. 1, Instituto de Investigaciones Sociales, UNAM, Mexico, January–March 1988.

Embriz, Arnulfo (coordinator) (1993) *Indicadores socio-económicos de los pueblos indígenas de México, 1990*, Instituto Nacional Indigenista, Direccíon de Investigación y Promoción Cultural, Subdirección de Investigación, Mexico.

Madrazo Cuéllar, Jorge (1995) 'Derechos Humanos, cultura y reforma indígena', *Revista del Senado de la República*, no. 2, Mexico, January–March 1995, p. 155.

Margain, Hugo B. (1968) 'Mexico, fusión de las culturas indígenas y españolas', *Boletín Bibliográfico de la Secretaría de Hacienda y Crédito Público*, no. 395, Mexico, 15 July 1968.

Havel, Václav (no date) 'La responsabilidad como destino', Fondo de Cultura Económica (FCE), Mexico.

PART IV
Solutions from
a Human Rights Perspective

9

Poverty and Social Justice
in Latin America

Economic and Social Rights and the Material Conditions
Necessary to Render them Effective

HÉCTOR GROS ESPIELL

Creating the necessary material conditions for the realization of economic
and social rights in the context of the current situation in Latin America
must first be contextualized in terms of the varying conceptions of the
region and the common elements, and vast differences, between all the
countries which go to make it up; second, they must be shaped by the
varying conceptions of poverty and justice applicable to the Latin
American reality.

What do we mean when we speak of Latin America in this context?
Perhaps the most accessible definition proceeds initially by way of
exclusion. When we speak of Latin America we are not speaking of the
United States or Canada, the region's most important English-speaking
countries. Although both belong to the Organization of American
States (OAS) – which currently consists of 34 member nations, plus
Cuba whose membership has been suspended since 1962 – neither is
Latin American, whether in terms of origin, culture or type of legal
system, nor according to linguistic criteria, level of economic development or membership of the North Atlantic Treaty Organization
(NATO). Nor does Latin America include the English-speaking
countries of the Caribbean. These are also members of the OAS but not
part of Latin America. On the other hand the Dominican Republic,
Haiti and Cuba, although all are Caribbean island nations, do fall within
the definition of Latin America employed here. They are part of Latin
America, for all of the reasons described above, along with Puerto Rico,
despite the latter's colonial status. Neither Suriname nor Guyana, independent nations which are also member states of the OAS, fall within
my definition, nor do French Guiana and the other territories in the
region possessed by the Netherlands, France or the United Kingdom,
regardless of whether their colonial status is formally acknowledged.

All of the Latin American states share common characteristics of history and culture, as well as similar legal systems. Despite important differences between them, all can be classified as developing countries in social and economic terms. The differences cannot be ignored, however, and are expressed in varying rates of poverty, ethnic composition, variations in distribution of income and social inequality, varying degrees of institutionalization of the rule of law and of social justice, and in varying regional characteristics.

Poverty is a common characteristic shared by these countries even though it varies in intensity from country to country. In my own country, Uruguay, for example, it does not have the terribly negative character that it does in others. But in addition to poverty we must add injustice to our measure of social and economic rights, the injustice of the breach between the richest and the poorest as well as the injustice of polarized distribution.

As Jorge Castañeda (1994) has noted, Latin America is not the poorest region in the world, but there is surely 'none that is more unjust'.[1] This reality has grave implications for the political, social and economic future of the region, given the evident relationship between inequality and governability, and thus between poverty, injustice and the sustainability and viability of political democracy under such conditions (Castañeda 1999). It is this reality which generates the grave contemporary concern about how much poverty is tolerable in a democracy in the Latin American context.

The relationship between social conditions, politics, human dignity and ethics is an unavoidable aspect in this whole discussion. This will not be focused on in this chapter, but its importance must be noted, remembering the recent words of Pope John Paul II in the post-Synodal Apostolic Exhortation *Ecclesia in America* (p. 207), which he signed in Mexico City in January 1999:

> Not infrequently, this leads some public institutions to ignore the actual social climate. More and more, in many countries of America, a system known as 'neo-liberalism' prevails; based on a purely economic conception of the human being, this system considers profit and the laws of the market as its only parameters, to the detriment of the dignity of and respect due to individuals and peoples. At times this system has become the ideological justification for certain attitudes and behaviour in the social and political spheres leading to the neglect of the weaker members of society. Indeed, the poor are becoming ever more numerous, victims of specific policies and structures which are often unjust.[2]

According to the Pope, 'the rule of law is the necessary condition for the establishment of an authentic democracy' (ibid., p. 209). For democracy to develop, there is a need for civic education and the promotion of public order and peace. In effect:

> there is no authentic and stable democracy without social justice. Thus the Church needs to pay greater attention to the formation of consciences, which will prepare the leaders of society for public life at all levels, promote civic education, respect for law and human rights, and inspire greater efforts in the ethical training of political leaders (ibid., p. 210).

Justice, as an essential element of all humane political and legal approaches to the issue of poverty, necessarily implies respect for the dignity of the person as a human being and as a member of a human community. It also implies equality before the law of all individuals as well as respect for their right to non-discriminatory treatment and to the promotion of their individual and collective development in association with others. Such a commitment to justice, which should be immanent throughout and guide governmental policies, implies compensatory measures when necessary. Different situations must be addressed differently in order for the end result to be itself equitably just. This is what is meant by distributive or retributive justice that corrects and conditions the absurd and blind application of the law and of the equality principle, which can have aberrant consequences. The correct way to conceive of the application of an equality principle whose conceptualization is parallel to the idea of justice leads to the conclusion that we must 'rattraper par la loi les inégalités foncières de la nature' (compensate legally for the inherent inequalities of nature) (Robert 1993: 41).

Justino Jiménez de Aréchaga (1946: 158) has commented accurately on the Uruguayan Constitution:

> What its norms require is that human beings who are equal, in similar circumstances, receive equal treatment. In this way the equality principle, or principle of equal protection by the laws, appears to be susceptible to a definition akin to that of retributive justice…But a democratic system of governance and the political philosophy on which such a democratic system is based do not impede the recognition of certain secondary degrees of inequalities between individuals. In fact, democratic philosophy demands that the state recognizes the existence of certain inequalities and that it seeks to re-establish effective equality between individuals by means of unequal treatment under such circumstances.

This point, which has been the object of political and philosophical thought since the origins of ethical reflection,[3] will not be developed here, but we would do well to remember the words of Uruguay's national hero, José Artigas, who said as long ago as 1815: 'Let the most abandoned ones become those who most benefit'.[4]

In this way, although natural equality and juridical equality – equality before the law – are different concepts, they are intimately related to each other; both converge and condition each other's translation into reality. Juridical equality implies the equal application of laws without any discrimination but does not suppose that it is not legitimate to legislate for specific groups or sectors of society in order to treat them in a singular fashion in pursuit of justice, with the ultimate objective of bringing about an equitable result. Nor can we forget what José Enrique Rodo (1956: 161–2) expressed so magnificently:

> The most truly dignified concept of equality rests upon the idea that all rational beings are endowed by nature with the capacity to develop towards a higher, more noble plain. The duty of the state lies in assuring all members of the society the equitable conditions necessary to evolve towards the perfection of their development. The duty of the state is to provide the means necessary so that the unveiling of superior stages of human development can unfold uniformly. In this way, beyond the initial conditions of equality provided for, all subsequent inequalities would be justified because they would be in effect the fruit of the mysterious choices of Nature or of wilful, meritorious effort. When conceived of in this way, democratic equality is far from being the enemy of the natural selection of customs and ideas, and is in fact the most effective instrument of spiritual selection.[8]

To be realized in practice, juridical equality implies a certain degree of natural equality, and in order to get closer to the always relative but desirable level of material equality, the recognition and effective application of juridical equality is required. In addition, equality in the material sense, or at least the negation of the most aberrant extremes of manifest natural inequality, in other words of poverty and injustice, demands that 'the state assures to those who need it protection', and the guarantee 'of those determinate juridical standards that are indispensable for the development of human persons and for the effective enjoyment of their remaining fundamental rights (Risso Ferrard 1998: 97).

> With respect to economic, social and cultural rights, the state has the essential but not exclusive obligation of acting: the obligation to provide the material means so that economic, social, health and cultural services are effective vehicles for their satisfaction. These are rights inherent in the human person, in accord with the legal system within which they arise, and which imply the ability to demand that the state respect these rights by providing the means necessary for their realization. (Gros Espiell 1991: 53)

In this sense juridical and material equality both require the prevalence of certain conditions of liberty (de Tocqueville 1963: 463).

What we generally refer to as social justice is based on certain ideas of distributive or retributive justice and consists of the application of the concept of equality. Social justice recognizes and is based on the need to legislate with due regard to the conditions of deprivation prevailing among certain social groups or sectors in order to compensate for these inequalities at their root by means of appropriate measures of special treatment. At the same time it implies an acceptance and promotion of the duty of law itself in the interests of community development, taking into account naturally existing conditions.

Individual and collective or social justice are two aspects or two manifestations of the underlying unity of justice itself. They are applied and integrated in reciprocal ways. If we fail to consider the collective dimensions, overall justice is incomplete and individual justice unachievable, because the individual human being, in her or his intimate and unreproduceable individuality, can only exist in the framework of a larger social reality. An unjust society implies the existence of individual human beings who have been treated unjustly.

Social Justice and Human Rights

A social approach to justice is a necessary component of the politics and conceptualization of law in the modern world. This is why one of the essential objectives of social justice is to combat poverty, which is fundamentally incompatible with a humane and convivial notion of society. This kind of justice, which cannot fail to be realistic in its emphases but which at the same time has to be idealistic in its objectives, must strive, through law, both directly and indirectly, against poverty itself. There is not, and cannot be, a meaningful social policy which accepts social justice as one of the legitimate aims of the exercise of contemporary state power, that does not have the combating of poverty as a central objective.

There has always been a predominant tendency in Latin American philosophical, juridical and political thought that has affirmed the essential unity of all human rights as the expression of the dignity of the human being, as well as the need for them to be vindicated through legal means. One always starts from the recognition of the indivisibility of civil, political, economic, social and cultural rights (see Gros Espiell 1991: 119). This Latin American doctrine of human rights has at the same time argued that economic, social and cultural rights 'are necessarily and unavoidably connected in terms of their possible effectiveness and realization in practice to broader issues of social and economic development' (Gros Espiell 1986: 103).

Economic, Social and Cultural Rights

What is the current state of economic. social and cultural rights in Latin America in terms of both domestic and international law? Since the path-breaking adoption of the world's first constitution to recognize social, economic and cultural rights, in Mexico in 1917 as the result of its revolution, and steps along similar lines taken by several European states after the first and second world wars, many American countries have followed suit. From the Latin American perspective, especially influential constitutions which followed the Mexican approach were those of Spain's Second Republic in 1931, prior to that country's civil war, and Cuba's of 1940. In the American continent today this trend has become virtually universal and in the last few years has taken on a more profound, integral and generalized character in more recently adopted constitutions such as those of Brazil, Paraguay, Argentina and Colombia.

In terms of international law, there is a universal set of standards, which includes the UN's International Covenant on Economic, Social and Cultural Rights of 1966, to which all Latin American nations are state-parties, in addition to the standards of international labour law and social rights which stem from the Conventions of the International Labour Organization (ILO) (see Gros Espiell 1978). In addition, we have the entitlements which flow from the internationally recognized rights to adequate nutrition and health, as well as cultural rights under the aegis of the UN's Food and Agriculture Organization (FAO), the World Health Organization (WHO) and the United Nations Educational, Scientific and Cultural Organization (UNESCO).

There is also a set of regional organizations and instruments which add to this overall international framework and which, in the American continent, flow from the American Declaration of Rights and Duties of Man as well as the Inter-American Charter of Social Guarantees, which were both adopted at the ninth Pan-American Conference in Bogotá in April 1948 (see Gros Espiell 1989). It is interesting to add, however, that the original charter of the Organization of American States (OAS), which was also adopted in Bogotá in April 1948, and which preceded the adoption of the Universal Declaration of Human Rights by the UN General Assembly in December of that year, did not contain norms recognizing economic, social and cultural rights. But the charter was amended as a result of the adoption of the Protocol of Buenos Aires in February 1967, and now includes, in its current Chapter VII ('Economic Standards'), a set of norms enunciating such rights. Issues of social justice and basic economic conditions are considered prerequisites for their realization. The two key provisions are in articles 30 and 34. Article 30 provides that the member states 'pledge themselves to mobilize their own national human and material resources through suitable programs, and recognize the importance of operating within an efficient domestic structure as fundamental conditions for their economic and social progress and for assuring effective inter-American co-operation'. Article 34 provides that the member states 'should make every effort to avoid policies, actions or measures that have serious adverse effects on the economic or social development of another Member State'.

The American Convention on Human Rights, adopted at San José, Costa Rica, in November 1969 – also known, and referred to here, as the San José Pact – provides in Chapter III (Economic, Social and Cultural Rights), Article 26 ('Progressive Development') that:

> The States Parties undertake to adopt measures, both internally and through international cooperation, especially those of an economic and technical nature, with a view to achieving progressively, by legislation or other appropriate means, the full realization of the rights implicit in the economic, social, educational, scientific and cultural standards set forth in the Charter of the Organization of American States as amended by the Protocol of Buenos Aires.

Article 26 and the overall issue of the status of economic, social and cultural rights in the San José Pact have led to the following observation:

> The draft text proposed by the Inter-American Council of Jurists of 1959 had included economic, social and cultural rights in its proposal and provided for a system guaranteeing their protection. The same approach was reflected in the Chilean and Uruguayan drafts proposed in 1965. Unfortunately during the final stages of the drafting process in the Interamerican Commission on Human Rights a different approach was adopted. The argument that prevailed was that, since the 1967 Protocol of Buenos Aires had incorporated economic, social and cultural norms into the OAS Charter, and since the 1966 International Covenant on Economic, Social and Cultural Rights had been adopted by the United Nations, no specific recognition of such rights was necessary in the Americas, and that there was no need to establish a regional system for their protection. This decision was a grave error which led to the inclusion in the San José Pact of its current Article 26. The only affirmative recognition of economic, social and cultural rights is in Article 42 of the American Convention which requires States Parties to refer copies of the annual reports which they submit to the Executive Commissions of the Inter-American Economic and Social Council and to the Inter-American Council for Education, Science and Culture to the Inter-American Commission on Human Rights. This article

fails to ensure direct international regional protection for economic, social and cultural rights. (see Gros Espiell 1991a: 118)

In 1988, the OAS adopted the Protocol of San Salvador, which is an additional protocol to the American Convention on Human Rights, concerning economic, social and cultural rights. It has to date been ratified by nine member states of the OAS but has not yet entered into force since the minimum number of ratifying states required by the charter is eleven. This protocol is in effect a treaty which is complementary to the San José Pact and which would establish a truly regional system for the protection of economic, social and cultural rights.

In any case the issue of the unfulfilled need for regional protection has been in part overcome by the adoption of the Protocol of San Salvador which upon taking effect would create a regional ombudsman to oversee the implementation of the economic, social and cultural rights which it recognises. This is a *sui generis* solution distinct from that provided for in the Charter with respect to compliance with the civil and political rights which it recognizes. This Protocol reiterates the approach taken in Article 26 of the American Convention, without referring back to the amended OAS Charter itself, reproduces Article 2 of the San José Pact, establishes a duty of non-discrimination (Article 3) and the criteria pursuant to which certain limitations and restrictions of these rights can be undertaken (articles 4 and 5), enumerates and defines these rights (articles 5 through 18), and defines the means for their protection and for the development and operative and technical implementation of Article 42 of the Pact (Article 19). This Protocol, which reflects progress in this area, but which is still insufficient, must be completed in the future, specifically by means of the establishment of a regional system of protection for at least some of the economic, social and cultural rights recognized in the Convention, which would include them within the machinery of the Interamerican Commission for Human Rights together with the civil and political rights already recognized and protected (Gros Espiell 1991a: 119)

Chasm between Norm and Reality

But what relationship is there today between the formal legal recognition of economic, social and cultural rights and the practical realization of these rights? There is, in truth, an abyss between the two, not only distancing the formal declaration of these rights from actual compliance with them in reality, but also, and what is perhaps worse, between the recognition of these rights and the policies and efforts of governments and of society as a whole in rendering them effective. This is the general situation in Latin America despite important differences in other spheres and between the region's varying political regimes.

What has not been understood is that these rights are not merely distant, arguably plausible objectives. Legal and social doctrine has accepted their juridical status and the consequent extent to which they may be vindicated through legal proceedings, without failing to recognize their differing status from those of civil and political rights. Governmental policies in most, but fortunately not all, cases have failed to undergo the necessary process of ideological and mental transformation required to synchronize the various government machines with the efforts needed to guarantee economic, social and cultural rights.

This chasm between norm and reality, between what is and what ought to be, must be breached as soon as possible, taking into account the nature of these rights and the challenges imposed by prevailing economic realities, without detriment to their realization.

Creating the Right Conditions

Beyond the necessary and unavoidable effort to implement and respect economic, social and cultural rights lies the fundamental question of assuring the material conditions essential for their realization. In the same sense in which the effective exercise of civil and political rights demands certain political conditions, especially those which flow from a democratic state where the rule of law prevails, so economic, social and cultural rights require the existence of material conditions capable of translating them into reality. The relationship between these two categories of indivisible and interdependent rights implies that adequate respect for economic, social and cultural rights demands not only conditions of an economic nature but also minimum political conditions. From the perspective of the dominant regional school of thought summarized here, the realization and effectiveness of economic, social and cultural rights demands the underlying framework of a democratic state where the rule of law prevails, together with a commitment to social justice, and in which, as a result, both the necessary material and political conditions prevail. Without the transformation and improvement of underlying economic, social and political conditions at the base of society, compliance with human rights can never be complete, remaining in the best of cases incomplete and formalistic.

If this is so with respect to all human rights, it is all the more evident with respect to economic, social and cultural rights which require a material underpinning expressed in patterns of public spending and the provision of publicly funded services. But the issue here is of even greater significance. Beyond budgetary considerations, material conditions of this kind provide the necessary basis for the translation of theoretical rights into actual social certainties which have a direct reference to individual human beings living in a concrete society.

The same goes for the realization of these rights on a global scale. It is in this broader context that we must consider the question of the effectiveness of these rights together with the framework of struggle against destitution, hunger, ignorance and underdevelopment. Under currently prevailing conditions in Latin America this implies an understanding of the intimate relationship linking the issue of human rights with the problem of underdevelopment, exploitation and injustice, not only as internal matters within a particular country but also on a global scale, as part of the division of humanity into a developed world on the one hand, and another world, trapped in underdevelopment, which is exploited and marginalized.

International law recognizes and affirms the unavoidable necessity of securing adequate conditions for the enjoyment of economic, social and cultural rights as objective realities. In 1948, the Universal Declaration of Human Rights proclaimed in Article 28: 'Everyone is entitled to a social and international order in which the rights and freedoms set forth in this Declaration can be fully realized'. And the two international human rights covenants of 1966 recognized and reaffirmed the guiding thread stressed here regarding the need for material conditions as the underpinning of compliance with declarations of rights. In the introductory part to the Covenant on Economic, Social and Cultural Rights it is, for instance, recognized that 'in accordance with the Universal Declaration of Human Rights, the ideal of free human beings enjoying freedom from fear and want can only be achieved if conditions are created whereby everyone may enjoy his economic, social and cultural rights, as well as his civil and political rights'. And the Covenant on Civil and Political Rights uses identical language to that cited above but with a reciprocal mention of the way in which compliance with civil and political rights also depends on respect for those of an economic, social and cultural character.

The above-mentioned Inter-American Charter of Social Guarantees expresses the following:

> It is recognized that the advancement of such rights and the progressive improvement of the standards of living of the community in general depended to a great degree on the development of economic activities,

increases in productivity and cooperation between workers and employers, expressed in the harmoniousness of their relations and in the respect for and reciprocal compliance with rights and duties.

It also proclaims what it describes as 'fundamental principles that must protect workers of all kinds', and 'sets forth the minimum rights workers must enjoy in the American states, without prejudice to the fact that the laws of each state may extend such rights or recognize others that are more favourable', since 'the state attains its goals not only by recognizing the rights of citizens alone, but also by concerning itself with the fortunes of men and women, considered not only as citizens but also as human beings'. As a result states must guarantee 'respect for political and spiritual freedoms, together with the realization of the postulates of social justice'.

In this same line of thought the Preamble to the 1969 American Convention on Human Rights reiterates that 'in conformity with the Universal Declaration of Human Rights the achievement of the ideal of a human being free from fear and misery is only realisable if conditions are created which permit each person to enjoy their economic, social and cultural rights as well as those of a civil and political character'. The Protocol of San Salvador expresses the same idea in similar terms, as does, for instance, the European Social Charter, adopted in Turin in October 1961, in a differing but parallel regional context, in the introductory paragraph to Part I: 'The Contracting Parties accept as the aim of their policy, to be pursued by all appropriate means, both national and international in character, the attainment of conditions in which the following rights and principles may be effectively realized...'.

It is clear that in a situation where generalized poverty prevails, in an economic setting characterized by scarcity and underdevelopment, in a state without resources, sunken in impotence and financial chaos and in the context of a society in which ignorance reigns, economic, social and cultural rights cannot be a reality despite their formal juridical recognition. Their realization under such conditions is impossible.

At the same time we have to recognize that law, that is to say the law of a democratic state committed to social justice, is the necessary but perhaps insufficient condition to promote the economic and social change necessary for rights be realized. A state's social and economic policies, implemented lawfully, are the unavoidable but not exclusive elements necessary for the development and transformation of negative conditions capable of enabling economic, social and cultural rights to begin to become a reality. Such a democratic state, committed to social justice, where the rule of law prevails, must itself also be the great vehicle for the transformation and betterment of society and for its economic, social and cultural development. It is not enough to be a manager of change. Without the combined effort of the society as a whole, including the state organs, nothing deep, transcendent and lasting can be achieved.

Notes

1. See also Juan Antonio Ocampo, 'Distribución del ingreso, pobreza y gasto social en América Latina', and Andrés Solimano, 'Crecimiento – Justicia Distributiva y Política Social', *Revista de la CEPAL*, August 1998.
2. Published by Libreria Editrice Vaticana, Vatican City.
3. Hans Kelsen (1945) 'La Justicia Platónica', in *La Idea del Derecho Natural y Otros Ensayos*, Losada, Buenos Aires; Hans Kelsen (1956) *Qué es la Justicia?*, Imprenta de la Universidad, Córdoba; Alf Ross (1963) *Sobre el Derecho y la Justicia, Capítulo XII, La Idea de Justicia*, Eudeba, Buenos Aires; Gustav Radbruch (1967) 'El fin del Derecho', in *Los Fines del Derecho*, UNAM, Mexico, 4th ed.
4. Article 60 of the 'Reglamento Provisorio de la Provincia Oriental para el Fomento de su Capaña y de Seguridad de sus Hacendados', 10 September 1815.

References

de Aréchaga, Justino Jiménez (1946) *La Constitución Nacional*, Tomo I, Montevideo.
Castañeda, Jorge (1994) *La utopia desarmada*, Ariel, Buenos Aires.
Casteñeda, Jorge (1999) 'Davos y el pos neoliberalismo', *La República*, Montevideo, 21 February,
Gros Espiell, Héctor (1978) *La Organización Internacional del Trabajo y los Derechos Humanos en América Latina*, UNAM, Instituto de Investigaciones Jurídicas, Mexico.
Gros Espiell, Héctor (1986) 'Los Derechos Económicos, Sociales y Culturales', in *El Sistema Interamericano*, Libro Libre, San José, Costa Rica.
Gros Espiell, Héctor (1989) 'La Declaración Americana sobre Derechos y Deberes del Hombre, Raices Conceptuales y Políticas en la Historia, la Filosofia y el Derecho Americano', *Revista IIDH*, special ed., San José, Costa Rica.
Gros Espiell, Héctor (1991a) *Derechos Humanos*, Instituto Peruano de Derechos Humanos, Lima.
Gros Espiell, Héctor (1991b) 'La Convención Americana y la Convención Europea de Derechos Humanos, Análisis Comparativo', *Jurídica de Chile*, Santiago.
Risso Ferrand, Martin I. (1998) 'Derecho Constitucional', in *Estado Social y Democrático de Derecho, Derechos, Deberes y Garantías*, Tomo III, Montevideo.
Robert, Jacques (1993) *Droits de l'Homme et Libertés Fondamentales*, 5th ed., Montchristien, Paris.
Rodó, José Enrique (1956) 'Ariel', in *Obras Completas*, Tomo II, Edición Oficial, Montevideo.
de Tocqueville, Alexis (1963) *La Democracia en América*, 2nd edition, Fondo de Cultura Económica, Mexico.

10

The Right to Development
as a Programming Tool
for Development Cooperation[1]

PATRICK VAN WEERELT

Article 1, Paragraph 3 of the UN Charter, signed on 26 June 1945, described respect for human rights and fundamental freedoms for all without distinction as to race, sex, language or religion as one of the purposes and principles of the United Nations. To this end the Charter attributed several powers to the UN General Assembly,[2] the Economic and Social Council (ECOSOC)[3] and the Trustee system.[4] On 10 December 1948, the General Assembly, meeting in Paris, adopted and proclaimed the Universal Declaration of Human Rights (UDHR). It was the first time the world community agreed upon 'a common standard of achievement for all peoples and all nations' in the field of human rights. Since that historic occasion, the UDHR has served as a moral imperative guiding the relationship between individuals and their governments and as a bulwark safeguarding the human rights, fundamental freedoms and inherent dignity of all members of the human family. At the time the UDHR was adopted, the general assembly requested ECOSOC to ask the Commission on Human Rights to prepare, as a matter of priority, a draft covenant on human rights and draft measures of implementation, and to examine further the question of the right to petition.

In 1950 the general assembly declared that 'the enjoyment of civic and political freedoms and of economic, social and cultural rights are interconnected and interdependent', and that 'when deprived of economic, social and cultural rights, man does not represent the human person whom the Universal Declaration regards as the ideal of free man'. It decided 'to include in the covenant on human rights economic, social and cultural rights and an explicit recognition of men and women in related rights as set forth in the Charter of the United Nations'.[5]

At its subsequent session in 1951, the Commission on Human Rights drafted 14 articles on economic, social and cultural rights reflecting the proposals made by governments and suggestions by the specialized agencies.[6] It then formulated ten articles on measures for implementation. The draft covenant on human rights was discussed by ECOSOC at its thirteenth session, also in 1951. The question was raised whether two different categories of rights could be embodied in one covenant, as initially decided by the General Assembly. Due to the international ideological controversies of the Cold War in prioritizing a particular set of rights, the General Assembly requested the Commission 'to draft two covenants on human rights…one to contain civil and political rights and the other to contain economic, social and cultural rights'. It specified, however, that the two covenants should contain as many similar provisions as possible, in order to emphasize the unity of the aim in view and to ensure respect for and observance of human rights. Although the Commission completed the preparation of the two covenants in 1953/4, and the article-by-article discussion by the General Assembly began as scheduled, it was not until the twenty-first session of the General Assembly, in 1966, that the elaboration of the covenants was completed.[7]

This description of the drafting process of the International Bill of Human Rights – the 1948 Universal Declaration of Human Rights and the 1966 Covenants on Civil and Political Rights and on Economic, Social and Cultural Rights – shows that the quest for an integral approach to human rights could not be answered fully at that time. In the following decades this quest became of paramount importance to human rights practitioners in the world, resulting, *inter alia*, in the solemnly adopted 1993 Vienna Declaration and Programme of Action (VDPA). In the VDPA, the World Conference on Human Rights (WCHR) recognized and affirmed that all human rights are universal, indivisible, interdependent and interrelated; that they derive from the dignity and worth inherent in the human person; that the human person is the central subject of human rights and fundamental freedoms and consequently should be the principal beneficiary; and that the human person should participate actively in the realization of these rights and freedoms.

The right to development also found clear guidance in the VDPA. The Vienna World Conference reaffirmed the right to development, established in the 1986 Declaration on the Right to Development,[8] as a universal and inalienable right and integral part of fundamental human rights, and declared that while development facilitates the enjoyment of all human rights, the lack of development may not be invoked to justify the abridgement of internationally recognized human rights. A key issue of the WCHR, however, was the possible reference to the establishment of the post of High Commissioner for Human Rights. After intense and long discussions, the World Conference on Human Rights recommended to the General Assembly that when examining the report of the conference at its forty-eighth session, it began, as a matter of priority, consideration of the question of the establishment of a High Commissioner for Human Rights for the promotion and protection of all human rights.

Mandate of the High Commissioner for Human Rights

In Resolution 48/141 of 20 December 1993, the General Assembly decided to create the post of High Commissioner for Human Rights. The assembly decided, *inter alia*, that the High Commissioner should be guided by the indivisibility and interrelatedness of all human rights as well as by the importance of promoting a balanced and sustainable development for all people. Moreover, the assembly decided that the High Commissioner for Human Rights should be the UN official with principal responsibility for UN human rights activities under the direction and authority of the Secretary-General, and that within the framework of the overall competence, authority and decisions of the General Assembly, ECOSOC and the Commission on Human Rights, the High Commissioner's responsibilities should be, amongst other things:

- to promote and protect the effective enjoyment by all of all civil, cultural, economic, political and social rights;

- to promote and protect the realization of *the right to development* and enhance support from the relevant bodies of the United Nations system for that purpose;

- to enhance international cooperation for the promotion and protection of all human rights.[9]

The General Assembly, ECOSOC and the Commission on Human Rights have since adopted several resolutions pertaining to the mandate of the High Commissioner in respect of the implementation of the right to development. For example, in its Resolution 1996/15 of 11 April 1996 the commission requested 'the United Nations High Commissioner for Human Rights, in his capacity as overall co-ordinator of United Nations human rights activities, to continue his dialogue with appropriate specialized agencies and bodies of the United Nations system with regard to the impact of their programmes and activities on the implementation of the right to development'. The Commission on Human Rights Resolution 1997/72 once more underlined the important role of the High Commissioner in the promotion and protection of the right to development, as mandated in paragraph 4(c) of General Assembly Resolution 48/141.

The Right to Development as a Human Right

For over 20 years, the international community has attached importance to the universal realization of the right to development. In 1977, the Commission on Human Rights requested the UN Secretary-General to undertake a study on the international dimensions of the right to development as a human right. The request was based on the idea that a relationship exists between human rights and economic and social development. In the following year, the Commission recognized the right to development as a human right for the first time and asked the Secretary-General to undertake a study on the conditions requested for the effective enjoyment by all peoples and all individuals of the right to development.

In 1981, the Commission on Human Rights decided to establish a working group of 15 governmental experts who were to submit a report with concrete proposals for the implementation of the right to development and for a draft international instrument on this subject. The draft Declaration on the Right to Development was adopted in final form by the General Assembly in its Resolution 41/128 of 4 December 1986, by a vote of 146 to 1 (the United States) and 8 abstentions. The adoption of this declaration marks the point of departure for the deliberations taking place, at the time of writing, on the implementation of the right to development.

In adopting the Declaration the General Assembly recognized that development is a comprehensive economic, social and political process which aims at the constant improvement of the well-being of the entire population and of all individuals on the basis of their active, free and meaningful participation in development and in the fair distribution of benefits resulting therefrom (see the 1986 resolution). As such there is a responsibility for the creation of national and international conditions favourable to the realization of the right to development.

The Declaration itself proclaims:

> The right to development is an inalienable human right by virtue of which every human person and all peoples are entitled to participate in, contribute

to, and enjoy economic, social, cultural and political development, in which all human rights and fundamental freedoms can be fully realized. (Article 1, paragraph 1)

And:

1. The human person is the central subject of development and should be the active participant and beneficiary of the right to development.

2. All human beings have a responsibility for development, individually and collectively, taking into account the need for full respect for their human rights and fundamental freedoms as well as their duties to the community, which alone can ensure the free and complete fulfilment of the human being, and they should therefore promote and protect an appropriate political, social and economic order for development.

3. States have the right and the duty to formulate appropriate national development policies that aim at the constant improvement of the well-being of the entire population and of all individuals, on the basis of their active, free and meaningful participation in development and in the fair distribution of the benefits resulting therefrom. (Article 2)

In 1987, the UN Secretary-General organized a global consultation on the fundamental problems posed by the implementation of the Declaration and the criteria which might be used to identify progress in the realization of the right to development. Subsequently, in 1993, building on the consensus of the Vienna World Conference where the right to development was reaffirmed as 'a universal and inalienable human right and integral part of fundamental human rights', the Commission on Human Rights decided to establish for a three-year period a new working group on the right to development, composed of 15 governmental experts with a mandate to identify obstacles to the implementation and realization of the right to development by all states and other appropriate sources; and to recommend ways and means towards the realization of the right to development by all states.[10]

In 1996, the Commission reaffirmed that the implementation of the Declaration on the Right to Development requires perseverance and concrete efforts and that this dynamic process should be pursued at all appropriate levels, including through the elaboration of international and national strategies, which requires the effective contribution of states, organs and organizations of the UN as well as of non-governmental organizations active in this field. To that end, the Commission decided, amongst other things, to establish yet another inter-governmental group of experts with a mandate to elaborate a strategy for the implementation and promotion of the right to development in its integrated and multidimensional aspects. It decided on this step bearing in mind the conclusions of the previous working group and the conclusions of the World Conference on Human Rights and of the four world conferences: the UN Conference on Environment and Development (Rio de Janeiro, 1992), the International Conference on Population and Development (Cairo, 1994), the World Summit for Social Development (Copenhagen, 1995), and the Fourth World Conference on Women (Beijing, 1995). In its report on its second session, the group of experts submitted suggestions for a global strategy for the promotion and implementation of the right to development. Its suggestions are directed at the UN, other international organizations, states and civil society.[11]

In its 1998 session, the Commission on Human Rights recommended to ECOSOC the replacement by a double mechanism of the above-mentioned working group: an open-ended inter-sessional working-group and an independent expert 'with a high competence in the field of the right to development' who is going to report to the working group on the 'current stage of progress in the implementation of the right to development'.[12] The expert appointed in 1998 was Mr Arkun Sengupta from India.

The Multidimensional Character of the Right to Development

The World Conference on Human Rights proclaimed democracy, development and human rights to be interlinked and mutually supportive. It reaffirmed the right to development as a universal and inalienable right and as an integral component of fundamental human rights, and, following the Declaration on the Right to Development, reiterated that the human person is the central subject of development.

In Resolutions 1997/72 and 1998/72 the Commission on Human Rights recognized that the Declaration on the Right to Development constitutes an integral link between the UDHR and the VDPA through its elaboration of an holistic vision integrating economic, social and cultural rights with civil and political ones. An outspoken definition of the right to development was provided by Secretary-General Kofi Annan in his statement to the 53rd session of the Commission on Human Rights on 9 April 1997:

> [T]ruly sustainable development is possible only when the political, economic and social rights of all people are fully respected. They help to create the social equilibrium which is vital if a society is to evolve in peace. *The right to development is the measure of the respect of all other human rights.* That should be our aim: a situation in which all individuals are enabled to

maximize their potential, and to contribute to the evolution of society as a whole.[13]

In other words, the human right to development is related to all human rights but cannot be identified just as the sum total of civil, political, economic, social and cultural rights. It allows for the recognition of ties between various human rights and enables integration of the body of rights from the perspective of the individual's participation in sustainable development. For example, economic growth can be a requirement for the realization of economic, social and cultural rights. Development is, however, more than just economic growth. Not all forms of growth would be compatible with development. As Asbjørn Eide, member of the UN Sub-Commission on the Prevention of Discrimination and Protection of Minorities, described, as early as 1987, the distinguishing criteria should be whether the processes of growth are such that they do not negatively affect civil and political rights and give better protection in terms of economic, social and cultural rights to the most vulnerable and impoverished.[14] The right to development encompasses the place of individuals in civil society, their personal security and their capacity to determine and realize their potential.

As in the case of all other human rights, the implementation of the right to development requires first and foremost its translation to the domestic level. Former UN Secretary-General Boutros Boutros-Ghali pointed out in his Agenda for Development[15] – and the Copenhagen Declaration, adopted at the 1995 World Summit for Social Development clearly concurs with him – that each state continues to bear primary responsibility for its own development. Furthermore, the World Conference on Human Rights underscored that while development facilitates the enjoyment of all human rights, the lack of development may not be invoked to justify the abridgement of internationally recognized rights. Whether expressed in the language of a state's responsibility or that of international human rights, development requires a competent government leadership, coherent national policy and strong popular commitment. It is a means of ensuring democracy at the national and international levels, the improvement of incomes, health and social services, and generally of the living conditions of all people. International cooperation is needed to facilitate and support activities to that end. In this respect, the right to development and its implementation have created a number of opportunities for the High Commissioner for Human Rights to give new impetus to the comprehensive human rights approach as foreseen in the purposes and principles of the UN Charter.

The Right to Development as a Programming Tool

With the passing of the 50th Anniversary of the Universal Declaration of Human Rights it seems that the universality and indivisibility of all human rights can be finally realized. By linking the normative standards of human rights law with other developmental processes, the right to development contains all the necessary components to guide the human rights system in the new millennium.

Taking into account the large number of opportunities created by the establishment of the Office of the High Commissioner for Human Rights (OHCHR) as well as by the evolution of the understanding of the right to development, but also accepting the limitations of the small UN human rights component, it will be essential for the High Commissioner to prioritize the following strategic and substantive programming tools if the human rights programme as a whole is to make a sound and sustainable impact on development planning.

Inter-agency cooperation

Probably the most important but at the same time least developed tool for a real impact of human rights on the larger development system is participation in inter-agency fora. The work carried out by all UN programmes and specialized agencies has a bearing on the implementation of the right to development, making it an inherent part of an homogeneous approach to human rights, for example, the United Nations Development Program (UNDP), the UN Conference on Trade and Development (UNCTAD), the International Labour Organization (ILO), and the World Bank. Bodies such as the economic commissions and the World Tourism Organization also have a role to play.

The UN human rights programme does not have the financial and human resources to enter into cooperation with many programmes and agencies on a bilateral basis. Inter-agency targeting is therefore of vital importance. Already-existing, broader inter-agency entities are probably the most important. As such, the human rights programme should be taken up by the executive committees on peace and security, economic and social affairs, development operations, and humanitarian affairs at headquarters level (within the realm of the UN Development Group – UNDG). At the same time, the Consultative Committee on Programme and Operational Questions (CCPOQ), the operational arm of the Administrative Committee on Co-ordination (ACC),[16] should be targeted for operational purposes. The CCPOQ advises ACC on ways of promoting complementary activities and mobilizing the UN's analytical, normative and operational capacities for economic and social development.

Whereas in the past, inter-agency cooperation was focused primarily at headquarters level, it is presently country-level cooperation that attracts most attention. Programmes and agencies in the field are directed towards one another. In his report to the UN General Assembly, *Renewing the United Nations: A Programme for Reform*,[17] Secretary-General Kofi Annan announced that:

> All United Nations entities with ongoing missions at the country-level will operate in common premises…and operate under a single UN flag. In countries where there is a Resident Co-ordinator [RC], all Funds and Programmes as well as UN Information Centres will become part of a single UN office under the Resident Co-ordinator.

THE COUNTRY STRATEGY NOTE[18]

Field level cooperation increasingly takes place through the formulation of a coherent action plan (a Country Strategy Note, or CSN) implemented at the request of a particular country. A CSN is formulated by interested recipient governments with the assistance of and in cooperation with the UN in accordance with General Assembly Resolution 47/199 of 1992. The CSN then becomes a government document. A CSN must be based on the priorities and plans of recipient countries and should be designed to ensure the effective integration of UN assistance into the development process of countries.

A CSN will be developed in all countries where a government so chooses. It should be a mechanism for substantive assessment of key development issues of concern to the country and, above all, for mobilizing UN assistance in a collaborative manner. It should focus on areas where the UN could make a significant difference to development. In accordance with Paragraph 9 of Resolution 47/199, the UN's contribution to a CSN should be formulated under the leadership of the Resident Coordinator (RC), to ensure greater cooperation at field level. The RC exercises team leadership among the UN organizations system at country level. In consultation with the other UN representatives, she/he assumes overall responsibility for, and coordination of, the UN's operational development activities at country level. This is to ensure their consistency with the plans, priorities and strategies of the country; to ensure effective, complementary and synergistic UN contributions; and to foster a collegial team approach to leadership.[19]

The RC has a special responsibility to ensure the coherence of the contribution of the UN system to the CSN. To this end he/she should form subgroups focused on the key themes of the plan. These subgroups should be chaired by the organization or individual best suited to the task, and should operate under the overall guidance of the RC. In order to cooperate with and support the government in preparing a CSN and to accommodate the fact that not all agencies or UN bodies are represented at country level, the RC should invite those organizations not represented to submit a written input or send a representative to participate in the drafting of a CSN.

THE UN DEVELOPMENT ASSISTANCE FRAMEWORK

Whereas the CSN is supposed to be the governments' lay-out for development planning, the UN Development Assistance Framework (UNDAF) has been designated as the centrepiece of UN development cooperation at country level, serving as a common framework for all development funds, programmes and agencies.[20] Entities such as the Bretton Woods institutions are also encouraged to join in the preparation of UNDAF.

UNDAF will serve, amongst other things, as a basis for follow-up at country level to recent international conferences and decisions of the general assembly. UNDAF will reflect CSN strategic priorities and, as appropriate, complement the CSN in establishing the UN parameters of operations. UNDAF will also serve as a basis for the preparation of the individual country programmes or projects of the various funds, programmes and agencies. UNDAF will, therefore, strategically link all individual country programmes in a more coherent and complementary manner.

As appropriate, the UN country team would initiate the UNDAF preparation process with a Common Country Assessment (CCA), based on the selection and use of indicators which reflect national priorities. The CCA will highlight the trends related to national development goals and suggest strategic issues to be considered for UNDAF.

During the UNDAF cycle, the UN country team should periodically review the programme implementation experiences of the participating Funds and Programmes. These periodic reviews would assess the collective impact of UN development cooperation at country level in relation to the objectives of UNDAF. The reviews would also provide a key opportunity for the UN country team to improve the complementarity and coherence of the individual and collaborative contributions of the Funds and Programmes in relation to national development priorities.

The Common Country Assessment

As mentioned before, a significant step in the UNDAF process is the CCA, the core purpose of which is to provide the UN country team with an assessment process that promotes team work. The CCA provides an overview of national development based on the compilation and review of a common set of indicators. These indicators will reflect the priorities and mandates of UN organizations as well as internationally agreed goals set by various world conferences held during the 1990s, adapted to the particular characteristics of the country.

The objectives of the CCA are to provide an holistic and analytic summary of the current level of national development; to identify trends in the improvement or deterioration of the relevant indicators; and to identify areas requiring priority attention in development assistance. As such the CCA provides a common set of demographic, practical, social, economic and cultural indicators. Its current eight-component framework is organized as follows: (i) population; (ii) mortality and fertility; (iii) health; (iv) education; (v) income and employment; (vi) habitat and infrastructure; (vii) environment; (viii) human security and social justice.

Based on the above-mentioned components, the CCA entails the development and maintenance of a database of specific indicator-data at country level, which is updated on a periodic basis. The indicator list has two components: indicators identified by headquarters which are to be used for all countries (global), and additional indicators specific to each country (local). A headquarters Working Group on Indicators is defining the core set of global indicators that will eventually be used as a minimum in each country.

Having touched upon the continuing development of inter-agency fora and tools such as the UN Development Group, the CSN, the UNDAF, and the CCA, it needs no further in-depth explanation to show what a tremendous impact the UN human rights programme would have when it actively participates in these development planning fora/tools/systems. It is through these initiatives that the application of human rights norms and standards can make a sound and sustainable difference in the development processes of countries concerned.

In order to mark progress in this area it would be advisable that the High Commissioner for Human Rights uses the following stepping-stones:

- appoint a team of experts exclusively responsible for mainstreaming human rights at country level;

- persuade RCs to incorporate a human rights expert within the RC unit structures;

- follow up on the request incorporated in the Vienna Declaration and Programme of Action to assign human rights officers to field offices;

- develop human rights training modules for UN country teams;

- compose a strong human rights research team on indicators, notably for the global indicators within the CCA;

- take serious action with respect to the call by the World Conference on Human Rights for universal ratification of all human rights treaties;

- provide the UN system with a comprehensive overview of the universal minimum core contents of all human rights.

Strengthening the legal notion of human rights

Despite the fact that human rights are the birthright of all human beings they have too often been relegated to a mere social aspiration. Human rights are, however, legal rights. They retain their legal notion even when some of these rights are (presently) not amenable to judicial enforcement. Strengthening this legal notion is of the utmost importance since rights carry greater weight than aspirations. Amongst other things, the following substantive programming tools can be pursued in this respect.

UPGRADING ECONOMIC, SOCIAL AND CULTURAL RIGHTS

One of the most important tools in promoting the implementation of the right to development is to be found in the indivisibility of all human rights. The World Conference on Human Rights reaffirmed that all human rights are universal, indivisible, interdependent and interrelated, and that the international community must treat human rights in a fair and equal manner, on the same footing and with the same emphasis. If this is to mean more than paying lip-service to all categories of rights, it should be clear that steps have to be taken in respect of economic, social and cultural rights. Although no set of rights should be prioritized as a component of the right to development, the implementation process pertaining to economic, social and cultural rights should be fostered. Although universality and indivisibility are proclaimed, in practice there is no question as to the difference in treatment of the whole set of civil, cultural, economic, political and social rights. Whereas clear standards have been set as to the contents of civil and political rights, the precise meaning of a number of economic, social and cultural rights remains vague in many instances. If one is to treat all human rights on an equal footing, more attention needs to be paid to clarifying the universal minimum core contents of economic, social and cultural rights.

The idea of defining the universal minimum core content was already advocated by the UN Committee on Economic, Social and Cultural Rights in its General Comment (1991) on the Right to Housing. The choice for the establishment of a universal minimum core content as opposed to a minimum level per country was made in order to avoid too much relativism.

The question of a universal minimum core content is often treated by the Committee on Economic, Social and Cultural Rights in connection with the possible establishment of a complaints procedure under the 1966 covenant. Even so, the committee has argued that it is 'of great importance that economic, social and cultural rights should be further defined at international level within the context of a complaints procedure'.[21] Although the steps advanced in order to achieve both the definition of universal minimum core contents of economic, social and cultural rights as well as the possible establishment of a complaints procedure are commendable, reality demands that the issues be separated. Apart from the fact that the Committee on Economic, Social and Cultural Rights will not be capable of setting the universal minimum core content of the rights contained in the Covenant, it would be unthinkable that any government will voluntarily attribute undefined powers with large financial implications to a treaty monitoring body. If a complaints procedure is to become a success, the minimum threshold should already be established. It will in particular be the High Commissioner for Human Rights who, within his or her mandate, will have to trigger the debates and discussions to that end. The approach that should be followed in this respect is that currently taken by the Food and Agriculture Organization (FAO) and the OHCHR in response to commitment 7 of the World Food Summit held in Rome in 1996. This invited the High Commissioner, in consultation with relevant specialized UN agencies and programmes and appropriate intergovernmental mechanisms, to better define the rights related to food in Article 11 of the Covenant on Economic, Social and Cultural Rights, and to propose ways to implement and realise these rights as a means of achieving the commitments and objectives of the World Food Summit, taking into account the possibility of formulating voluntary guidelines for food security for all.

OPERATIONALIZING THE RIGHTS APPROACH TO DEVELOPMENT

The right to development as a programmatic right requires a crucial change in conceptual thinking with respect to development planning. This changed mind-set will impact heavily on programming tools such as the ones described in Chapter 12. The OHCHR will once again have to lead the process in order to preserve the holistic nature of the right to development and to avoid standard-setting not in conformity with the current human rights regime. The High Commissioner for Human Rights should subsequently vigorously promote and protect this approach towards all UN and other development partners.

In terms of policies and strategies, the critical change that has to take place is the adjustment of basic-needs strategies to a rights-based approach. A basic-needs strategy incorporates a certain element of charity, whereas a human rights-based approach not only defines beneficiaries and the nature of their needs but recognizes beneficiaries as active subjects and claim-holders and establishes duties or obligations for those against whom a claim can be brought to ensure that needs are met. The concept of claim-holders and duty-bearers introduces an important element of accountability. Increased accountability holds the key to improved effectiveness and transparency of action and as such offers the potential for added value flowing from the application of a rights-based approach.[22]

The operationalization of the rights approach will be a continuing exercise, particularly with respect to the implementation of economic, social and cultural rights. One only has to think of the efforts by the United Nations Children Fund (UNICEF) to operationalize the 1989 Convention on the Rights of the Child. Many difficulties were/are encountered in linking this convention with technical assistance programmes. If UNICEF has difficulties in operationalizing one convention, one can imagine the difficulties in operationalizing all core human rights treaties.

A first step in operationalizing the indivisible set of human rights would be to incorporate the typology of Asbjørn Eide, as elaborated in his study on the right to food,[23] as standard practice in all human rights technical-assistance and development programmes. Eide's typology – 'respect', 'protect' and 'fulfil' human rights – can be seen as an instrument for analysing states' accountability and as an important tool for assessing social progress. The typology should be understood as follows:

- *the obligation to respect*: this obligation requires all sectors of government to refrain from interfering with the enjoyment of the rights contained in the International Bill of Rights;

- *the obligation to protect*: this obligation requires all sectors of government to prevent violations of such rights by third parties;

- *the obligation to fulfil*: this obligation requires all sectors of government to take appropriate legislative, administrative, budgetary, judicial and other measures towards the full realization of such rights.

In addition, a division must be made between 'obligations of conduct' and 'obligations of result'. The obligation of conduct requires action reasonably calculated to realize the enjoyment of a particular right. The obligation of result requires government to achieve specific targets to satisfy a detailed substantive standard.

Applying the Eide typology to human rights law and its subsequent governmental consequences will most likely shed some light on the extent of human rights realization at country level. It would be highly suited, therefore, to be incorporated into the CCA as one of the development indicators.

Enhancing a cross-sectoral profile

Flowing from both the inter-agency and legal strategies, an enhanced cross-sectoral political profile of the OHCHR is also needed in order to strengthen the implementation process of the right to development. Based on sound research and the acknowledgement of the particular mandates of the respective UN programmes and agencies, the OHCHR will have to become a visible participant in inter-governmental fora such as the Commissions for Social Development, on Prevention and Criminal Justice and on the Status of Women. The OHCHR should no longer hide behind repetitive contributions to these fora, but should be inventive, guiding and acting as an advocate for change. As such, it could for example be a giant step forward if the OHCHR was to prove the usefulness of incorporating the rights approach to development into the concept of 'sustainable livelihoods', as elaborated since its acceptance at the 1992 United Nations Conference on Environment and Development.

The High Commissioner for Human Rights should take up all issues relevant to the office's mandate contained in the respective documents of the UN world conferences. The Commissioner has the authority and potential to remind governments of their commitments undertaken at the World Conferences on Human Rights, Environment and Development, Population and Development, Social Development, Women, Children, Housing and Food. Emphasizing the importance of an improved implementation process relating to economic, social and

cultural rights once more as one of the essential elements for the realization of the right to development, the High Commissioner could, for
example, strongly support the 20/20 compact as endorsed by the conferences on social development and women. The implementation of
this concept would give the elements pertaining to the quality of life a
more prominent place on the development agenda. Paragraph 88 of the
Programme of Action as adopted by the World Summit for Social
Development reads:

> Implementation of the Declaration and the Programme of Action in develop-
> ing countries, in particular in Africa and the least developed countries, will
> need additional financial resources and more effective development co-
> operation and assistance. This will require:...Agreeing on a mutual commit-
> ment between interested developed and developing country partners to
> allocate, on average, 20 per cent of ODA [Official Development Assistance]
> and 20 per cent of the national budget, respectively, to basic social pro-
> grammes.[24]

Although the 20/20 compact does not cover all economic, social and
cultural rights, it could serve as a useful tool in monitoring the seriousness of governmental intentions to implement such rights.

Conclusion

According to the 1986 declaration, the right to development is 'an
inalienable right by virtue of which every human person and all peoples
are entitled to participate in, contribute to and enjoy economic, social,
cultural and political development, in which all human rights and fundamental freedoms can be fully realized'. States have the subsequent
right and duty to formulate appropriate national development policies to
that end. At the time of writing, the provisions of the 1986 Declaration
on the Right to Development have still not proved to be sufficient to
achieve real progress. But with the evolution of the programmatic
nature of the right in recent years and, moreover, through the important
decision by the international community to establish the post of High
Commissioner for Human Rights, having an explicit mandate in the
field of the realization of the right to development, the opportunities for
a better implementation of the right to development have received a
new impetus.

The High Commissioner for Human Rights should use the right to
development as a strengthened normative foundation for tackling fundamental issues related to poverty and other aspects of sustainable
human development. By, amongst other things, vigorously supporting

efforts to define the universal minimum core content of economic, social and cultural rights, the concept of right to development will shed fresh light on a possible complaints procedure under the Covenant on Economic, Social and Cultural Rights and on the opportunities for incorporating human rights law notions within the CCA and UNDAF, while other agencies that would like to pursue a rights-based approach to their development planning would also benefit. No-one, however, should ever be forced to choose between freedom and bread. The High Commissioner should forcefully protect and promote the holistic approach to human rights, incorporating the whole range of civil, cultural, economic, political and social rights, as foreseen in the Universal Declaration on Human Rights.

Notes

1. The opinions expressed in this article are those of the author and should not be taken to reflect, in whole or in part, the opinion of the United Nations. Chapter 10 is an amended and updated version of the paper presented in Santiago.
2. Article 13, UN Charter.
3. Article 62, UN Charter.
4. Article 76, UN Charter.
5. UN General Assembly Resolution 421 E (V) of 4 December 1950.
6. Commission on Human Rights; seventh session 16 April–19 May 1951.
7. In Resolution 2200 (XXI) of 16 December 1966, the assembly adopted and opened for signature, ratification and accession three instruments: (a) the International Covenant on Economic, Social and Cultural Rights; (b) the International Covenant on Civil and Political Rights; and (c) the Optional Protocol to the International Covenant on Civil and Political Rights.
8. Adopted as Resolution 41/128 of the General Assembly of the United Nations on 4 December 1986.
9. Italics added.
10. UN Doc. A/Conf.157/23, Para I/10.
11. UN Doc. E/CN.4/AC.45/1997/CRP.1; 10 October 1997, Draft Report of the Intergovernmental Group of Experts on the Right to Development at its second session.
12. Commission on Human Rights Resolution 1998/72.
13. Italics added.
14. Asbjørn Eide (1987) 'Linking human rights and development', in Kumar Rupesinghe (ed.) *Development Assistance in the Year 2000: Political and Social Conditions in Norway*, Institute for Social Research, Oslo: 200–35.
15. UN Doc. A/48/935.
16. The ACC was established by ECOSOC Resolution 13 (III) of 1996 and is composed of the UN Secretary-General and the executive heads of the special-ized agencies as well as of several other UN bodies. Its main function is ensuring the coordination of the programmes approved by the governing bodies of the

various UN organizations and, more generally, promoting cooperation within the UN in pursuit of the common goals of member

17. UN Doc. A/51/950, 14 July 1997.
18. CPOQ, A4, United Nations New York, March 1994.
19. UN Doc. ACC/1995/1; Statement on the Role and Functioning of the Resident Co-ordinator System.
20. Provisional Guidelines for the Formulation of the United Nations Development Assistance Framework (UNDAF), 19 August 1997, prepared by the Joint Consultative Group on Policy (JCGP) Sub-Group on Programme Harmonization for the Executive Committee, United Nations Development Group (UNDG).
21. Netherlands Advisory Committee on Human Rights and Foreign Policy (1994), *Economic, Social and Cultural Rights*, Advisory Report No. 18, The Hague: 15.
22. For an extensive elaboration on this approach in respect of the right to adequate food, see Uwe Kracht, *The Right to Adequate Food: Its Contents and Realization*, an issues paper prepared for consideration by the United Nations Committee on Economic, Social and Cultural Rights at its Day of General Discussion, 1 December 1997.
23. UN Doc. E/CN.4/Sub.2/1987/23.
24. UN Doc. A/Conf.166/9, 19 April 1995.

11
The Human Rights Challenge to Global Poverty

CHRIS JOCHNICK[1]

The end of the twentieth century is heralded as the age of rights, marked by a global interest in democracy and civil liberties. In its thirty years of active campaigning, the international human rights movement has made human rights a household term. At the same time, a billion people live in poverty, the gap between rich and poor is growing dramatically and globally more people die of hunger in a single day than of all the political killings over the course of a year. Rights have apparently won the day in spite of the dramatic dimensions of poverty, social marginalization and inequality. Is poverty simply irrelevant to human rights?

In fact, the human rights movement has much to offer the struggle against poverty, but it must first move beyond its unnecessarily narrow vision of these rights. The dominance of western governments and non-governmental organizations (NGOs) has produced a model of human rights advocacy that is mainly limited to civil liberties and state action.[2] While the narrow focus on civil liberties has been widely criticized and an increasing number of NGOs are now addressing economic, social and cultural rights, the singular focus on state action endures. This focus fails to address the roots of poverty-related rights violations, particularly violations of economic, social and cultural rights, that increasingly lie beyond national borders.

Moving human rights beyond its state-centric paradigm potentially serves two purposes: (i) it challenges the reigning neo-liberal extremism that trivializes much of the public discourse about development and poverty, providing a rhetoric and vision to emphasize that entrenched poverty is neither inevitable nor acceptable; and (ii) it provides a legal framework with which to begin holding the most influential non-state actors – corporations, financial institutions and third-party states – more accountable for their role in creating and sustaining poverty.[3]

This chapter outlines the role of other actors in rights violations and the extent to which these other actors are governed by human rights instruments. The focus on impact and accountability is meant to demonstrate the importance of, and the legal basis for, broadening human rights advocacy to address additional sectors.

The Need to Expand Understandings about Human Rights

The role of human rights discourse – an anecdote

Some years ago, the Center for Economic and Social Rights – CESR (1994) undertook an investigation of the impact of oil development on people in the Ecuadorian Amazon. The investigation initially focused on the government's human rights obligations despite the fact that a private company, Texaco, was responsible for the brunt of the damage. For decades, the affected Amazon communities had suffered Texaco's abuses largely in silence, having been repeatedly told, both explicitly and implicitly, that they had no rights against the oil company and that the damage was a natural and inevitable price to pay for the country's development. Human rights offered these communities a rare alternative to the dominant discourse, guaranteeing them a right to a healthy environment that was clearly being violated by Texaco's regular dumping of toxic wastes into their water supplies.

When CESR met with these communities, there was little sympathy for the legal nuance that private companies are technically immune to human rights claims, that they do not sign treaties guaranteeing human rights and that only the state is responsible for ensuring these rights. In the communities' eyes, Texaco was the villain. Texaco had operated for years in the Amazon as practically a state unto itself, with annual global earnings four times the size of Ecuador's GNP, and with the active support of the US government. Even if the Ecuadorian government had been disposed to control the company, few believed it could.

Under these circumstances, CESR's intended approach risked the uncomfortable prospect of doing more harm than good. Insisting solely on governmental obligations would have obscured the true nature of the violation, reinforced Texaco's impunity and, most importantly, detracted from the communities' long-overdue sense of injustice and resolve.

The principle of state responsibility as the basis for the human rights regime

As the heir to an international legal system dating back to the 1600s, the human rights regime is based on the enduring principle of state responsibility.[4] International law has long been considered the exclusive province of state actors, as treaties, the primary instruments of international law, existed to govern relations between states. The establishment of human rights instruments was revolutionary in the sense that it recognized a new subject of international law: private individuals. But this recognition was limited largely to individuals as the holders of rights, with states still considered the principle, if not exclusive, holders of duties.

The distinction between individuals as the holders of rights and states as the holders of duties was premised on a notion of the state as the ultimate guardian of its population's welfare. As described by the Commission on Global Governance (1995):

> When the United Nations system was created, nation-states, some of them imperial powers, were dominant. Faith in the ability of governments to protect citizens and improve their lives was strong...Moreover, the state had few rivals. The world economy was not as closely integrated as it is today. The vast array of global firms and corporate alliances that has emerged was just beginning to develop. The huge global capital market, which today dwarfs even the largest national capital markets, was not foreseen.[6]

Half a century ago, governments had far more control over the political, social and economic conditions within their countries. States had the responsibility of guaranteeing human rights on the presumption that they, and they alone, were capable of doing so.[5]

The danger of traditional interpretations: legitimization of the status quo

The narrow focus of human rights law on state responsibility is not only out of step with current power relations, it also tends to obscure them. The exclusive concern with national governments not only distorts the reality of the growing weakness of national-level authority, but also shields other actors from greater responsibility. The focus on state responsibility also creates a false sense of rigidity or inevitability about social and political hierarchies and existing inequities.[6] International human rights law perpetuates the notions that private actors are, and by implication should be, only accountable to states, not individuals, and that other states are, and should be, only accountable to their own populations.[7]

The real potential of human rights lies in its ability to change the way people perceive themselves *vis-à-vis* the government and other actors. Rights rhetoric provides a mechanism for reanalysing and renaming 'problems' as 'violations', and, as such, something that need not and should not be tolerated. As explained by Paulo Freire (1970), the move beyond a 'consciousness of internalized subordination' is the first step in the decision to take action. Rights make it clear that violations are neither inevitable nor natural but arise from deliberate decisions and policies. By demanding explanations and accountability, human rights expose the hidden priorities and structures behind violations. The demystification of human rights, both in terms of their economic and social content and their applicability to non-state actors, constitutes a critical step towards challenging the conditions that create and tolerate poverty.

Basis for a Broader Vision

Rooting human rights in human dignity

A broader conception of human rights is consistent with their original foundation in human dignity.[8] International law generally is understood to be based on a mix of customary practice and consent. States are bound either by those norms that achieve the distinction of customary law or by those that they explicitly consent to through treaties. However, human rights law has in large measure defied these narrow categories by suggesting an additional foundation: human dignity. Human dignity makes certain claims on all actors, state and non-state, regardless of custom or consent.

The Universal Declaration of Human Rights and the twin covenants of 1966 do not merely recognize those rights that are considered customary or to which states have previously consented, but also acknowledge that those rights derive 'from the inherent dignity of the human person'.[9] This is significant in so far as the emphasis on the human person places human rights beyond the narrowness of particular treaties or, at a minimum, suggests a broad interpretation of these treaties and their corresponding duties. Thus human rights obligations linked to human dignity may be violated by a host of actors including non-parties to the treaties; the exclusive focus on the state must be viewed as pragmatic and contingent, rather than necessary.

Legal support for a broader vision of human rights

Despite common perception to the contrary, international law has long contemplated duties for non-state actors.[10] Early treaties outlawing piracy and slavery were clearly directed at private parties.[11] The imposition of duties on private parties is also found in the 1948 Genocide Convention, which declares that 'persons committing genocide…shall be punished, whether they are constitutionally responsible rulers, public officials or private individuals'.[12] The Nuremberg Tribunal lent strong support to this principle by trying both state actors and private individuals: 'International law, as such, binds every citizen just as does ordinary municipal law. Acts adjudged criminal when done by an officer of the Government are criminal when done by a private individual...The application of international law to individuals is no novelty.'[13] The 1950 Principles of the Nuremberg Charter and Judgement state that: 'Any person who commits an act which constitutes a crime under international law is responsible therefor and liable to punishment.'[14]

Likewise, all of the major human rights treaties contemplate both private and state duties. As the Universal Declaration states: 'The General Assembly proclaims this Universal Declaration of Human Rights as a common standard of achievement for all peoples and all nations, to the end that every individual and every organ of society shall...promote respect for these rights and freedoms'.[15] The American Declaration of the Rights and Duties of Man, as suggested by the name, is even clearer about private duties: 'The fulfilment of duty by each individual is a prerequisite to the rights of all. Rights and duties are interrelated in every social and political activity of man.'[16] Both the International Covenant on Civil and Political Rights (ICCPR) and the International Covenant on Economic, Social and Cultural Rights (ICESCR) reaffirm the obligations of individuals: 'The individual, having duties to other individuals and to the community to which he belongs, is under a responsibility to strive for the promotion and observance of the rights recognized in the present Covenant.'[17]

Global changes supporting a broader human rights vision

Over the past half century, the vision of the powerful state sovereign has become increasingly anachronistic. Today's governments are besieged by a host of outside actors whom they have an ever-decreasing capacity to control. Rapid privatization, free trade agreements, economic integration and the explosion of transnational corporations (TNCs) have tremendously limited government prerogatives, particularly among the smaller, developing countries.

> No longer...can states pretend to be autonomous...The most important forces that affect people's lives are global in scale and consequences. Even the most powerful states recognize serious global constraints on their capacity to affirm their own national interest above all else...The organization of political life within a fragmented system of states appears to be increasingly inconsistent with emerging realities. (R.B.J. Walker and Saul H. Mendlovitz, *Integrating State Sovereignties*, cited in Steiner and Alston 1996: 151)

The global changes limiting state control are particularly relevant to the field of economic, social and cultural rights.[18] While civil liberties and formal political rights are generally consistent with the demands of the market-place, economic, social and cultural rights are often at odds with these demands.[19] Neo-liberal reforms have gradually whittled away at state authority over economic and social spheres. Human welfare and the environment have been increasingly left to the vagaries of the market, with governments playing almost a secondary role in trying to ensure basic levels of welfare for their populations. The UN Special Rapporteur on Economic, Social and Cultural Rights describes the changes in these terms:

> The flurry of many states romantically to embrace the market as the ultimate solution to all of society's ills, and the corresponding rush to denationalize and leave economics, politics and social matters to the whims of the private sector, although the theme of the day, will inevitably have an impact upon the full realization of economic, social and cultural rights.[20]

The application of human rights laws to non-state actors is thus well supported under international law, and all the more critical in today's world. Not surprisingly then, the movement to apply human rights to these actors, thought nascent, is already under way.

Human Rights and the Impact of Non-state and Third-party State Actors

As state authority declines, human rights advocates must look to those sectors that have filled the void. Non-state actors and third-party states play a direct and indirect role in a wide range of human rights violations, and their responsibilities have been alluded to in a growing number of human rights resolutions and legal codes.[21] These instruments provide a starting point from which to seek more concrete obligations that attach to non-state actors like TNCs and the International Financial Institutions (IFIs), as well as to third-party states.

Transnational corporations

The regulation of TNCs is perhaps the most pressing task for the promotion of economic, social and cultural rights. Most developing countries face individual TNCs with revenues many times larger than their domestic economies. TNCs account for almost half of the top one hundred economies in the world,[22] and a mere 200 of them are estimated to control a quarter of the world's productive assets.[23]

Grouped together in trade associations with the active support of their home countries, TNCs exercise an inordinate influence over local laws and policies. Their impact on human rights ranges from a direct role in violations, such as abuses of employees or the environment, to indirect support of governments guilty of widespread repression.[24] The conduct of TNCs can also have a dramatic impact on poverty, either by directly undermining human welfare (e.g., limiting a community's access to land or food) or influencing relevant government policies and laws (e.g., relating to agriculture, technology, employment and subsidies).

Corporations are established through special grants of their incorporating countries and are presumably subject to all of the national laws under which they operate.[25] To the extent that private businesses are involved in violations, most advocates would look to the government's failure to regulate. TNCs are thereby reachable indirectly through the government's obligations to protect human rights.[26] As explained by the Inter-American Court of Human Rights, a state violates the rights of its citizens 'when the State allows private persons or groups to act freely and with impunity to the detriment of the rights recognized by the Convention'.[27] The obligation to protect economic, social and cultural rights requires that governments regulate private parties like TNCs through legislation and effective enforcement.[28] The fact that corporate abuses are often systematic and in many ways sanctioned by the state make these violations ripe for examination by human rights bodies.

However, the overwhelming political and economic influence of TNCs requires more direct application of rights standards.[29] These standards may come either from international treaties or from specific codes of conduct for industries or individual companies. There have been numerous efforts to bring TNCs under international law. Thirty years ago, inter-governmental and non-governmental groups were already developing codes of conduct for TNCs.[30] Unfortunately, none of these codes has proved effective beyond a very limited sphere of corporate activities. More recently, the UN Commission on Transnational Corporations produced a comprehensive code for TNCs after twenty years of drafting and negotiating.[31] While the code was never adopted, its human rights provisions are relevant in so far as they are the product of lengthy consideration, and consensus, among the drafters.[32] These human rights provisions mandate, among other things, that transnational corporations should respect the social and cultural objectives, values and traditions of the countries in which they operate.[33] In addition, the transnational corporations shall respect human rights and fundamental freedoms in the countries in which they operate, while in their social and industrial relations, TNCs shall not discriminate on the basis of race, colour, sex, religion, language, social, national and ethnic origin or political or other opinion.[34]

Recent international conferences and UN-body resolutions continue to push for human rights and environmental accountability from corporations. For example, the Rio Declaration[35] and the Copenhagen Declaration on Social Development[36] both underscore the responsibilities of TNCs with regard to development and the environment. In addition, the UN Secretary-General has stated that TNCs have a duty to promote the right to development.[37] Likewise, both the UN General Assembly[38] and the Commission on Human Rights[39] have addressed the need for TNCs to promote human rights and prevent further violations. While specific duties have yet to be elaborated, these various resolutions and declarations evince a continuing interest in applying rights obligations directly to corporations.[40]

Additional efforts have been made by individual corporations, industry associations and NGOs to develop codes of conduct covering various human rights, though rarely by name.[41] These codes have covered a range of activities from working conditions, wages, free association, child labour, discrimination, environmental pollution and investment in countries deemed gross violators of human rights. While there is promise in some of these efforts, they carry a risk of legitimizing, and thereby facilitating as much as restraining, existing practices. The fact that the codes are voluntary and largely established through corporate initiative has tended to preclude them from impinging significantly on corporate interests, and certainly not sufficiently to address the massive violations of economic, social and cultural rights in which TNCs play a role.[42]

International financial institutions

A great deal of attention has been devoted to the human rights impacts of IFIs like the World Bank[43] and the International Monetary Fund (IMF). These institutions play a vital role in the ability of governments, particularly those of developing countries, to provide for the general welfare of their populations. For example, the World Bank is the largest source of international funding for development programmes, and the imprimatur of the IMF is often the critical condition for access to other sources of funding and investment (see Ranis 1997). In addition, the projects they fund often directly implicate violations of both civil and political rights and economic, social and cultural rights. Their potential for violations is directly related to the tremendous influence they exercise over the economies of developing countries.

Structural adjustment packages (SAPs) demanded by both the World Bank and the IMF often have widespread, serious impacts on human welfare.[44] The UN Special Rapporteur on Economic, Social and Cultural Rights lists the following components of SAPs that threaten human rights:

> (a) devaluation of local currency; (b) decrease of government expenditure on public services; (c) abolition of price controls; (d) imposition of wage controls; (e) reduction of trade and foreign exchange controls; (f) restrictions on domestic credit; (g) reduction of the role of the state in the economy; (h) increasing basis for the export economy; (i) decreasing imports; and (j) privatization of heretofore public enterprises.[45]

These policies have been particularly devastating to vulnerable sectors of the population, such as the poor, women and children.[46] Additionally, many of the development projects funded by the World Bank have involved gross human rights abuses, including forced evictions.[47]

Beyond the substantive impacts, IFI involvement in development decisions often moves the locus of decision-making further from affected communities, making policies less transparent, participatory and accountable to traditional democratic processes. Negotiations with the IMF over debt reduction and over SAPs, both of which have broad ramifications for development policies, are almost exclusively carried out behind closed doors with only the involvement of the finance ministries (see Bradlow 1996). The Special Rapporteur's study of IFIs concludes that

> the relative decline of national sovereignty and domestic control over local economic processes and resources and the corresponding growth in the level to which the international financial agencies directly influence domestic policy decisions are clearly aspects of the adjustment process which conclusively affect economic, social and cultural rights.[48]

While the World Bank and IMF readily concede their impact on human rights, they have refused to hold themselves accountable to human rights standards. They have justified this policy on the basis of their constitutive charters, which arguably limit their mandate to the consideration of economic factors, distinguishing human rights concerns as political.[49]

However, while these charter limitations provide the Bank and the IMF with a defence against obligations in the field of civil and political rights, they pose no ostensible limitation to economic, social and cultural rights obligations.[50] On the contrary, both the World Bank and the IMF increasingly consider poverty alleviation and a number of related welfare concerns (even going so far as to consider issues of income distribution) to be central to their missions.[51] As the president of the World Bank forcefully declared at the 1998 meeting of the World Bank and the IMF: 'We must address the issues of long-term equitable growth on which prosperity and human progress depend...We must focus on social issues...if we do not have greater equity and social justice, there will be no political stability and without political stability no amount of money put together in financial packages will give us financial stability.'[52] These goals are well supported by the respective Articles of Agreement. For example, the World Bank's authorized purposes include promoting 'the long-range balanced growth of international trade...thereby assisting in raising productivity, the standard of living and conditions of labor in their territories'.[53] The IMF's Charter refers to the 'expansion and balanced growth of international trade' and the 'promotion and maintenance of high levels of employment and real income'.[54] Since the early 1990s, the IMF has described its goals as 'high quality' growth, which the managing director contrasts with 'growth at the expense of the poor or the environment'.[55]

As specialized agencies of the United Nations, the World Bank and the IMF are obligated to promote the UN's human rights mission, and as international organizations they are at least responsible for not violating customary international human rights law.

> Both institutions [the IMF and the World Bank], like any other United Nations body or any other subject of international law, are bound by the Charter of the United Nations and have a duty to respect the postulates formulated in the Preamble to the Charter...the objectives of the Organization in the area of international economic and social co-operation (Articles 55 and 56), specific provisions aimed at their realization and which are contained in the Charter as well as in other international instruments including, *inter alia*, the International Covenants on Human Rights, international conventions, including the international labour conventions, and resolutions and declarations of the United Nations.[56]

The UN Committee on Economic, Social and Cultural Rights has underscored the human rights obligations of these institutions, noting that 'the international agencies should scrupulously avoid involvement in projects which, for example, involve the use of forced labour... or... large-scale evictions or displacement of persons',[57] and that 'international financial institutions promoting measures of structural adjustment should ensure that such measures do not compromise the enjoyment of the right to adequate housing'.[58]

These obligations are further highlighted and bolstered by recent UN conferences that have made explicit reference to IFIs, urging them to 'assess...the impact of their policies and programmes on the enjoyment of human rights'[59] and underscoring their 'special responsibility'[60] to promote human rights through international cooperation.[61] Additionally, the UN Commission on Human Rights has recently issued a number of resolutions touching on IFI responsibilities.[62]

Third-party states

Inevitably, as the world grows smaller and more tightly integrated, states will play an increasingly important role in human rights violations beyond their borders. The impact of third-party states comes through a variety of channels, including sanctions, development and military assistance, debt negotiations, trade agreements and diplomatic relations. States may also be implicated in violations abroad relating to actors, such as TNCs, or activities emanating from within their borders, such as environmental contamination.[63]

Recognizing that third-party states have impacts beyond their borders, several human rights instruments and bodies have been established to govern the consequences. The United Nations itself was established to promote international cooperation, and this intent is found in all of the major human rights documents.[64] For example, the UN Charter calls on members to take 'joint and separate action'[65] to promote the following UN purposes: '(a) higher standards of living, full employment, and conditions of economic and social progress and development; (b) solutions of international economic, social, health, and related problems;...and (c) universal respect for, and observance of, human rights.'[66] In addition, the Universal Declaration of Human Rights recognizes that 'everyone, as a member of society...is entitled to [the] realization, through national effort and international co-operation...of economic, social, and cultural rights'.[67] Similarly, the ICESCR underscores the 'essential importance of international co-operation' particularly in relation to the right to food.[68] Finally, the UN Committee on Economic, Social and Cultural Rights has made it clear that development assistance and cooperation are matters of human rights, stating that

> the Committee wishes to emphasize that in accordance with Articles 55 and 56 of the Charter of the United Nations, with well-established principles of international law, and with the provisions of the Covenant itself, international co-operation for development and thus for the realization of economic, social and cultural rights is an obligation of all States.[69]

Obligations relating to international cooperation are further bolstered by the UN Declaration on the Right to Development,[70] which speaks of both private and state duties:

> All human beings have a responsibility for development, individually and collectively, taking into account the need for full respect for their human rights and fundamental freedoms as well as their duties to the community, which alone can ensure the free and complete fulfilment of the human being, and they should therefore promote and protect an appropriate political, social and economic order for development.[71]

And states have the primary responsibility for the creation of national and international conditions favourable to the realization of the right to development.[72] The Working Group on the Right to Development underscored that the declaration 'should have a decisive influence not only on the domestic policies, but also on the foreign policies of states, either in their bilateral relations or in their contribution to regional and multilateral co-operation'.[73]

These international provisions are bolstered by regional legal regimes that further tie the fates and obligations of neighbouring countries. For example, the OAS Charter proclaims the 'consolidation on this continent…of a system…based on respect for the essential rights of man'[74] and describes the 'spiritual unity of the continent'[75] and the need for 'close co-operation'[76] in promoting the 'fundamental rights of the individual without distinction as to…nationality'.[77]

Analogous obligations are contained in those provisions of humanitarian law that hold third-party states responsible for the welfare of other civilian populations.[78] For example, under one such provision, occupying countries are required to 'facilitate…the care and education of children'[79] and to ensure the availability of 'foodstuffs, medical stores, and other articles' for the civilian population under their control.[80] Additionally, all parties to a conflict must ensure that their activities do not disproportionately harm non-combatants and must safeguard the free passage of medical supplies and foodstuffs for civilians.[81]

Governments have recognized some of these obligations by incorporating them into foreign assistance and trade relations. By law, if rarely in practice, US trade and foreign assistance is conditioned on an array of civil and political, and some labour rights.[82] The European Community conditions development assistance on a fuller range of human rights:

> Co-operation shall be directed towards development centred on man, the main protagonist and beneficiary of development, which thus entails respect for and promotion of all human rights. The rights in question are all human

rights, the various categories thereof being indivisible and inter-related... civil and political rights; economic, social and cultural rights.[83]

Governments, particularly those with significant international influence,[84] are also under obligation to respect economic, social and cultural rights in their multilateral assistance. The Maastricht Guidelines, one of the most authoritative texts on the ICESCR, declare that

> the obligations of States to protect economic, social and cultural rights extend also to their participation in international organizations, where they act collectively. It is particularly important for States to use their influence to ensure that violations do not result from the programmes and policies of the organizations of which they are members.[85]

States also have obligations relating to the activities of TNCs with headquarters under their jurisdiction. The 1975 Charter of Economic Rights and Duties of States provides that states should cooperate with each other 'in the exercise of every state to regulate and supervise the activities of TNCs within its national jurisdiction and take measures to ensure that such activities comply with its law, rules and regulations and conform with its economic and social policies'.[86] This principle was reiterated in the Rio Declaration which holds states responsible for ensuring that 'activities within their jurisdiction or control do not cause damage to the environment of other states'.[87] Furthermore, the Maastricht Guidelines hold that 'the obligation to protect includes the state's responsibility to ensure that private entities or individuals, including transnational corporations *over which they exercise jurisdiction*, do not deprive individuals of their economic, social and cultural rights'.[88]

Towards a Fuller Accountability

While this array of treaties, declarations and resolutions demonstrates the interest and potential of bringing human rights to bear on non-state and third-party state actors, real progress awaits more concrete acknowledgement of legal accountability. Non-state actors are only too eager to trumpet the importance of human rights but will rarely broach actual human rights obligations. The literature of the World Bank is replete with commentary about its role in promoting economic, social and cultural rights, but never suggests actual legal obligations.[89] TNCs are equally adept at appropriating the language of human rights to their benefit.[90] The whole concept of human rights is undermined by the notion that institutions will promote them at their own discretion.

Defining a human right as such allows for a process of developing reciprocal duties, monitoring conduct and holding actors accountable. Codes of conduct, policy directives and legislation must be tied to the larger framework of human rights in order to ensure the positive and integrated contribution of these legal obligations to human development. Furthermore, tying legal obligations to human rights imbues these laws with the necessary sense that rights and obligations derive from human dignity, and not generosity or whim.

Beyond pushing for explicit acknowledgement of accountability, the challenge for human rights advocates lies with the elaboration of specific duties. Towards that end, the following principles should be considered:

(1) Responsibility should correspond roughly to an actor's influence and proximity to violations. The human rights system allots almost total responsibility to the state based on the presumption that the state has control over violations. However, because other actors have assumed much of this influence and control they should assume some of the corresponding duties. The US Supreme Court's recognition of state-like obligations for certain private corporations with state-like authority provides an illuminating example.[91] Likewise, humanitarian law places responsibility on non-state forces and third-party states based on their influence and control over the welfare of occupied or threatened populations. For example, international law implicates states in the activities of terrorist groups that they harbour or finance. Thus, the International Court of Justice's decision holding the US government responsible for the acts of the Nicaraguan Contras was based on the government's proximity and degree of influence over the Contras' violations of Nicaraguan sovereignty.[92] Such an imposition of state responsibility suggests interesting parallels for the legalization, headquartering, subsidization and general promotion of TNCs abroad.

(2) All parties must be held to the most basic level of obligation, that of respect.[93] At a minimum, the UN Charter and the various human rights treaties require that states and specialized agencies ensure that their economic and political relations with other countries neither significantly threaten the ability of a country to provide for its population nor encourage or facilitate violations.

The duty to respect must be understood to encompass government initiatives and activities that play a significant role in violations. Free trade agreements that fail to incorporate human rights concerns, foreign assistance that has negative impacts on certain sectors of the population, structural adjustment programmes, excessive debt-repayment schedules and the facilitation of TNC activities without corresponding controls may all implicate this duty to respect. Given the dramatic and growing gap between the richest and poorest countries, the duty to respect may implicate a wide range of state policies that undergird the current global economy.[94]

(3) Given the lack of legal precedents and guidelines, procedural obligations, such as transparency, monitoring, impact statements, consultation, participation and remedies, may provide the most effective starting point for advocacy around economic, social and cultural rights, particularly with non-state and third-party state actors. Compared to other substantive components of economic, social and cultural rights, these obligations, such as requiring impact statements and an accounting, are less threatening and at the same time more crucial because of their capacity to bring affected populations into the process of defining and ensuring rights.

Conclusion

Economic, social and cultural rights are drawing a far broader and more grassroots constituency than that represented by the traditional human rights movement. For these new human rights advocates, poverty and inequality are central issues, and human dignity and basic needs are as relevant to the definition of rights as international treaties. This broader approach to human rights has opened the door to holding other actors accountable, and human rights are now regularly manifest in campaigns against corporations and multilateral banks. While changes to the human rights dogma will be resisted in many quarters, in a world of growing poverty and marginalization the constituency for a broader and truer vision of human rights grows ever larger and, thanks to new communications technology, ever more united.

Notes

1. The author is Legal Director of the Centro de Derechos Económicos y Sociales (Quito), an affiliate of the Centre for Economic and Social Rights. This article draws from the ideas and experience of both organizations, over the course of eight years working in the field of economic and social rights.
2. See, for example, Legia Bolivar (1986) and Chris Jochnick (1997): 3–5.
3. The term third-party states is meant to describe all other states beyond the one in question.
4. See generally H. Lauterpacht (1946), and Rosalyn Higgins and Christopher Greenwood (1996).

5. See Rosalyn Higgins and Christopher Greenwood (1996): 39–55 and 146–59.
6. The psychological and sociological effects of such legal distinctions as state/ individual and public/private have been described by scholars associated with Critical Legal Studies. See Karl Klare (1982): 'The primary effect of the public/ private distinction is thus to inhibit the perception that the institutions in which we live are the product of human design and can therefore be changed'. See also Phillip R. Trimble (1990), and Chris Jochnick and Roger Normand (1994).
7. Feminist scholars have gone far towards debunking the public/private distinction in human rights. See, e.g., Catherine MacKinnon (1993).
8. See, e.g., the Universal Declaration of Human Rights (UDHR), adopted 10 December 1948 (GA Resolution 217A (III)); the International Covenant on Civil and Political Rights (ICCPR), adopted 16 December 1966 (GA Resolution 2200 (XXI)); the International Covenant on Economic, Social and Cultural Rights (ICESCR), adopted 16 December 1966 (GA Resolution 2200 (XXI)).
9. ICCPR, preamble; ICESCR, preamble. 'The American states have on repeated occasions recognized that the essential rights of man are not derived from the fact that he is a national of a certain state, but are based upon attributes of his human personality.' See also the American Declaration of the Rights and Duties of Man, signed 2 May 1948, OEA/Ser.L/V/II.71, Introduction (1988).
10. See Andrew Clapham (1993); see also Jordan J. Paust (1992).
11. See Paust (1992): 56-57.
12. Convention on the Prevention and Punishment of the Crime of Genocide, adopted 9 December 1948, Article IV.
13. Transcript of Proceedings, Nuremberg Tribunal, 41 *American Journal of International Law* 172 (Supp. 1947). The 1945 Charter of the International Military Tribunal (IMT) enshrined the idea that individuals have duties under international law. The Charter is reprinted in Dietrich Schindler and Jiri Toman (1988): 825–31.
14. Principles of International Law Recognized in the Charter of the Nuremberg Tribunal and in the Judgement of the Tribunal, adopted 2 August 1950, UN Doc. A/1316.
15. UDHR, preamble.
16. American Declaration, preamble. The American Declaration elaborates specific duties of the individual in Articles 19–38. See comparable provisions in both the African Charter, Articles 27–9, and Article 17 of the European Convention for the Protection of Human Rights and Fundamental Freedoms, opened for signature 4 November 1950.
17. ICCPR, preamble; ICESCR, preamble.
18. As the UN Committee on Economic, Social and Cultural Rights cautions, 'full realization of human rights can never be achieved as a mere by-product, or fortuitous consequence, of some other developments, no matter how positive. For that reason, suggestions that the full realization of economic, social and cultural rights will be a direct consequence of, or will automatically flow from, the enjoyment of civil and political rights are misplaced'. *Statement to the World Conference on Human Rights on Behalf of the Committee on Economic, Social and Cultural Rights,* UN ESCOR, Committee on Economic, Social and Cultural Rights, 7th session, Supp. No. 2: 82.
19. While the positive/negative distinction between civil and political rights and economic, social and cultural rights should not be exaggerated, the promotion of the latter would seem to require a stronger state with greater resources.

Moreover, the legal norms and most powerful institutions governing international relations are more amenable to civil and political rights than to economic, social and cultural rights.

20. Danilo Türk, Special Rapporteur of the Sub-Commission on Prevention of Discrimination and Protection of Minorities, *The Realization of Economic, Social and Cultural Rights* (Final Report), UN ESCOR, Commission on Human Rights, Sub-Commission on Prevention of Discrimination and Protection of Minorities, 44th session, Provisional Agenda Item 8: 27.

21. See the Report of the Secretary-General, n. 24 below (providing a list of UN resolutions and related codes directed at TNCs).

22. See Tony Clarke (1996); see also Sarah Anderson and John Cavanagh (1996), noting that 51 of the world's 100 largest economies are corporations.

23. See *The Economist*, 27 March 1993: 5–6, cited in Sarah Anderson and John Cavanagh (1996): n.10; see also Anderson and Cavanagh (1996), at Introduction.

24. See generally, *The Realization of Economic, Social and Cultural Rights: the impact of the activities and working methods of transnational corporations on the full enjoyment of all human rights, in particular economic, social and cultural rights and the right to development, bearing in mind existing international guidelines, rules and standards relating to the subject-matter*, Report of the Secretary-General, E/CN.4/Sub.2/1996/12 (2 July 1996); Richard J. Barnet and John Cavanagh (1994); Diane Orentlicher and Timothy Gelatt (1993).

25. It is worth noting that originally the licence to establish a corporation was considered a privilege that bound the incorporators to conduct business in a socially conscious manner. As one US court declared in 1809, if the applicants' purpose 'is merely private or selfish; if it is detrimental to, or not promotive of, the public good, they have no adequate claim upon the legislature for the privileges'. See Richard L. Grossman and Frank T. Adams (1996): 378, citing the Supreme Court of Virginia's reasoning in an unnamed 1809 case. Today, there are only the most minimal social obligations attached to incorporation, and governments are even less inclined to impose restrictions on TNCs operating abroad.

26. Human rights obligations are commonly broken down into three levels: 'respect' (abstain from interference), 'protect' (prevent others from interfering), and 'fulfil' (take the necessary steps to ensure satisfaction). See Summary Record of the 20th Meeting of the Committee on Economic, Social and Cultural Rights, UN ESCOR, Committee on Economic, Social and Cultural Rights, 3rd session, 20th Meeting, E/C.12/1989/SR.20 (1989) (discussing Asbjørn Eide's report).

27. Velásquez Rodríguez Case, Case 7920, Ser. C, No. 4, Inter-American Court of Human Rights 35, OAS Doc. OEA/Ser.L/V/III.19, Doc. 13 (1988) (judgement of 29 July 1988), reprinted in 28 *International Legal Materials* 291. See also Case 7615, Inter-American Court of Human Rights (10 October 1985), holding the state accountable for violations against Yanomami Indians caused by private persons. The Inter-American Commission has also recently held the Cuban government responsible for deaths caused by the acts of a private shipping company (decision not yet released).

28. See Matthew Craven (1995).

29. According to the UN Secretary-General: 'the emergence of an integrated international production system, increased locational mobility of TNCs and their monopolistic and oligopolistic tendencies have increased the bargaining power of TNCs and have been associated with a loss of decision-making capacity by

states, especially in developing countries. Increasing pressures to compete inter-nationally for capital, markets and labour contribute to reducing the margin of manoeuvre available to states'. *The Realization of Economic, Social and Cultural Rights. the relationship between the enjoyment of human rights, in particular, interna-tional labour and trade union rights, and the working methods and activities of transna-tional corporations,* Background document prepared by the Secretary-General, E/CN.4/Sub.2/ 1995/11, 24 July 1995 (Article 99).

30. Codes have been produced by the International Labour Organization (ILO), the Organization for Economic Cooperation and Development (OECD), the European Economic Community (EEC), the Organization of American States (OAS), the International Chamber of Commerce (ICC) and the International Confederation of Free Trade Unions (ICFTU), among others. See generally Peter Muchlinski (1995); see also Norbert Horn (1980): 407–49.

31. 'Development and International Economic Co-operation: Transnational Corporations', Letter Dated 31 May 1990 from the Chairman of the Recon-vened Special Session of the Commission on the Transnational Corporations to the President of the Economic and Social Council, UN ESCOR, Commission on Transnational Corporations, 2nd session, Agenda Item 7, UN Doc. E/1990/94 (1990).

32. See generally Barbara A. Frey (1997).

33. Draft Code of Conduct on Transnational Corporations, adopted 1 February 1988, UN ESCOR: 13; UN Doc. E/1988/39/Add.1 (1988).

34. Ibid.: 14.

35. Rio Declaration on Environment and Development, adopted 13 June 1992, UN Conference on Environment and Development, UN Doc. A/CONF.151/26 (Vol. I) (1992), [hereinafter Rio Declaration], reprinted in 31 *International Legal Materials* 874 (1992).

36. *Copenhagen Declaration on Social Development and Programme of Action,* Report of the World Summit for Social Development, adopted 12 March 1995, UN Doc. A/CONF.166/9 (1995) [hereinafter Copenhagen Declaration].

37. Report of the Secretary-General, n. 24 above, Para 80.

38. See The Impact of Property on the Enjoyment of Human Rights and Fundamental Freedoms, adopted 11 February 1988, GA Resolution 42/115, UN GAOR, 42nd Session, Agenda Item 105: 2, UN Doc. A/42/115 (1988).

39. See Commission on Human Rights Resolutions 1987/18 and 1988/19.

40. The UN Sub-Commission on Prevention of Discrimination and Protection of Minorities has recently begun to focus attention on TNCs and human rights. See Resolutions 1995/34, 1996/39.

41. The most well-publicized codes include those of Levi's, Reebok, Sears and Philips, among others. See generally, Lance A. Compa and Tashia Hinchliffe (1995).

42. See Gerry Spence (1989): 'Most see the in-house ethics efforts of corporations being adopted more for public relations than for the good of the public. The truth is, corporations are no more capable of acting ethically than they are of acting lovingly'.

43. Reference to the World Bank is intended to include both the International Bank for Reconstruction and Development and the International Development Association.

44. As one former Bank official states, 'everything we did from 1983 onward was

based on our new sense of mission to have the South "privatized" or die; towards this end we ignominiously created economic bedlam in Latin America and Africa'. Davison Budhoo, cited in Diana E. Moller (1995).

45. *The Realization of Economic, Social and Cultural Rights*, Second Progress Report submitted by Mr Danilo Türk, Special Rapporteur, UN ESCOR, Commission on Human Rights, Sub-Commission on Prevention of Discrimination and Protection of Minorities, 43rd session, Agenda Item 8: 85, UN Doc. E/CN.4/Sub.2/1991/17 (1991) [hereinafter *The Realization of ESCR*].

46. Ibid: 113–65.

47. See generally Bruce Rich (1994), describing the history of ill-advised Bank projects and their impact on local communities.

48. *The Realization of the ESCR*, Final Report submitted by Mr Danilo Türk, Special Rapporteur, E/CN.4/Sub.2/1992/16.

49. Articles of Agreement of the International Bank for Reconstruction and Development, 7 December 1945, Article IV, para. 10, as amended, 17 December 1965 [hereinafter IBRD Articles] ('The Bank and its officers shall not interfere in the political affairs of any member…Only economic considerations shall be relevant'); Articles of Agreement of the International Monetary Fund, 27 December 1945, as amended, 1 April 1978 [hereinafter IMF Articles], ('respect the domestic social and political policies of members, and in applying these principles…pay due regard to the circumstances of members'). The Bretton Woods institutions (the IBRD and the IMF) were originally conceived as the economic partner to the 'political' UN institution. However, both institutions have already broadened the interpretation of economic considerations to include 'good governance' and environmental concerns on the grounds that these issues have economic impacts. The Inter-American Development Bank Charter contains similar provisions against considering human rights. The European Bank for Reconstruction and Development, on the other hand, considers human rights to be central to its purposes.

50. See Ibrahim F.I. Shihata (1988): 'While…there are limits on the possible extent to which the World Bank can become involved with human rights, especially those of a civil and political nature, the Bank certainly can play, and has played, within the limits of its mandate, a very significant role in promoting various economic and social rights.…The right to development …is one human right which the World Bank has been promoting throughout its history'. There are strong arguments for rejecting these interpretations against civil and political rights. See Sigrun I. Skogly (1993); Balakrishnan Rajagopal (1993).

51. For information on the World Bank's consideration of poverty alleviation, see Ibrahim F.I. Shihata (1991). See generally World Bank (1996). For information on the IMF's consideration of welfare concerns, see Enrique R. Carrasco and M. Ayhan Kose (1996).

52. 'Excerpts from Remarks at Global Lenders' Talks', *New York Times*, 7 October 1998; http://www.nytimes.com/library/world/global/100798imf-text.html.

53. IBRD Articles, n. 49 above, Article I (iii).

54. IMF Articles, Article I (ii).

55. Michel Camdessus, cited in Jacques J. Polak (1991).

56. *Question of the Realization in All Countries of the Economic, Social and Cultural Rights contained in the Universal Declaration of Human Rights and in the International Covenant on Economic, Social and Cultural Rights, and Study of Special Problems which*

the Developing Countries Face in their Efforts to Achieve these Human Rights; ways and means to carry out a political dialogue between creditor and debtor countries in the United Nations system, based on the principle of shared responsibility, Report of the Secretary-General, Para 50, E/CN.4/1996/22 (5 February 1996).

57. *International Technical Assistance Measures*, General Comment No. 2, UN ESCOR, Committee on Economic, Social and Cultural Rights, 4th session, UN Doc. E/C.12/1990/23 (1990).

58. *The Right to Adequate Housing*, General Comment No. 4, UN ESCOR, Committee on Economic, Social and Cultural Rights, 6th session, UN Doc. E/C.12/1991/4 (1992). See also 'Globalization and Economic, Social and Cultural Rights: Statement by the Committee on Economic, Social and Cultural Rights', May 1998, Committee on Economic, Social and Cultural Rights. ('The Committee wishes to emphasize that international organizations, as well as the governments that have created and manage them, have a strong and continuous responsibility to take whatever measures they can to assist governments to act in ways which are compatible with their human rights obligations and to seek to devise policies and programmes which promote respect for those rights.')

59. *Vienna Declaration and Programme of Action*, UN GAOR, World Conference on Human Rights, 48th session, 42nd plenary meeting, Part II, UN Doc. A/CONF.157/23 (1993), reprinted in 32 *International Legal Materials* 1667 (1993).

60. *Report of the United Nations Conference on Environment and Development*, UN Conference on Environment and Development, Agenda 21: 38 and 41, A/Conf. 151/26 (Vol. III) (1992).

61. See generally *Copenhagen Declaration*, n. 36 above.

62. *The Realization of Economic, Social and Cultural Rights. Preliminary set of basic policy guidelines on structural adjustment programmes and economic, social and cultural rights*, Report of the Secretary-General prepared in pursuance of Resolution 1994/37, E/CN.4/Sub.2/1995/10 (4 July 1995).

63. See, e.g., Trail Smelter Arbitration (US v. Canada) (1941).

64. See, e.g., International Co-operation for Economic Development of Under-developed Countries, GA Resolution 13/1316 (XIII), UN GAOR, 13th session, Supp. No. 18 (1958); Permanent Sovereignty Over Natural Resources, GA Resolution 21/2158 (XXI), UN GAOR, 21st session, Supp. No. 16 (1966); Charter of Economic Rights and Duties of States, GA Res. 32/3281 (XXIX), UN GAOR, 29th session, Supp. No. 31 (1974), cited in Advisory Committee on Human Rights and Foreign Policy (1994) (concluding that 'an obligation to provide international aid may in general be said to exist when another state is no longer capable of independently realizing the absolute minimum norms of ESC rights').

65. UN Charter, Article 56, signed 26 June 1945.

66. Ibid, Article 55 (A)–(C).

67. UDHR, n. 49 above, Article 22.

68. ICESCR, n. 49 above, Article 11. Third-party states' obligations are reaffirmed in the Universal Declaration on the Eradication of Hunger and Malnutrition, adopted by the World Food Conference, Rome, UN Doc. E/CONF.65/20, at 1, 2, 8 and 11 (1974) ('All countries, and primarily the highly industrialized countries… should [*inter alia*] make all efforts to disseminate the results of their research work to governments and scientific institutions of developing

countries'. Parties should cooperate to promote 'a more equitable and efficient distribution of food between countries' and to 'improve access to markets').

69. The Nature of States Parties Obligations, General Comment No. 3, adopted 13–14 December 1990, UN ESCOR, Committee on Economic, Social and Cultural Rights, 5th Session, UN Doc. E/C.12/1990/8 (1990).

70. Declaration on the Right to Development, adopted 4 December 1986, GA Resolution 41/128, UN GAOR, 41st session, Supp. No. 53, Agenda Item 101: 186, UN Doc. A/41/53 (1987). The president of the International Court of Justice calls the right to development 'the *core right* from which all others stem...In reality the international dimension of the right to development is nothing other than *the right to an equitable share in the economic and social well-being of the world*. It reflects an essential demand of our time since four-fifths of the world's population no longer accept that the remaining fifth should continue to build its wealth on their poverty'. Mohammed Bedjaoui, quoted in Henry J. Steiner and Philip Alston (1996): 1117. See also Copenhagen Declaration, n. 8 above, at Para. 17(c); Charter of Economic Rights and Duties of States, Article 2 (2)(b) (maintaining that states should cooperate in the exercise of the right of every State 'to regulate and supervise the activities of TNCs within its national jurisdiction').

71. Declaration on the Right to Development, Article 2(2).

72. Ibid., Article 3 (1).

73. *Question of the Realization of the Right to Development*. Report of the Working Group on the Right to Development on its third session, E/CN.4/1995/27 (11 November 1994), para. 71.

74. Charter of the Organization of American States, 30 April 1948, Introduction, reprinted in 33 *International Legal Materials* 981 (1994).

75. Ibid., Article 3(l).

76. Ibid.

77. Ibid., Article 3(k). The Inter-American Commission on Human Rights recently ruled that 'conduct on the part of one state...[can have] the effect of violating the rights of persons in another OAS state'. Case 10,573, Inter-Am Court of Human Rights (1993).

78. See generally, the four 'Geneva Conventions', Geneva 1949.

79. Geneva Convention relative to the Protection of Civilian Persons in Time of War ('Geneva IV'), Article 50.

80. Ibid., Article 55.

81. Ibid., Article 23.

82. See the Foreign Assistance Act of 1961, para. 502 (b). A 1984 amendment to the Trade Act of 1974 incorporated the following items to be covered by the Act: '(A) right of association; (B) right to organize and bargain collectively; (C) a prohibition on the use of any form of forced or compulsory labor; (D) a minimum age for the employment of children; and (E) acceptable conditions of work with respect to minimum wages, hours of work, and occupational safety and health'. *Public Law* No. 98–573, 98 Stat. 3019.

83. African, Caribbean and Pacific States – European Economic Community Convention (Lomé IV), concluded 15 December 1989, Article 5, reprinted in 29 *International Legal Materials* 783 (1990). The Lomé conventions govern trade cooperation, foreign aid and technical assistance of the European Community. The European Community operates under the principle that measures against a

government 'should avoid penalizing the population of the country in question and particularly its poorest sections'. See Demetrios Marantis (1994).

84. For instance, in the World Bank's weighted voting scheme, a few individual countries like the United States can exercise decisive influence.

85. *Maastricht Guidelines on Violations of Economic, Social, and Cultural Rights,* para 19 (January 1997) [hereinafter Maastricht Guidelines], reprinted in 20 *Human Rights Quarterly* 691, 698 (1998). The Maastricht Guidelines were elaborated by a group of more than 30 experts under the auspices of the International Commission of Jurists, the Urban Morgan Institute for Human Rights and the Centre for Human Rights of the Faculty of Law of Maastricht University. Under US law, executive directors to multilateral development banks are prohibited from voting for any action or proposed loan that would have a significant effect on the human environment, unless an environmental impact assessment has been provided to the director by the bank at least 120 days in advance of the vote and a comprehensive summary is provided to the public. Pelosi Amendment, 103 Stat: 2511. Other legislation covers human rights and poverty, though only weakly. See 22 USC, para. 262d (1994).

86. GA Resolution 3281 (XXIX), Charter of Economic Rights and Duties of States, Article 2 (2)(b).

87. Rio Declaration, n. 35 above, Principle 13.

88. Maastricht Guidelines, para 18 (emphasis added).

89. The Bank's submission to the World Conference on Human Rights is typical. In 13 pages devoted to the importance of human rights and the many ways in which the Bank 'is helping developing countries to make the enjoyment of economic and social human rights a reality' there is a studious avoidance of legal obligation. World Bank, *The World Bank and the Promotion of Human Rights*, UN Doc. A/Conf.157/PC/61/Add.19 (1993).

90. A number of corporations have directed grants and awards to human rights organizations. Reebok, for instance, is strongly associated with human rights for its annual awards given to human rights defenders and its support for particular human rights programmes.

91. These cases have involved a requirement on the part of corporations to respect First Amendment free speech rights even when they infringe upon private property rights. See, e.g., Marsh v. Alabama, 326 US 501 (1946).

92. Military and Paramilitary Activities (Nicaragua v. US), 1986 International Court of Justice 4 (June 27), paras 107–9. The Inter-American Commission has recently held the Cuban government responsible for deaths caused by the acts of a private shipping company.

93. See n. 26 above and accompanying text for discussion of Asbjørn Eide's 1989 report.

94. See generally the *Provisional Report on the Relationship between the Enjoyment of Human Rights, in Particular Economic, Social and Cultural Rights, and Income Distribution, Submitted by Mr José Bengoa, UN Special Rapporteur on Income Distribution,* UN Commission on Human Rights, Sub-Commission on the Prevention of Discrimination and Protection of Minorities, 48th session, Agenda Item 8, para. 9, UN Doc. E/CN.4/Sub.2/1996/14 (1996) (showing that the global percentage of GDP of the richest 20 per cent of countries has risen from 89.33 per cent in 1980 to 92.42 per cent by 1994, while the poorest 20 per cent has fallen from 0.13 to 0.07 per cent during the same time period).

References

Anderson, Sarah and John Cavanagh (1996) *The Top 200: The Rise of Global Corporate Power*, Institute for Policy Studies, Washington.

Barnet, Richard J. and John Cavanagh (1994) *Global Dreams: Imperial Corporations and the New World Order*, Simon & Schuster, New York.

Bedjaoui, Mohammed (ed.) (1991) *International Law: Achievements and Prospects*, UNESCO, Paris; M. Nijhoff Publishers, Dordrecht, Boston.

Bolivar, Legia (1986) 'Derechos Económicos, Sociales y Culturales: Derribar Mitos, Enfrentar Retos, Tender Puentes: una Vision desde la (in) Experiencia de America Latina', *Estudios Básicos de Derechos Humanos,* Vol. 5, Instítuto Interamericano de Derechos Humanos, Costa Rica.

Bradlow, Daniel D. (1996) 'The World Bank, The IMF, and Human Rights', *Transnational Law and Contemporary Problems,* Vol. 6.

Carrasco, Enrique R. and M. Ayhan Kose (1996) 'Income Distribution and the Bretton Woods Institutions: Promoting an Enabling Environment for Social Development', *Transnational Law and Contemporary Problems,* Vol. 6.

Cassesse, Antonio (1990) *Human Rights in a Changing World*, Polity Press, Cambridge.

Center for Economic and Social Rights (1994) *Rights Violation in the Ecuadorian Amazon: The Human Consequences of Oil Development*, Center for Economic and Social Rights, New York.

Clapham, Andrew (1993) *Human Rights in the Private Sphere*, Clarendon Press, Oxford; Oxford University Press, New York.

Clarke, Tony (1996) 'Mechanisms of Corporate Rule', in Jerry Mander and Edward Goldsmith (eds) *The Case against the Global Economy: and for a Turn Toward the Local*, Sierra Club Books, San Francisco.

Commission on Global Governance (1995) *Our Global Neighbourhood*, Oxford University Press, Oxford.

Compa, Lance A. and Tashia Hinchcliffe (1995) 'Private Labor Rights Enforcement Through Corporate Codes of Conduct', *Columbia Journal of Transnational Law*.

Craven, Matthew C.R. (1995) *The International Covenant on Economic, Social and Cultural Rights: A Perspective on its Development*, Oxford Monographs in International Law series, Clarendon Press, Oxford; Oxford University Press, New York.

Freire, Paulo (1970) *Pedagogy of the Oppressed*, trans. Myra B. Ramos, The Seabury Press, New York.

Frey, Barbara A. (1997) 'The Legal and Ethical Responsibilities of Transnational Corporations in the Protection of International Human Rights', *Minnesota Journal of Global Trade,* Vol. 6.

Grossman, Richard L. and Frank T. Adams (1996) 'Exercising Power over Corporations Through State Charters', in Jerry Mander and Edward Goldsmith (eds) *The Case against the Global Economy: and for a Turn Toward the Local*, Sierra Club Books, San Francisco.

Henkin, Louis (1995) 'Human Rights and State "Sovereignty"', *The Georgia Journal of International and Comparative Law,* Vol. 25, Nos 1–2.

Higgins, Rosalyn and Christopher Greenwood (1996) 'Problems and Process: International Law and How We Use It', *The International and Comparative Law Quarterly*, Vol. 45, No. 3.

Hoof, G.J.H. van (1984) 'The Legal Nature of Economic, Social and Cultural

Rights: A Rebuttal of Some Traditional Views', in P. Alston and K. Tomasevski (eds) *The Right to Food*, International Studies in Human Rights series, M. Nijhoff Publishers, Boston; Stichting Studie- en Informatiecentrum Mensenrechten, Utrecht.

Horn, Norbert (ed.) (1980) *Legal Problems of Codes of Conduct for Multinational Enterprises*, Studies in Transnational Economic Law series, Vol. 1, Kluwer, Boston.

Jochnick, Chris (1997) *A New Generation of Human Rights Activism*, Carnegie Council, New York.

Jochnick, Chris (1999) 'Confronting the Impunity of Non-State Actors: New Fields for the Promotion of Human Rights', *Human Rights Quarterly*, Vol. 21, No. 1, February.

Jochnick, Chris and Roger Normand (1994) 'The Legitimation of Violence: A Critical History of the Laws of War', *Harvard International Law Journal*, Vol. 35, Issue 1: 49–96.

Klare, Karl (1982) 'The Public/Private Distinction in Labor Law', *University of Pennsylvania Law Review*, Vol. 130.

Lauterpacht, H. (1946) 'The Grotian Tradition in International Law', *British Yearbook of International Law*, Vol. 23.

MacKinnon, Catherine (1993) 'On Torture: A Feminist Perspective on Human Rights', in Kathleen E. Mahoney and Paul Mahoney (eds) *Human Rights in the Twenty-first Century: A Global Challenge*, M. Nijhoff Publishers, Dordrecht, Boston.

Marantis, Demetrios (1994) 'Human Rights, Democracy and Development: The European Community Model', *Harvard Human Rights Journal*, Vol. 7.

Moller, Diana E. (1995) 'Intervention, Coercion or Justifiable Need? A Legal Analysis of Structural Adjustment Lending in Costa Rica', *Southwestern Journal of Law And Trade in the Americas*, Vol. 2.

Muchlinski, Peter (1995) *Multinational Enterprises and the Law*, Blackwell Publishers, Oxford and Cambridge, Massachusetts.

Mutua, Makau (1996) 'The Ideology of Human Rights', *Virginia Journal of International Law*, Vol. 36, No. 3.

Orentlicher, Diane and Timothy Gelatt (1993) 'Public Law, Private Actors: The Impact of Human Rights on Business Investors in China', *Northwest Journal of International Law and Business*, Vol. 14.

Paust, Jordan J. (1992) 'The Other Side of Right: Private Duties under Human Rights Law', *Harvard Human Rights Journal*, Vol. 5.

Polak, Jacques J. (1991) *The Changing Nature of IMF Conditionality*, Essays in International Finance series, No. 184, International Finance Section, Dept. of Economics, Princeton University, Princeton.

Rajagopal, Balakrishnan (1993) 'Crossing the Rubicon: Synthesizing the Soft International Law of the IMF and Human Rights', *Boston University International Law Journal*, Vol. 11, No. 1.

Ranis, Gustav (1996) 'The World Bank Near the Turn of the Century', in Roy Culpeper, Albert Berry and Frances Stewart (eds) *Global Development Fifty Years after Bretton Woods: Essays in Honour of Gerald K. Helleiner*, St. Martin's Press, New York.

Rich, Bruce (1994) *Mortgaging the Earth: The World Bank, Environmental Impoverishment and the Crisis of Development*, Beacon Press, Boston.

Schindler, Dietrich and Jiri Toman (eds) (1988) *The Laws of Armed Conflicts: A Collection of Conventions, Resolutions and Other Documents*, 3rd revised and completed ed., M. Nijhoff Publishers, Dordrecht, Boston.

Shihata, Ibrahim F. I. (1988) 'The World Bank and Human Rights: An Analysis of the Legal Issues and the Record of Achievements', *Denver Journal of International Law and Policy,* Vol. 17.

Shihata, Ibrahim F.I. (1991–95) *The World Bank in a Changing World*, M. Nijhoff Publishers, Dordrecht, Boston.

Skogly, Sigrun I. (1993) 'Structural Adjustment and Development: Human Rights – An Agenda for Change', *Human Rights Quarterly*, Vol. 15.

Spence, Gerry (1989) *With Justice for None: Destroying an American Myth*, Times Books, New York.

Steiner, Henry J. and Philip Alston (1996) *International Human Rights in Context: Law, Politics, Morals: Text and Materials*, Clarendon Press, Oxford; Oxford University Press, New York.

Trimble, Phillip R. (1990) 'Review Essay: International Law, World Order and Critical Legal Studies', *Stanford Law Review,* Vol. 42.

Walker, R.B.J. and Saul H. Mendlovitz (eds) (1990) *Contending Sovereignties: Redefining Political Community*, Lynne Rienner Publishers, Boulder.

World Bank (1996), *Poverty Reduction and the World Bank*, World Bank, New York.

12

Human Rights as a Source of Inspiration and an Instrument for the Eradication of Extreme Poverty

The Need for an Integrated Economic, Political and Legal Approach

WILLEM VAN GENUGTEN AND CAMILO PEREZ-BUSTILLO

In 1995, CROP organized a workshop on Law, Power and Poverty, which resulted in a book with the same title (Kjønstad and Veit Wilson 1997). In her preface to the book, Else Øyen, Chair of CROP, said that 'law is one of the important means of combating poverty' (ibid.: i). And Asbjørn Eide, a well-known Norwegian scholar in the field of human rights, added that 'if the internationally recognized human rights in their entirety had been fully implemented, poverty would not have existed' (ibid.: 118). Human rights were described as 'the expression of a specific social goal: creating the legal, economic and social conditions in which persons all over the world can live a life worthy of a human being' (van Genugten, in Kjønstad and Veit Wilson 1997: 100).

> [T]his – highly ambitious – goal immediately links human rights protection to specific situations in specific countries. In some of these countries there will be an enormous need for legal protection against torture and political killings, in other situations the primary problem will be the right to adequate food or health care, and in many cases there will be a combination of such needs, often reflecting the levels of extreme and structural poverty. The international human rights instruments are supposed to evolve according to the changing needs which have to be met worldwide. Law is not a static phenomenon. (ibid.)

'Living a life worthy of a human being' – this approach has been expressed in, *inter alia*, Article 25 of the 1948 Universal Declaration of Human Rights:

> everyone has the right to a standard of living adequate for the health and well-being of himself and his family, including food, clothing, housing, medical care and necessary social services, and the right to security in the event of unemployment, sickness, disability, widowhood, old age or other lack of livelihood in circumstances beyond his control.

184

If we take this (complex) right seriously it is obvious that living in circumstances of (extreme) poverty means a violation of many internationally recognized human rights (Kjønstad and Veit Wilson 1997). According to one commentator: 'Virtually all the energy of the extremely poor is devoted to the struggle for survival, leaving little room for an enriching cultural and social life'. This is the 'vicious circle of poverty'.[1]

The 1997 (Santiago de Chile) and 1999 (Mexico City) CROP workshops which led to this book can be seen as a follow-up to the 1995 meeting, addressing a series of issues: the need for special protection of indigenous peoples; the negative sides of the free market; the role of transnational corporations and other actors; the need for participation by the poor; and the relation between human rights, poverty and the environment, to mention only a few examples. In this final chapter, some major issues in the field of human rights and poverty will be raised, linking our approach to the other contributions to the book.

Participation by the Poor

One of the conclusions of the 1994 United Nations seminar on Extreme Poverty and the Denial of Human Rights (New York, 12–14 October 1994) was that families and groups living in situations of extreme poverty make constant and important efforts to improve their living conditions but that such efforts 'tend to go unnoticed by the dominant society, which seems unable to build upon them or upon the fragile solidarity that can exist among persons, families and groups living in situations of extreme poverty'.[2] The same conclusions were drawn at the 1995 World Summit for Social Development. The summit identified the following as manifestations of poverty: lack of income and productive resources sufficient to ensure sustainable livelihoods; hunger and malnutrition; ill-health; limited or lack of access to education and other basic services; increased morbidity and mortality from illness; homelessness and inadequate housing; unsafe environments; and social discrimination and exclusion; but added, in its Final Document, that poverty is also 'characterized by a lack of participation in decision-making and in civil, social and cultural life'.[3] The document continues: 'the aim of social integration is to create "a society for all", where every individual, each with rights and responsibilities, has an active role to play',[4] while recommending, amongst (many) other things, the need to strengthen 'popular political participation, and…the transparency and accountability of political groupings at the local and national levels'.[5]

Popular participation, and its reflected image, exclusion, was one of the central and recurring issues at the 1997 and 1999 workshops. In Chapter 2 of this book Patricia Helena Massa Arzabe states that 'the exclusion of parts of the society enlarges the levels of extreme poverty', while Eduardo S. Bustelo in Chapter 1 discusses the concept of 'emancipated citizenship', being 'by definition a socially inclusive project'. The same author discusses the expansion of citizenship from civil to political and finally to social rights, adding:

> If there are poor and marginalized people, they do not enjoy the status of citizens, because civil and political rights are merely formal recognitions. What difference would recognition of the right to property make to those who are poor if they possess nothing, or the right to vote if its exercise is ineffectual in changing the situation of social exclusion? (p. 5).

The convergence of civil and political rights on the one hand and economic, social and cultural rights on the other forms, for several authors, the cornerstone of what a decent, human rights-based society is all about. Without such a convergence being taken into consideration and realized in practice, there will be no human dignity. In the words of Marco Aurelio Ugarte Ochoa (Chapter 4) 'human rights lose their meaning and their force if we separate them from each other'. A series of testimonies by poor persons, as presented by the same author, underlines this position.

An important aspect of the participation issue raised in several contributions relates to education. Lack of education is generally considered to be characteristic of poor families (see, for instance, the contribution by Maribel Gordon C., Chapter 5), while education is also seen as a way out of the misery (see, for instance, Claudio González-Parra's 'Quality of Life Improvement Plan' in Chapter 6). In the words of Eduardo S. Bustelo, Chapter 1: 'Participation and education in this sense are almost interchangeable terms: to participate is to educate and to learn, and equally to educate is to participate and learn'; 'Participatory democracy implies a "learning society" since education is the root of emancipation itself'.

Indigenous Peoples

The issue of participation is also extremely relevant in relation to indigenous peoples, who often live under disproportionately poor conditions and are confronted with social, economic, political and cultural structures that exclude and marginalize them. The issues of poverty and participation are reflected in Chapter 8 by Luis Hernandez Navarro. As he says in relation to Mexico's indigenous peoples: 'it is virtually synonymous…to be indigenous and to be poor'; 'this overall situation is attributable in part to the lack of recognition of indigenous political institutions and to their lack of political representation in institutions which wield power at the municipal, state and federal levels'. The fact that representation and decision-making is mainly done through the channels of 'officially recognized political parties' and not through systems that indigenous peoples are using ('In most indigenous communities traditional forms of participation and organization prevail based on decision-making in community assemblies, by plebiscite or consensus, and according to systems of rotation of responsibilities') is in Hernandez Navarro's opinion (Chapter 8) one of the major root causes for this disadvantaged position. As he asks, more or less rhetorically: what about the right to self-determination, as formulated in the two major (1966) UN covenants (on Civil and Political Rights and on Economic, Social and Cultural Rights) in the field of human rights, which in their common first Article, say that 'all peoples have the right to self-determination', by virtue of which 'they freely determine their political status and freely pursue their economic, social and cultural development'?

As also noted by the Chilean indigenous scholar and activist Claudio González-Parra, in Chapter 6, it is indeed a misconception to think 'that development can be created without the active participation of the communities'. He concludes that 'the implementation of mega-projects [like the Hydroelectric Dams in the land of the Pehuenches in Chile] and the process of resettlement without active participation of the communities is a violation of the rights of the communities and of the [Chile's] Indigenous Law'.

Several contributions draw attention to the need for further legal protection for indigenous peoples, be it on the national or the international level (see especially the contribution by Camilo Perez-Bustillo, Chapter 7). It may be recalled that since the 1970s the UN has been involved in initiatives, frequently in cooperation with the International Labour Organization and the Organization of American States, concerning the development of specific standards for the protection of indigenous peoples as a result of which the UN Working Group on Indigenous Populations was, in 1982, created as a body of the Sub-Commission for the Prevention of Discrimination and Protection of Minorities, one of its commitments being the drafting of a Declaration on the Rights of Indigenous Populations. The draft was adopted by the Sub-Commission in August 1994, and handed over to the UN Commission on Human Rights for further deliberation (see Chapter 7).

The draft declaration consists of 45 articles, related to such issues as the right of indigenous populations to self-determination (Article 3), the right not to be 'forcibly removed from their lands or territories' (Article 10), the right 'to practise and revitalize their cultural traditions and customs' (Article 12), the right 'to establish their own media in their own languages' (Article 18), and the right 'to determine and develop priorities and strategies for the development or use of their lands, territories and other resources' (Article 30). Since 1995, a Working Group of the UN Human Rights Commission has been involved in a debate on similar issues, discussing the draft declaration on an article-by-article basis. A number of indigenous peoples' organizations are involved in the debate. The general feeling is that, after some initial skirmishes, the working group debate is becoming more constructive. The problems to be resolved are, however, still enormous, and results are awaited. In the words of Camilo Perez-Bustillo, 'it is unlikely to move quickly into the next phases of adoption by the UN General Assembly'. Nevertheless, according to the plans, the Declaration has to be adopted by the General Assembly before the end of the International Decade of the World's Indigenous People (December 2004).

One of the major problems relates to the issue of collective rights.[6] For some decades there has been extensive debate both within the UN system and, more generally, in the field of international law and international human rights as to whether entities like national minorities and indigenous peoples should be protected as such, that is to say, as collectivities, or whether the international community should stick to protection of the individual members belonging to these groups.[7] The previously mentioned draft Declaration on the Rights of Indigenous Populations seeks to incorporate aspects of both lines of argument: 'Indigenous individuals and peoples are free and equal to all other individuals and peoples in dignity and rights' (Article 2). The draft also recognizes a series of collective rights, such as those related to the right to self-determination:

> Indigenous peoples, as a specific form of exercising their right to self-determination, have the right to autonomy or self-government in matters relating to their internal and local affairs, including culture, religion, education, information, media, health, housing, employment, social welfare, economic activities, land and resource management, environment and entry by non-members, as well as ways and means for financing these autonomous activities. (Article 31)

For many indigenous peoples represented in the drafting process, the right to self-determination fundamentally means autonomy ('internal self-determination'). This is a concept which can be defined in several ways. For these indigenous peoples the broad way it has been done in the draft Declaration is adequate. But another group of representatives demands incorporation into the draft of a full acceptance of the right to self-determination, including the right to secession ('external self-determination').

In the debates on the draft Declaration as well as in various national legal practices it would in our opinion be best for states fully to accept the concept of autonomy, as a road towards the solution of problems which otherwise might not be solved. In Chapter 8 of this volume, Luis Hernandez Navarro emphasizes the need to accept autonomy agreements as 'the means by which organized indigenous communities can free themselves from the influence of mestizo landowners and middlemen...In this way the struggle for the self-determination and autonomy of indigenous peoples, and for the construction of a differentiated citizenship are elements which act in favour of the substantive democratization of the whole nation'. In our opinion a 'differentiated citizenship' also means that the human rights of individual members of indigenous peoples have to be secured in case these individuals want something which might contradict the wishes of the collectivity. This is an approach which is reflected in the wording of the draft Declaration, and which is in conformity with existing international law.[8] From this perspective a multiculturalist approach, based on respect for individual human rights and on tolerance towards all kinds of ethnic backgrounds and identities, and the recognition of group rights do not in fact have to be in conflict. Such an approach harvests thinking in terms of self-determination and autonomy for indigenous peoples as concepts which create room for them in addition to the legal status states and individuals already have in international (human rights) law.

Apart from the draft Declaration, the UN Human Rights Commission is at the time of writing considering the possibility and desirability of a permanent forum for indigenous peoples. At its 1998 session, the commission decided 'to establish an open-ended inter-sessional ad hoc working group, from within existing overall United Nations resources, to elaborate and consider further proposals for the possible establishment of a permanent forum for indigenous people within the United Nations system'.[9] In the meantime, the previously mentioned Working Group on Indigenous Populations of the Sub-Commission, having as its task, *inter alia*, 'to review developments pertaining to the promotion and protection of the human rights and fundamental freedoms of indigenous people', is still active, waiting for a more permanent successor. There is a broadly felt need to strengthen the position of indigenous peoples in the international arena, but many steps have to be taken before that international protection becomes acceptable to them as well as instrumental in their national struggles. Several contributions to the present book deal with the extremely disadvantaged position of indigenous communities, as well as of their individual members. This is a central issue in the sphere of poverty eradication.

Human Rights and the Environment

A key aspect of poverty, for indigenous peoples as well as others, is the absence of a clean, healthy environment, that is to say, a decent physical environment for all as a condition for living as a human being. More concretely, a decent physical environment has to do with protection against, for instance, noise, air pollution, pollution of surface waters, and the dumping of toxic substances. Some 350 multilateral and 1,000 bilateral conventions, to say nothing of numerous declarations, action programmes and resolutions, have already been drawn up across the world to regulate and protect in areas which have a bearing on the environment.[10] These instruments generally impose obligations on states to make efforts to further the relevant objectives. This means that individual citizens cannot invoke them in law. This situation is, however, beginning to change, as could be seen, for instance, in the judgement of the European Court of Human Rights in the case of López Ostra v. Spain (judgement 09/12/94), in which the Court held that Article 8 of the 1950 European Convention for the Protection of Human Rights and Fundamental Freedoms had been violated because the applicant had not been indemnified by the state against damage resulting from environmental pollution.

Meanwhile the UN Human Rights Commission made progress in the field of supervision and implementation of the right to a clean environment by appointing, in 1995, a Special Rapporteur on The Adverse Effects of Illicit Movement and Dumping of Toxic and Dangerous Products and Wastes on the Enjoyment of Human Rights. Discussing the Rapporteur's report in 1998, the Commission again underlined the importance of

> the increasing rate of illicit movement and dumping by transnational corporations and other enterprises from industrialized countries of hazardous and other wastes in African and other developing countries that do not have the national capacity to deal with them in an environmentally sound manner which constitutes a serious threat to the human rights to life, good health and a sound environment for everyone.[11]

In addition, the Commission decided to renew the mandate of the Special Rapporteur for a period of another three years, giving the Special Rapporteur the possibility of making 'a global multidisciplinary and comprehensive study of existing problems of and solutions to illicit traffic in and dumping of toxic and dangerous products and wastes, in particular in developing countries'.[12] The resolution was adopted by a roll-call vote of 33 votes in favour, 14 against and 6 abstentions, showing the still controversial character of the issue.[13]

The human right to a clean environment is controversial because, among other things, it has individual as well as collective aspects. This is especially the case where environmental problems are related to protection of indigenous habitats. In the words of the above-mentioned UN Special Rapporteur 'the human rights problems facing indigenous peoples due to environmental factors are rapidly increasing', while 'the situation of indigenous peoples, especially as it relates to human rights and the environment, is at a critical point'.[14]

The present book has many examples of problems fitting into the matrix of human rights and environmental problems, with an individual and collective aspect. For example, in Chapter 6 Claudio González-Parra quotes the Chilean Indigenous Law of October 1993 which says that indigenous lands 'shall not be alienated, seized, nor acquired by limitation, except between communities or indigenous persons belonging to the same ethnic group'. He goes on to state that:

> A large number of indigenous communities are facing such situations, due to the implementation of a number of mega-projects such as the Coast Road, the Temuco By-Pass, urban expansion, exploitation of forest, and privatization of coastal areas and their waters. All these projects plunge Chile's most needy ever deeper into poverty, leading to enormous social and cultural problems amongst them. The disastrous environmental consequences of the projects barely need mention. (p. 79)

In Chapter 3, Cuban scholar and human rights advocate Juan Antonio Blanco deals fundamentally with the issue of human rights and the environment. He speaks in terms of the uncertainty 'of continuing survival for our species', and human society having achieved 'technological powers comparable only to those traditionally attributed to God', followed by his call 'to reveal the critical existent nexus between natural history and social history'. 'More of the same' cannot be the solution. Blanco also brings together, on p. 43, some of the issues being dealt with so far (participation, environment) as well as some of the issues to be discussed in the rest of this final chapter (such as the right to development):

In the struggle for human rights we cannot restrict ourselves to softening the hard edges of the tensions dominant in the world today, but must instead promote the conceptualization and implementation of new models of social organization. We urgently need a new civilizational and cultural paradigm that is politically participatory, economically inclusive, culturally pluralist, environmentally responsible, ethically rooted in notions of solidarity and equitable in terms of assuring equal access to opportunities for social advancement. The fundamental challenge of our times is to define and bring about the prevalence of this new paradigm. This is the only guarantee we have that we will be able to find a holistic and simultaneous solution to the needs we must confront in terms of both the environment and human rights.

Human Rights and Development

Many of the above-mentioned aspects come together in the 1986 Declaration on the Right to Development (see especially Chapter 10) where the emphasis is on both the basic needs of individuals and the need to assist peoples as a whole. Issues such as participation are considered from a developmental perspective. Article 1 of the Declaration states that: 'The right to development is an inalienable human right by virtue of which every human person and all peoples are entitled to participate in, contribute to, and enjoy economic, social, cultural and political development in which all human rights and all fundamental freedoms can be fully realized'.

The right to development was reaffirmed at the World Conference on Human Rights in Vienna in 1993 'as a universal and inalienable right and an integral part of fundamental human rights',[15] while the UN Commission on Human Rights spoke in its 1998 session of an important right 'for every human person and all peoples in all countries',[16] thereby underlining once again the individual as well as the collective aspects of the right to development. In this session the Commission also underlined the importance of structural measures to tackle the problems developing countries have to overcome: 'international co-operation is acknowledged more than ever as a necessity deriving from recognized mutual interest, and therefore ... such co-operation should be strengthened in order to support the efforts of developing countries to solve their social and economic problems and to fulfil their obligations to promote and protect all human rights'.[17] This position is supported by Héctor Gros Espiell in Chapter 9, where the author speaks about linking together 'the issue of human rights with the problem of underdevelopment, exploitation and injustice, not only as internal matters within a particular country, but also on a global scale, as part of the tragic division of humanity into a developed world, on the one hand, and another world trapped in underdevelopment which is exploited and marginalized'.

Patrick van Weerelt argues in Chapter 10 that the right to development is a programmatic tool which can be used to strengthen the 'normative foundation for tackling fundamental issues related to poverty and other aspects of sustainable human development'. There needs to be a shift from a 'basic needs strategy', which incorporates 'a certain element of charity', to a human rights–based approach.

In Van Weerelt's as well as in other contributions to this book, the notion of development is subjected to serious inquiry, not taken as a concept whose meaning can be assumed. Claudio González-Parra states, for instance, in Chapter 6, that 'the fallacy exists…that development can be created without the active participation of the communities', and that 'many argue that the development which the dam will bring [the Hydroelectric Dam in the land of the Pehuenches in Chile] will justify whatever violations of human rights have occurred in the process'. In Chapter 5, Maribel Gordon C. argues that it is imperative 'that we create awareness of an economic policy to be maintained on the basis of sustainable economic development, not only on the growth of the economic aggregates that are generating social exclusion'. In Chapter 11, Chris Jochnick, quoting the UN Committee on Economic, Social and Cultural Rights, states that 'many activities undertaken in the name of "development" have subsequently been recognized as ill-conceived and even counterproductive in human rights terms'.

In its 1998 session, the UN Commission on Human Rights spoke about 'the unacceptable situation of absolute poverty, hunger and disease, lack of adequate shelter, illiteracy and hopelessness' being 'the lot of over one billion people', about the 'gap between developed and developing countries' remaining unacceptably wide, and about the difficulties developing countries have to face when 'participating in the globalization process', as a result of which they face being 'marginalized and effectively excluded from its benefits'.[18] This brings us to the matter of globalization and the role of the free market, another major issue in the present book.

Globalization, Free Markets and the Role of the State

The world is involved in a process of globalization and creating free markets for all kinds of economic interests, be it in the field of capital flows, the manufacturing of products or the exchange of information, symbolized by the creation of the World Trade Organization (WTO) on 1 January 1995,[19] an organization dealing amongst other things with agriculture, textiles and clothing, banking, telecommunications, government purchases, industrial standards, food-sanitation regulations, and intellectual property.[20]

As a starting point, one might argue that more trade is good for productivity, that more productivity will lead to more welfare, that more welfare will lead to social stability, and that social stability is an important basic requirement for the full realization of human rights. In the words of the WTO itself:

> The data show a definite statistical link between freer trade and economic growth. Economic theory points to strong reasons for the link. All countries, including the poorest, have assets – human, industrial, natural, financial – which they can employ to produce goods and services for their domestic markets or to compete overseas. Economics tells us that we can benefit when these goods and services are traded. Simply put, the principle of 'comparative advantage' says that countries prosper first by taking advantage of their assets in order to concentrate on what they can produce best, and then by trading these products for products that other countries produce best. [21]

Reading such a proclamation, several questions come to the fore: what about the negative side-effects of the free market, and what about ensuring that everybody benefits from the economic welfare created by globalized economic activities? Isn't *the* basic presumption behind the free market idea that you will be a loser if you cannot compete? Of course, the WTO has a series of special programmes and activities for Third World countries, an issue which will not be dealt with here at length, but is this enough to repair the negative side-effects?

Many of the authors of the present book would likely consider the quote taken from the WTO website to be nothing more than free-market rhetoric. In Chapter 2, Patricia Helena Massa Arzabe asks herself, for instance, 'how much *laissez faire* in "globalization days" is worth deep inequality', and states that 'a capitalist system which aims at more and more profit above all other interests is centred in what can be called the paradigm of continuous economic growth'. Eduardo S. Bustelo states in Chapter 1 that 'market mechanisms have been reinstituted not just as a means of optimizing resources but as a hegemonic economic logic in processes of public decision-making'. In other words, the free-market language far exceeds the sphere of economic activities. The same author argues explicitly that capitalism produces deep social inequalities, leading, for instance, to more power for those who have the money:

> In the case of the political market, the only effective demand is that by those who have purchasing power and not the consumers as such. The dominant

interests are those of the sectors with the money necessary to organize a political party or pressure group, finance an electoral campaign or buy promotional spots in the mass media. Similarly this formulation does not take into account the various different kinds of restrictions which frequently arise in the spaces of activity of consumer-citizens confronted by obstacles such as oligopolistic political parties, or packets of prefabricated desires promoted by sophisticated political marketing techniques.

This is no longer then a discussion about the side-effects of the free market only, but rather touches upon the core of the concept of capitalism itself. In that respect many authors also question the role of the state, which is inclined to withdraw itself from the scene, or to fill its role in an unbalanced way. So Partricia Helena Massa Arzabe argues, in Chapter 2, that the state has undertaken policies to promote more employment by strengthening the market, but at the same time worsens 'the conditions for workers and potential workers, that is, the major part of the world's population', while Eduardo S. Bustelo, in Chapter 1, discusses the rising imbalance between the public and the private sphere. He speaks in terms of an 'increasing concern about the loss and near-disappearance of public spaces: education, health and different forms of social protection. A vigorous current of public opinion is re-emerging which demands a serious discussion about the public character of education, health and other key public areas as spheres for democratization of the overall society'. He adds:

> Public services which have been privatized with continued monopoly guarantees have left consumers in virtual helplessness in terms of verifying the costs of their services (e.g., that of telephones and electricity) so as to be able to justify rate hikes. In Latin America, efforts at organized forms of consumer protection have not yet attained the vigour or the power that they have in the developed world, although they have begun to emerge. The idea here is not of a return to the former state role as such, but rather of an increased popular perception of the need to define adequate public regulatory frameworks for the protection of consumers rights. (pp. 15–16)

Juan Antonio Blanco seems to adopt the same approach in Chapter 3: he states that 'the false dichotomy that some propose to impose upon us between the market and the state must be transcended so that there can be a redefinition of their functions and limits, as well as their reciprocal connections'.

The role of the state is further commented upon by Héctor Gros Espiell who discusses, in Chapter 9, the problem of realizing human rights under bad conditions such as: underdevelopment, the absence of resources and the existence of financial chaos. One can agree with the author that under such conditions the realization of economic, social and cultural rights is impossible. Gros Espiell discusses the role of the state which, in his words, has 'the essential but not exclusive obligation' to realize economic, social and cultural rights. 'Essential but not exclusive' – as Gros Espiell underlines, the state can never be made responsible for all this on its own. Without strong support from society itself, human rights will never be realized:

> A state's social and economic policies, implemented lawfully, are the unavoidable but not exclusive elements necessary for the development and transformation of negative conditions capable of enabling economic, social and cultural rights to begin to become a reality. Such a democratic state, committed to social justice, where the rule of law prevails, must itself also be the great vehicle for the transformation and betterment of society and for its economic, social and cultural development. It is not enough to be a manager of change. Without the combined effort of the society as a whole, including the state organs, nothing deep, transcendent and lasting can be achieved. (pp. 139–40)

Wise words, written by a man with outstanding and long experience in the field of the realization of (economic, social and cultural) human rights.

The Role of Transnational Corporations

The issue of the 'reciprocal connections' (Blanco) is also related to the role transnational corporations (TNCs) can and should play in the field of human rights protection and, thus, in poverty eradication. It is an issue with a serious history. In the 1970s the debate concerning the influence of TNCs on the economic, political and social conditions of host states, especially developing countries, resulted, *inter alia*, in attempts by the latter and by workers' organizations to regulate TNC activities. The immediate cause was the well-documented efforts by the International Telephone and Telegraph Corporation (ITT), and other US corporations with significant investments in the country, such as the Kennecott and Anaconda copper companies, to overthrow the popularly elected leftist coalition (Popular Unity) government headed by Salvador Allende in Chile. Similar examples from the recent past in Latin America include those of the United Fruit Company in Guatemala, culminating in a successful US-backed coup in 1954; the counter-revolutionary activities of the sugar, telephone, railroad and tourist sector interests in Cuba after Fidel Castro seized power in 1959; the role played by Gulf and Western's mining interests in supporting the US invasion of the Dominican Republic in 1965; the invasion of

Panama in 1989 to secure continued protection of US commercial and military interests in the canal zone; and, finally, the role played currently by massive US investments and growing interventionism in Mexico in the wake of the North American Free Trade Agreement (NAFTA).

Many concluded that ITT's actions in Chile showed that TNCs were able and willing to exert inadmissible forms of political coercion on lawful governments.[22] As a result, during a meeting of the United Nations' Economic and Social Council (ECOSOC) in July 1972, the Chilean representative requested the establishment of a group of experts which was to undertake a comprehensive study of the activities of all TNCs, irrespective of their origin or influence.[23] Also in the 1970s, several international organizations – especially the Organization for Economic Co-operation and Development (OECD), the International Labour Organization (ILO) and the International Chamber of Commerce (ICC) – undertook studies with the objective of developing codes of conduct for TNCs, leading finally to the adoption of the ICC 'Guidelines for International Investment' (1972; in 1990 modified into 'The Business Charter for Sustainable Development'), the OECD 'Guidelines for Multinational Enterprises' (1976; presently again in revision) and the ILO 'Tripartite Declaration of Principles Concerning Multinational Enterprises and Social Policy' (1977). All these codes contain a series of obligations and possibilities that TNCs (should) have in the field of human rights and related issues. To mention only one example: according to the Preamble to the ILO code, TNCs 'can make an important contribution to the promotion of economic and social welfare; to the improvement of living standards and the satisfaction of basic needs; to the creation of employment opportunities, both directly and indirectly; and to the enjoyment of basic human rights, including the freedom of association, throughout the world'.

It is sometimes argued that these codes have no legal importance because they are of a voluntary and non-legally enforceable nature. It would be incorrect, however, to suggest that the absence of legal regulation necessarily outlaws a code. Although voluntary codes of conduct cannot be enforced by a court of law, their underlying principles may render them a normative force. Consequently, the actors will feel obliged to adapt their behaviour to the requirements ensuing from normative principles, based on self-regulation. Behaviour will be brought into conformity with the principles not because the actors feel they are legally obliged to do so, but because they feel that their behaviour ought to be in conformity with the norm and because consumers so require (van Dijk 1987: 9).[24] In addition, it can be said that in the course of time, the principles may be translated into a rule which is legally enforceable. When applied by courts, provisions of the OECD, ILO and ICC codes may pass into the general corpus of customary international law, even for TNCs which have never accepted them.[25] It is important to stress that several international organizations have their own monitoring procedures for the implementation of their codes of conduct. The ILO, for instance, has a system of questionnaires, asking governments for information about the implementation of the ILO Tripartite Declaration. It's seventh full-scale survey, covering the years 1996–99[26] is currently in preparation.

During the 1980s, the interest in regulating TNC behaviour declined.[27] Attention shifted instead to the liberalization of the international economy and to the attraction of international direct investment. During the 1990s, however, the quest for regulating instruments such as codes of conduct has been revitalized, albeit with a different point of departure. While the approach of the 1970s was primarily motivated by the wish to combat international economic inequality and to prevent TNCs from intervening in the domestic affairs of states, presently the aim is to take up the challenges brought about by globalization. TNCs are the main actors within the globalized economy, and as such are gaining influence in global policy-making. They have distinctive responsibilities and are increasingly invited to take up this challenge. In the words of the Commission on Global Governance (1995: 3):

> business must be encouraged to act responsibly in the global neighbourhood and contribute to its governance…The international community needs to enlist the support of transnational business in global governance and to encourage best practices, acknowledging the role the private sector can play in meeting the needs of the global neighbourhood. Wider acceptance of these responsibilities is likely if the business sector is drawn to participate in the processes of governance.

In the present book, the role of TNCs is most specifically discussed by Chris Jochnick in Chapter 11. He touches upon the issue, by pointing to the enormous influence TNCs' activities can have on societies, thereby underlining that the legal responsibility for negatively influencing the realization of human rights lies with the states concerned and not with the corporations themselves. This is according to the orthodox prevailing view of international relations and international law in which nation-states are the key actors and subjects, with some exceptions for individuals in the sphere of human rights.

One can add, however, that in this field much is changing rapidly. To some extent TNCs have already been given the status of international legal personalities. For instance, at the Iran–United States Claims

Tribunal, created in 1981 as part of the settlement of the Teheran hostage crisis and established to deal with claims between nationals of and companies from the two states, individuals and companies which are nationals of one of the two parties have, under certain conditions legal standing (Malanczuk 1997: 101). Another example is to be found in the United Nations Convention on the Law of the Sea of 10 December 1982 together with its 1994 Implementation Agreement.[28] The 'Seabed Dispute Chamber' has been given jurisdiction over disputes between parties to a contract, specifically states parties, state enterprises and natural or juridical persons which carry out activities with regard to deep sea-bed mining.[29] The conclusion can be that the old scheme to which we referred earlier is not absolute any more. As Peter Malanczuk (1997: 103–4) rightly says, however: 'it should be noted that the international legal personality of…companies…is still comparatively rare and limited'. Nevertheless, one can also say that the perspective is changing, be it step by step. And apart from a set of hard legal obligations, one can in any case point to the previously mentioned codes of conduct, guidelines which are made in the presence and with the support of TNCs.

Concerted Action Required

The eradication of poverty in all its aspects (many of which have been presented and discussed in the present book) requires joint efforts by actors on all kind of levels, employing all kinds of political, economic and legal means. In addition to the actors already mentioned, several others should be noted, for instance the Bretton Woods institutions (the World Bank and the IMF). They are both criticized in the present volume – by Camilo Perez-Bustillo, in Chapter 7, amongst others, who states that the World Bank has until recently displayed an 'apparent lack of interest in the issue of the impact of its policies on indigenous peoples' – as well as recognized for their evolving stance. See, for instance, Chris Jochnick, Chapter 11, who states that 'both the World Bank and the IMF increasingly consider poverty alleviation and a number of related welfare concerns (even going so far as to consider issues of income distribution) to be central to their missions'.

In addition, one can think of all kinds of other UN-related agencies and programmes, such as the United Nations Development Programme (UNDP), the UN Development Fund for Women (UNIFEM), the World Health Organization (WHO), the UN Food and Agricultural Organization (FAO) as well as, for instance, the UN Educational, Scientific and Cultural Organization (UNESCO), the International

Labour Organization (ILO) and the UN Development Assistance Framework (UNDAF). They are all active in the field of poverty eradication,[30] and as Patrick van Weerelt notes, in Chapter 10, they should all incorporate human rights law notions and standards more fully into all of their activities.

The need for involvement by so-called third-party states in tackling these kinds of issues must also be considered. They are not free to lean back and wait to see whether their colleagues in the field of sovereign states are able to solve the problems caused by the poverty of their citizens. The key is to organize their societies in such a way that their citizens can, as far as possible, solve their own problems. As Chris Jochnick stresses in Chapter 11, third-party states have clear obligations in this field, in terms of refraining from violations, for instance, through active support for the full realization of human rights and through rescinding sanctions which violate the rights of innocent citizens. Examples of the latter include the long-standing US economic embargo against Cuba, and its latest expression in the form of the Helms-Burton law, or the embargo against Iraq, which continues to have devastating consequences for the country's undernourished children. Arguably successful examples of the former affirmative commitment are those of UN sanctions against the former apartheid regime in South Africa, current international NGO campaigns calling for disinvestment and/or sanctions against the Taliban regime in Afghanistan or the dictatorship in Myanmar (Burma), as well as similar controversies regarding ostensibly transitional and often poverty-creating regimes in countries such as Indonesia, Nigeria or Mexico, to cite only a few.

Finally, one should again think of the many NGOs, active in the field of human rights, development and environment, as well as related organizations such as consumers' groups and trade unions. Governments as well as international governmental organizations attach increasing importance to the contribution of NGOs in achieving their objectives, particularly in the field of poverty eradication. In recent years, the role of NGOs has been poignantly underlined on many occasions. See, for instance, the Vilnius Declaration, where the participants (parliamentarians, local representatives, NGOs, economic and political experts of the Member Countries of the Council of Europe, meeting in Vilnius in November 1995) stated that NGOs are 'an essential part of the system of "checks and balances" in a modern democracy; they can bring about or accelerate social change and help to reinforce solidarity and coherence in society'. The participants therefore 'recalled the eminent role of NGOs, notably in the field of human rights, environmental protection…

supporting the emergence of a new sense of civil responsibility, which is the foundation of democracy'.[31] In the present book, the importance of NGOs in the field of poverty eradication is clearly underlined, for instance in the contribution by Marco Aurelio Ugarte Ochoa, Chapter 4, dealing with Father Joseph Wresinski's ATD/Fourth World Movement.

Final Remarks

There is a widespread tendency in the western world towards the juridification of all kinds of social issues, as if law were the only means available, or desirable, for their solution. In the field of poverty eradication it would also be a mistake to expect legal means to be a panacea. Nevertheless, the use of human rights instruments, and other legal means and strategies not discussed in the present volume, can make a positive contribution to the elimination of poverty. The redefinition of key aspects of policy analysis of poverty issues and research in terms of human rights discourse and terminology is necessary in order to give these problems a somewhat higher status than they are typically accorded. Lacking adequate health care, for instance, is then not only a social problem, but also a human rights violation (Arambulo 1999; Toebes 1999). This enhanced status of the problem in question provides a more compelling basis for advocacy on behalf of those affected, before multiple kinds of fora, as a matter of compliance with the international human rights norms of the global juridical order.

It should be borne in mind that many contemporary human rights instruments are not legally binding or justiciable in the same way that domestic (national) laws might be: they consist, for example, of declarations which are primarily politically and morally binding; resolutions adopted by the UN General Assembly or, to mention another example, ILO recommendations, which can be used in a national debate but not as a source of law in a legal process. However, major parts of the 1948 Universal Declaration of Human Rights, for instance, have in the meantime acquired the status of international customary law, which means that over the years the declaration has developed from a political and moral standard of achievement into an instrument which can be used in legal proceedings. The same goes for many conventional human rights instruments. Almost all human rights conventions have created special procedures, giving individuals and NGOs access to relevant supervisory bodies, while they can often also be used within national legal procedures. This is especially so where nations have elected specifically to incorporate international human rights norms into their constitution (see, for example, the recently adopted constitutions of South

Africa or Colombia) or have provided for international legal norms from treaties and conventions that they have ratified to be considered 'self-executing' in terms of their actionability in domestic courts. The legal proceedings initiated against former Chilean dictator Augusto Pinochet in the United Kingdom (as the result of a petition for extradition and a warrant issued by a magistrate in Spain investigating systematic human rights abuses and acts of international state terrorism committed by his regime) raised many issues of this kind as to the ultimate justiciability of international norms in domestic courts.

Additional obligations flow from the duty of state parties to human rights conventions periodically to present reports on the national implementation of the obligations contained in the instruments, while the reactions and responses by the international supervisory bodies can be used for debates within the national context. The same applies to such things as the international debate on strengthening the rights of indigenous peoples; here again, the relevant discussions can be relied upon within the national context. One can reiterate in sum that law is not a static phenomenon. If and as far as the present instruments and solutions do not fit with the problems to be solved, the law will have to change, as it has historically, perhaps at the level of redefining prevailing standards, but at least, and in any case, in terms of procedures. In that respect there is a clear need for fashioning more effective legal vehicles for 'collective action' ('class actions' in the US context), a highly underdeveloped instrument in the field of international human rights protection.

What is needed in the field of poverty eradication is concerned and concerted action, by all the above-mentioned actors employing the various means discussed in this book, with all of this steered by the common conviction and resoluteness to eradicate, or at least seriously reduce, the unacceptable problem of increasingly globalized poverty. The problem of global poverty is inherently multidimensional and can only be tackled (eradicated or reduced) by coalitions of effort and through the use of a variety of means. NGOs, states, intergovernmental bodies, TNCs, trade unions and local grassroots social movements all have their specific responsibilities, capabilities and approaches. What they sometimes require are bridges, that is to say the preparedness to understand and discuss with each other and to cooperate where this is useful. None of the actors has a monopoly on potential strategies and solutions either on a psychological level or as to actual activities, nor are they capable of single-handedly solving a problem of this kind on such a global scale. This goes for the grassroots NGO as well as for the international lawyer, the state as well as the TNC, and at the national as well as the international level.

Human rights instruments are not panaceas and there are no uni-dimensional solutions. But for some cases and situations legal means of struggle might well be the most appropriate. International human rights norms are both a source of inspiration and an instrument for the eradication of extreme poverty.

Notes

1. Quotes taken from UN Document E/CN.4/Sub.2/1994/19: 10.
2. UN Document E/CN.4/1995 /101: 19.
3. *Copenhagen Programme of Action*, adopted by the World Summit for Social Development (Copenhagen, 6–12 March 1995), Chapter II, Paragraph 19.
4. Ibid., Chapter IV, Paragraph 66.
5. Ibid., Chapter IV, Paragraph 71 (h).
6. For an overview of the debate at the 4th session of the Working Group (30 November–11 December 1998) see Andrew Gray (1999) *The United Nations' Declaration on the Rights of Indigenous Peoples is Still Intact*, Report, IWGIA and Forest Peoples' Programme.
7. See, for instance, the General Comment on Article 27 of the UN Covenant on Civil and Political Rights, adopted by the UN Human Rights Committee in April 1994, and the Framework Convention for the Protection of National Minorities (and the Explanatory Memorandum to it), adopted by the Council of Europe in November 1994.
8. See, for instance, the view of the UN Human Rights Committee in the case of the Indian woman Sandra Lovelace versus Canada (case no. 24/177).
9. UN Commission on Human Rights, Resolution 1998/20.
10. UN Document E/CN.4/Sub.2/1994/9: 8.
11. UN Commission on Human Rights, Resolution 1998/12.
12. Ibid.
13. The introduction to the section on 'Human Rights and Environment' of the UN Sub-Commission on Prevention of Discrimination and Protection of Minorities is based on: Advisory Committee on Human Rights and Foreign Policy (1995) *Collective Rights*, report, The Hague, and W.J.M. van Genugten (1999) *Human Rights Reference Handbook*, 2nd revised ed., SDU, The Hague.
14. UN Document E/CN.4/Sub.2/1994/9: 22 and 27.
15. UN Document A/CONF.157/23, Chapter I, Paragraph 10.
16. Resolution 1998/72.
17. Ibid.
18. Ibid.
19. The Agreement to establish the World Trade Organization was signed on 15 April 1994 in Marrakech, Morocco. As of 1 January 1995, the actual date of the organization's creation, it had 76 members, and at the beginning of 1999, some 130 members, about 100 of them developing countries.
20. See: http://www.wto.org/wto/about/facts2.htm.

21. See http://www.wto.org/wto/about/facts3.htm.

22. The role played by ITT was disclosed during hearings before the Subcommittee on Foreign Affairs of the US House of Representatives: *United States House of Representatives: United States and Chile During the Allende Years, 1970–1973*; Hearings before the Subcommittee on Foreign Affairs of the House of Representatives, US Government Printing Office, Washington, 1975.

23. ECOSOC, Official Records, 53rd session, 3–28 July 1972, 1822nd meeting, 5 July 1972: 22.

24. For a more detailed analysis of the difference between legal and normative force, see S.C. van Eyk (1995) *The OECD Declaration and Decisions Concerning Multinational Enterprises: An Attempt to Tame the Shrew*, Ars Aequi Libri, Nijmegen, pp. 49 *et seq.*

25. The introduction is based on S.C. van Eyk, W.J.M. van Genugten and E.G.Ch. Wesselink (eds) (1998) *Multinational Enterprises and Human Rights*, report written for Amnesty International and Pax Christi, Amsterdam/Utrecht; W.J.M. van Genugten and S.C. van Bijsterveld (1998) 'Codes of Conduct for Multinational Enterprises: Useful Instruments or a Shield Against Binding Responsibility', *Tilburg Foreign Law Review*, Vol. 7, No. 2: 161–77.

26. See the report of the Governing Body, April 1997: 79.

27. See S.C. van Eyk, *op. cit.*: 243 *et seq.*

28. United Nations Convention on the Law of the Sea, Montego Bay, 10 December 1982. Agreement Relating to the Implementation of Part XI of the United Nations Convention on the Law of the Sea of 10 December 1982, 16 November 1994.

29. Ibid., 1982 convention, Article 187 (C), section Part XI, section 5.

30. For a recent overview of their activities see UN Document A/53/1, 1998: 10–11 and the report *Social Watch*, NOVIB, The Hague, 1996, passim.

31. Council of Europe, Conference on Non-Governmental Organizations and Civil Society, Vilnius, 23–4 November 1995.

References

Arambulo, Kitty (1999) *Strengthening the Supervision of the International Covenant on Economic, Social and Cultural Rights*, Hart/Intersentia, Antwerp/Groningen/ Oxford.

Commission on Global Governance (1995) *Our Global Neighbourhood*, Chapter 5: Reforming the United Nations, Oxford University Press, Oxford: 3.

Kjønstad, Asbjørn and John H. Veit Wilson (eds) (1997) *Law, Power and Poverty*, CROP, Bergen.

Malanczuk, P. (1997) *Akehurst's Modern Introduction to International Law*, 7th revised ed., Routledge, London/New York.

Toebes, Brigit C.A. (1999) *The right to Health as a Human Right in International Law*, Hart/Intersentia, Antwerp/Groningen/Oxford.

van Dijk, P. (1987) 'Normative Force and Effectiveness of International Norms,' *German Yearbook of International Law*, Vol. 30: 9.

Index

Zed Books titles on Poverty

Many Zed Books titles on international and Third World issues deal, one way or another, with the question of poverty. The following titles, however, deal with the question specifically.

Housing the Urban Poor: A Guide to Policy and Practice in the South
BRIAN C. ALDRICH AND RANVINDER S. SANDHU (EDS)

The Globalization of Poverty: Impacts of IMF and World Bank Reforms
MICHEL CHOSSUDOVSKY

In the Land of Poverty: Memoirs of an Indian Family, 1947-97
SIDDHARTH DUBE

The International Glossary on Poverty
DAVID GORDON AND PAUL SPICKER (EDS)

Poverty: Human Consciousness and the Amnesia of Development
RAJNI KOTHARI

Big Business, Poor Peoples: The Impact of Transnational Corporations on the World's Poor
JOHN MADELEY

Gender and Slum Culture in Urban Asia
SUZANNE THORBEK

The Poverty of Rights: Human Rights and the Eradication of Poverty
WILLEM VAN GENUGTEN AND CAMILO PEREZ-BUSTILLO (EDS)

Poverty Reduction: What Role for the State in Today's Globalized Economy?
FRANCIS WILSON, NAZNEEN KANJI AND EINAR BRAATHEN (EDS)

•••

For full details of this list and Zed's other subject, area studies and general catalogues, please write to:
The Marketing Department, Zed Books, 7 Cynthia Street, London N1 9JF, UK
or email Sales@zedbooks.demon.co.uk
Visit our website at: http://www.zedbooks.demon.co.uk